TALKING
TO THE GIRLS

Intimate and Political Essays
on the Triangle Fire

Edited by

Edvige Giunta

and

Mary Anne Trasciatti

New Village Press, 2022

Published in the United States by New Village Press
bookorders@newvillagepress.net www.newvillagepress.org
New Village Press is a public-benefit, nonprofit publisher
Distributed by NYU Press

Publication Date: March 2022

First Edition

We are grateful for the permission to quote from Woody Guthrie's song: PLANE WRECK AT LOS GATOS (DEPORTEE), Words by Woody Guthrie; Music by Martin Hoffman WGP/TRO-© Copyright 1961 (Renewed), 1963 (Renewed) Woody Guthrie Publications, Inc., & Ludlow Music, Inc., New York, NY, administered by Ludlow Music, Inc. International Copyright Secured.

We are also grateful for permission to quote from Francesca Incudine's song, "No Name," from the album *Tarakè*, text by F. Incudine and M. Vacanti, music by F. Incudine and M. Tumminello.

Library of Congress Cataloging-in-Publication Data

Names: Giunta, Edvige, editor. | Trasciatti, Mary Anne, editor.
Title: Talking to the girls : intimate and political essays on the Triangle fire / edited by Edvige
    Giunta and Mary Anne Trasciatti.
Description: First edition. | [New York] : New Village Press, 2022. | Includes bibliographical
    references. | Summary: "Candid and intimate accounts of the factory-worker tragedy that
    shaped American labor rights. On March 25, 1911, a fire broke out on the eighth floor of
    the Asch Building in Greenwich Village, New York. The top three floors housed the Trian-
    gle Waist Company, a factory where approximately 500 workers, mostly young immigrant
    women and girls, labored to produce fashionable cotton blouses, known as "waists." The fire
    killed 146 workers in a mere 15 minutes but pierced the perpetual conscience of citizens
    everywhere. The tragedy of the fire, and the resulting movements for change, were pivotal in
    shaping workers' rights and unions. This book is a collection of stories from writers, artists,
    activists, scholars, and family members of the Triangle workers. Nineteen contributors offer
    a collective testimony: a written memorial to the Triangle victims"—Provided by publisher.
Identifiers: LCCN 2021057740 (print) | LCCN 2021057741 (ebook) | ISBN 9781613321508
    (paperback) | ISBN 9781613321515 (hardcover) | ISBN 9781613321522 (ebook) |
    ISBN 9781613321539 (ebook other)
Subjects: LCSH: Triangle Shirtwaist Company—Fire, 1911. | Labor movement—New York
    (State)—New York | Clothing factories—New York (State)—New York. | Women immi-
    grants—New York (State)—New York—Social conditions.
Classification: LCC HD8083.N7 T35 2022 (print) | LCC HD8083.N7 (ebook) |
    DDC 331.809747/1—dc23/eng/20211222
LC record available at https://lccn.loc.gov/2021057740
LC ebook record available at https://lccn.loc.gov/2021057741

Cover design: Lynne Elizabeth
Cover image: Eighth-grade students from J. Taylor Finley Middle School, Huntington,
    New York, at the Triangle fire commemoration in 2019. Photo by Kimberly Schiller
Interior design and composition: Leigh McLellan Design

For Brigida Trasciatti, Imelda Gilboy,
Ruth Gilboy Trasciatti, Lawrence Trasciatti,
Frances Anne Musto, Michael Caslowitz,
Sam Caslowitz, Bridget Caslowitz,
Erin Stymacks Caslowitz, and Sophie Ruth Caslowitz

For Dorotea Favitta, Concetta De Caro,
Nunziatina Nuncibello, Cettina Minasola,
Diego Giunta, Claudia Giunta, Dalila Urbano,
Emily Alice Cutts, and Matteo Giunta Fausty

And for the girls

Venite sorelle comu stiddi avvampati,
Vi insignu a vulari 'ncapu all' America,
Siamo comete nere precipitate,
Il fumo la cenere ammenzu a li strati.

Come, sisters like stars on fire
I will teach you to fly above America
We are fallen dark comets
Smoke and ash in the middle of the street.

Francesca Incudine, "No Name"

Contents

List of Illustrations

Talking to the Girls

▼

A Story That Calls to Us

A factory fire that occurred in New York City at the beginning of the twentieth century has broken through the wall of silence and disinterest that has so often hidden the stories of workers—especially women and girls—and their fight for justice. From New York to California, from Italy to Bangladesh, people remember the 146 workers who died in the Triangle Shirtwaist Factory fire, the largest workplace disaster in the history of New York City prior to 9/11. Most of these workers were women and girls, some as young as fourteen. The majority had emigrated from Eastern Europe and Italy; some had been in the United States less than a year. Their lives were cut short by capitalist greed. With *Talking to the Girls: Intimate and Political Essays on the Triangle Shirtwaist Factory Fire*, we want to show how these workers are remembered today, and how their stories have inspired people, and even changed lives. A diverse group of writers, artists, activists, scholars, and teachers tell us when and where they first heard the call of the Triangle workers and how that call has shaped them, their work, and their communities.

Talking to the Girls is not a book about the fire, but about the ways Triangle continues to call to us. It does not tell the stories of Triangle workers, at least not only. Instead, their stories are remembered, evoked, coaxed out of a distant, often obscure past. They are entwined with the stories of a son, a grandson, a granddaughter, a great-niece, a teacher, a scholar, an art historian, a labor historian, a writer, a poet, an architect, a labor organizer, an activist. The first anthology on the Triangle fire, *Talking to the Girls* illustrates the diversity of voices and experiences within the Triangle fire community, a community that transcends temporal, national, geographic, ethnic/racial, gender, and class boundaries.

The Fire and Its Aftermath

On Saturday, March 25, 1911, at 4:40 P.M., as the workers prepared to leave with their pay in hand, an alarm bell sounded at the Triangle Waist Company. Triangle was the flagship factory of Max Blanck and Isaac Harris, two Russian Jewish immigrants who had arrived in the United States in the late 1800s and, after working in the garment industry, had started their own factory. The factory was located on the eighth, ninth, and tenth floors of the modern Asch Building (now the Brown Building). Workers produced shirtwaists, an iconic item of clothing for the "new" American woman inspired by the Gibson Girl, created by illustrator Charles Dana Gibson. The ideal of feminine independence, exemplified by middle- and upper-class suffragists, appealed to the young women of Triangle, many of whom wore shirtwaists themselves.

The fire started on the eighth floor, likely caused by a live ash from a cigarette that fell into a bin of flammable cloth. Soon after, a call went from the eighth floor to the switchboard on the tenth floor, where the bosses' office was located (the eighth floor could not communicate directly with the ninth floor). Eighth-floor workers began to exit down the stairs; many workers, mostly on the tenth floor, escaped to the roof and climbed to safety to the adjacent building with the help of New York University law students. Ninth-floor workers were not so fortunate. The switchboard operator on the tenth floor fled—in the ensuing panic, she forgot to call the ninth floor. As a result, workers on that floor did not realize there was a fire until it was raging all around them.

Smoke, sirens, and screams drew hundreds of New Yorkers to the corner of Washington Place and Greene Street, one block east of

Washington Square Park, in Greenwich Village. Firemen arrived on the scene almost immediately. They began hosing the fire with limited water pressure. Their ladders reached only to the sixth floor. Desperate to escape, ninth-floor workers rushed to the exit doors on the Greene Street side of the building. Many of the women and girls were soon crushed up against the doors as they struggled to open them. When a barrel of machine oil near a doorway burst into flames, that exit was blocked altogether. Workers pounded desperately on the locked doors on the Washington Place side of the building, to no avail. Many packed into the passenger elevator on the Washington Place side and rode to safety with its operator, Joseph Zito, but that escape route closed when the elevator cable broke. Some threw themselves down the elevator shaft in a desperate attempt to get out. Those who fled on the fire escape died when the structure collapsed under their weight. Desperate to escape the flames, more than fifty women and girls jumped to their deaths from the ninth floor.

The reporter William Gunn Shepherd counted sixty-two bodies on the ground, almost all of them women and girls from the ninth floor. Firefighters, policemen, reporters, family members, union representatives, passersby, and those workers who had escaped were the horrified witnesses of the Triangle fire.

We do not know the exact number of workers who were at Triangle that day, because the records burned in the fire. There may have been as many as five hundred. We know, however, that there were 278 sewing machines on the ninth floor. No workers were found dead at their machines. All of them had tried to escape.

Much has been written about the dynamics of the fire: the three minutes that would have saved lives if the ninth floor had been alerted immediately, the panic that paralyzed some workers and propelled others to react quickly, the firefighters' short ladders, the nets that could not withstand the force of the falling bodies. Ultimately, the deaths of 146 workers, if not the fire itself, could have been prevented by adequate fire safety measures.

The Triangle Waist Company was technically not a sweatshop, notorious for its low pay and terrible working conditions, including lack of fire safety. It was a modern factory. It was driven, however, by the same impetus that had created the sweatshop: the relentless drive for profit predicated on the ruthless exploitation of workers. The Asch Building was certified fireproof, but fire safety precautions were minimal. Workers and machines were packed together to maximize productivity. The owners used the factory's high ceilings to calculate the overall square footage to fit a greater number of workers. Scraps of cloth lined the factory floor and particles of fiber filled the air. The bins stuffed with fabric were placed under the tables to save space. All these conditions accelerated the spread of the fire. In addition, the owners had not installed a working sprinkler system. Hoses were not connected to water. There were only buckets of water to extinguish fires. While the building code required three enclosed staircases for a structure of that size, there were only two enclosed staircases. The developers had petitioned successfully to have the fire escape (which collapsed during the fire) count as a third staircase. The factory doors opened inward and, according to the testimony of survivors, at least one set of doors was locked. When the firefighters finally extinguished the fire, the structure of the building was still standing. Blanck and Harris's factory had indeed proved to be fireproof. But its contents, and the workers trapped inside, were burned beyond recognition.

Triangle workers experienced firsthand the failure of an economic system focused on profit at the expense of human life. The Triangle factory would have been a safer place to work if it had been a union shop. There had been efforts to organize under the banner of the International Ladies Garment Workers Union (ILGWU). In September 1909, with the backing of Local 25 of the ILGWU, Triangle workers had gone on strike for better wages, shorter hours, and union representation. Their effort was met with verbal harassment, beatings, and arrests. Clara Lemlich, a twenty-three-year-old Ukrainian Jewish immigrant organizer for Local 25, was beaten by company goons. On November 22, 1909, she gave a brief but stirring speech during a union meeting at the Great Hall of Cooper Union. Her speech resonated with women garment workers and inspired a general strike in the industry. The largest strike of women workers until that time, it has come to be known as "the Uprising of the 20,000." The strike lasted until February 1910, when most factory owners met workers' demands, including union representation. Triangle was one notable exception. Although they granted an increase in wages and shortened hours, Blanck and Harris refused to recognize the union. The consequences of their refusal proved deadly.

After the fire, bodies lay on the sidewalk for hours as doctors looked for signs of life and authorities scrambled to find enough coffins. Mourners walked up and down Washington Place, weeping, wringing their hands, and calling out the names of loved ones. The dead were transported to a makeshift morgue at the pier on Twenty-sixth Street, where they were identified by family members and friends. In the days that followed, funeral processions for the dead who had been identified wound their way through the streets of the Village and the Lower East Side. On April 5, 1911, city officials held a funeral for seven unidentified victims, whom they had decided to bury at the Evergreens Cemetery in Brooklyn, where the city owned a plot. Women of the ILGWU and their allies observed their own mourning rituals. That same day, the union held its procession for the unnamed dead in Manhattan. Despite pouring rain, as many as 100,000 mourners, many of them women, marched silently for hours without hats or umbrellas while 300,000 people stood witness. The procession, which included empty hearses, was devoid of pageantry or display—political, religious, or otherwise—save for banners that read we mourn our loss.

A feeling of collective guilt clung to city officials. Fingers pointed and questions swirled. Who was responsible? The building department? The fire department? The factory owners? Elected officials? No one? Everyone? The most obvious culprits were the factory owners. New York State Labor Laws stipulated that doors should not be locked during working hours. Blanck and Harris had violated this stipulation so that workers could not leave without having their handbags inspected for stolen pieces of fabric, a measure that saved them only pennies, since cases of theft were rare. On April 11, a grand jury indicted the factory owners on seven counts and charged them with second-degree manslaughter. The trial began on December 4, 1911. It ended three weeks later. As New York City and the country watched, the jury acquitted

Blanck and Harris of any wrongdoing. The defense attorney, Max Steuer, had persuaded the jury that it could not be proved that the Triangle owners knew the doors of the factory were locked, in violation of regulations. Less than two years later, Blanck was fined for keeping the doors of yet another factory locked. This time, the judge apologized to Blanck for the fine he imposed.

It took three years for the twenty-three families of workers who filed a civil suit to receive seventy-five dollars for each life lost to the fire. Blanck and Harris, on the other hand, received about sixty thousand dollars from their insurance: four hundred dollars for each worker who had died in the fire. The fire had netted them a profit.

Triangle survivors and other factory workers did not need to ask questions to establish culpability. They felt the dangers of the factory system directly and understood that most New Yorkers were blissfully ignorant of the conditions in which their fashionable attire was made. Their resolve to organize and fight for better working conditions intensified. Jewish labor activists like Rose Schneiderman, Clara Lemlich, and Pauline Newman, who had themselves worked in clothing factories, channeled their grief and outrage about Triangle into their union organizing campaigns. After the fire, women joined the labor movement in greater numbers. Convinced that unions offered the best chance of securing good wages and safe workplaces, Italian women workers showed themselves to be militant rank and filers in mass strikes such as those led by the Industrial Workers of the World (IWW) in the textile mills of Lawrence, Massachusetts (1912), and Paterson, New Jersey (1913).

In some ways, the situation at Triangle was not unusual among industrial workplaces. Low pay, a twelve-hour workday, a six-day workweek, child labor, and potentially lethal accidents were standard elements of working life for many in the United States. As Erik Loomis reminds us, coal miners died from mine explosions and cave-ins; meat-packers were killed by electrocutions, meat hooks hitting them in the head, and tuberculosis; loggers were crushed to death by falling trees; timber-mill workers lost limbs and sometimes their lives when they were caught in saws and machines. Workers in these industries fought ceaselessly for their safety, but their cries were usually ignored by those in power. Unlike most labor disasters, however, the Triangle fire was impossible to ignore. It assaulted the senses of middle- and upper-class New Yorkers. People saw smoke, bodies plunging out the windows, to be smashed on the ground below, firemen standing around helplessly with broken nets. They heard fire bells, screams from the victims, gasps from the gathering crowd, and the awful sound of bodies hitting the pavement, recorded with stunning clarity by Shepherd: "THUD-DEAD, THUD-DEAD, THUD-DEAD." They smelled smoke, pavement wet from water, and burned human flesh. They felt their own hearts beating in their chests. The Triangle fire forced New York's rich and powerful to confront the reality of factory work. Before the fire, New Yorkers could easily walk past the Asch Building and other factory sites and still have no idea what went on inside. Now they had seen workers—mostly young women—die horrible deaths. This vision sparked moral outrage. The story of Triangle became part of the fight for women's suffrage, as well. Middle- and upper-class suffragists, many of whom had allied themselves with working-class women during the 1909 Uprising as part of the "mink brigade," recalled the bodies of the dead girls of Triangle in their arguments for the vote.

Following the recommendations of the Factory Investigating Commission, established after the Triangle fire and chaired by Robert Wagner and Alfred E. Smith, the New York State legislature adopted workers' compensation and radically revised most of the state's occupational safety and health codes along progressive lines. Thus, the fire became the catalyst for changes not only in fire safety but also in many areas of labor law, with historic effects on the lives of many Americans.

It's Personal—and Also Collective

The labor tragedy that killed 146 people in 1911 is personal not only for families, coworkers, and fellow citizens, but also for people who may have no direct relation to Triangle. Organizers, reporters, politicians, artists, writers, scholars, teachers—ask anyone who has been involved in Triangle fire activism, and they will tell you a story.

It became personal for William Gunn Shepherd that March 25. "I looked up—saw that there were scores of girls at the windows," he wrote. "The flames from the floor below were beating in their faces. Somehow I knew that they, too, must come down, and something within me—something that I didn't know was there—steeled me." It became personal for Frances Perkins, who later became the U.S. secretary of labor and the first woman to join a U.S. presidential cabinet. Perkins, a workers' rights advocate, was having tea with a friend the day of the fire. The commotion drew her to the factory. The horrors she witnessed drove her to dedicate her life's work to ensuring that tragedies like Triangle would never happen again. A century later, Susan Harris, the artist of the shirtwaist project "Remembering Their Prayers" and granddaughter of Triangle factory owner Blanck, experiences the memory of the fire as "a certain sorrow that's in your blood, your genes." Performer LuLu LoLo is overcome with emotion when she realizes that ten of the women who died in the fire came from the East Harlem neighborhood where she lived—as did her parents and immigrant grandparents: "We had family who worked in the factories," she says. "We knew this world." LoLo's Triangle-inspired performances, including her one-woman play *Soliloquy for a Seamstress*, resonate with this intimate knowledge, as does Harris's shirtwaist project.

The memory of Triangle exists in a space that is both personal and collective. Although there is no government-designated Triangle fire day or commemoration, the Triangle fire has been commemorated in public and community spaces for over a century. From the individuals and the crowd that witnessed the fire to the individuals and groups that have remembered it for over a century in the United States and elsewhere, this singular event has retained its historical and cultural specificity while also speaking to an ever-growing variety of individuals and constituencies. Here, the meaning of the Triangle fire—as articulated collectively by our contributors—emerges from something akin to John Bodnar's description of public memory: "Public memory emerges from the intersection of official and vernacular cultural expressions." While addressing the history of the fire, our contributors delve into its traces and permutations in the family, the community, the culture.

There is a collective spirit at the core of Triangle history and the community that has grown in its memory. From the union and labor organizing that led to the 1909 Uprising, to the funerals for the seven unidentified victims, to the political and commemorative efforts that have followed, the history of Triangle is the history of people coming together to mourn and fight for social justice.

In 1913, the Ladies' Waist and Dressmakers' Union of New York and Philadelphia remembered the dead at their union meetings. On March 25, 1914, Fire Commissioner Robert Adamson held a citywide drill in factories and schools from Brooklyn to the Bronx for "Triangle Day." For several years after the fire, the working classes of New York used the May Day parade as an opportunity to remember the Triangle dead. Their otherwise upbeat celebration turned solemn as it marched past the Asch Building. For the first fifty years after the fire, however, Triangle commemorations were not strongly attached to the site where the fire had happened, or, for that matter, to the date. Commemorations in the 1930s and 1940s involved trips to the Evergreens Cemetery. In 1951, an observance of the fortieth anniversary of the fire was held at the cemetery to coincide with "I Am an American" day—which in that year was May 20—instead of the anniversary day.

The fiftieth anniversary seemed a fitting occasion to return to the corner of Washington and Greene. Like so much in the history of Triangle, the impetus came from a woman. Esther Peterson, assistant secretary of labor and director of the U.S. Women's Bureau under President John F. Kennedy, suggested a major commemoration to ILGWU president David Dubinsky. Dubinsky notified Leon Stein, the editor of *Justice*, the official newspaper of the ILGWU. Stein seized on the idea and organized an event in front of the Brown Building. The event was attended by political and labor leaders, including Dubinsky, Peterson, Frances Perkins, Eleanor Roosevelt, and Rose Schneiderman, as well as by fourteen survivors of the fire. After the ceremony at Washington and Greene, participants took buses to the Evergreens Cemetery to remember the unidentified dead.

Commemoration was sporadic for the next twenty years. The fifty-third anniversary of the fire focused almost exclusively on fire prevention.

Since 1981, however, the ILGWU, in partnership with the Fire Department of New York (FDNY) and other labor and community groups, has organized a yearly commemoration at the site on or about March 25. The commemoration is held on a weekday around lunchtime so that people working nearby can attend. This commemoration links the events leading to and following the Triangle fire to contemporary struggles for workplace justice. Participants have expanded to include low-wage workers in the service economy, especially other workers' organizations, pro-worker advocacy groups, recent immigrants, farmworkers, construction workers, feminist activists, scholars, writers, artists, K–12 and college teachers and students. A call for action on a current labor issue—pending legislation or an organizing drive in a particular industry—is customarily part of the commemoration. During the ritual reading of names and laying of flowers, typically carnations, in memory of the dead Triangle workers, flowers are also laid for workers killed in other workplace disasters in the United States and around the world to call attention to the struggle for the safety of workers everywhere and the need for continued vigilance.

Since 2001, the memory of the fire has been amplified by a movement that has engaged in multiple cultural and political activities, which have succeeded in raising awareness, not only of that tragic event but also of the sweeping legal reforms and movements for social change that it inspired. In 2008, the newly formed Remember the Triangle Fire Coalition joined the community of Triangle memory guardians and dedicated itself to helping organize the annual commemoration and to making the 2011 centennial a major event that equaled or exceeded the 1961 commemoration. Despite frigid temperatures, the centennial drew thousands of people to the building. Many more participated via live stream. The program included a procession from Union Square to the Brown Building, where several speakers addressed the crowd, many of whom held union banners or shirtwaists with the names of the dead workers. The program culminated with "One Hundred Years After: The Triangle Fire Remembered and Rethought," a moving event at the Great Hall of Cooper Union, where Kalpona Akter, LuLu LoLo, Annelise Orleck, Cecil Roberts (president of the United Mine Workers Association), Gioia Timpanelli, Mary Anne Trasciatti, and others spoke. Subsequent commemorations have been much smaller, but they continue to attract people, and the anniversary of the fire is recognized every year in print and online media in the United States and elsewhere.

From the very beginning, Jewish American communities and organizations recognized Triangle as a chapter of Jewish history. Jewish American groups have held commemorative events to pay tribute to the Triangle workers, especially after the fiftieth anniversary. The centennial gave a new impetus to these commemorative activities. Mourners gathered on Staten Island at the cemetery run by the Hebrew Free Burial Association to recite the Kaddish over the graves of twenty-two Jewish Triangle workers who died in the fire on the anniversary of their deaths in the Hebrew calendar (25 Adar 1, 5771/March 1, 2011). On March 25, 2011, the historic Eldridge Street Synagogue hosted the Sweatshop Poets Literary Tribute, an afternoon of music and poetry where actors portrayed the 146 workers. Every year, the Yiddish-language newspaper *Forward,* one of the first to report on the fire in 1911, publishes commemorative articles. Other Jewish publications also regularly remember the fire. Paula Hyman has highlighted some of the ways in which "the fire captured the imagination of the immigrant Jewish community" already in its immediate aftermath, though with little or no emphasis on the gender of the workers. Things have changed over time, especially as feminist scholars and organizations have turned their attention to women's life narratives and histories. The Jewish Women's Archives, which held commemorative activities for the centennial, includes an array of resources on Triangle history as part of their online *Jewish Women: A Comprehensive Historical Encyclopedia.*

Jewish immigrants from Eastern Europe were the largest group of workers to die in the fire. Italian immigrants were the second. Until the 1990s, however, there was little or no effort on the part of Italian American groups to publicly embrace Triangle as a chapter of Italian American history. Yet the stories of those dead immigrant workers had not been forgotten. They had stayed mostly within the bounds of family grief. Fourteen-year-old Rosaria Maltese, her sister Lucia, and their mother, Caterina, were not forgotten by their descendants. Every year, their nephew and grandson, Vincent Maltese, laid flowers at the corner of Washington and Greene anonymously until 1986, when his identity became known to commemoration organizers and he joined the official union commemoration. In 1955, Vincent and his brother, New York State Senator Serphin Maltese, had founded the Triangle Survivors Group, later renamed the Triangle Fire Memorial Association. Survivors sometimes told their stories, like Paulina Pepe, an eighth-floor machine operator at Triangle, whose recollection of the fire was recorded in an interview in March 1986, in which her daughter can also be heard asking questions and reminding her mother of details she had heard from her over the years.

Public memory of the fire—both in Italian American culture and wider U.S. culture—has overlooked that approximately a third of the dead workers were Italian women. This gap is part of a larger erasure of key chapters of Italian American history, such as the involvement of early- twentieth-century Italian immigrants in the labor movement. This erasure can be understood in the context of the racialization of and discrimination against Italian immigrants in the early stages of their migration and during World War II, when Italian became an enemy language and Italian immigrants were deemed enemy aliens. This fraught history and the combination of pressure and aspiration to assimilate into mainstream U.S. culture has led to a pernicious amnesia, often accompanied by racist and conservative politics, which Italian American scholars have been working to historicize, understand, and dismantle. The reclamation of the Triangle fire in the annals of Italian American history complicates the simplistic narrative of immigrant struggle and success and illustrates how the excesses of capitalism have been borne by the bodies of women, including Italian women.

In 2001, on the ninetieth anniversary of the fire, the Collective of Italian American Women (CIAW, later renamed Malia) organized the first large Italian American Triangle commemoration. Sicilian American writer and storyteller Gioia Timpanelli told the story of the fire in front of the Brown Building. Her mournful chant, steeped in ancient southern Italian grief rituals, drew the crowd closer. Organizers passed around small cards, each inscribed with the name of one of the 146 workers and a reproduction of *Fire,* a collage created by artist Nancy Azara. In the silence, individual voices rose as, one by one, people called out the names of the dead workers.

Across the Atlantic, in Italy, the personal pull of Triangle has been felt intensely. The history of Triangle memory in that country captures the complex and sometimes mysterious interconnections among culture, memory, and imagination. As early as the 1970s, the memory of the fire was in the hearts of thousands of feminists and appeared in "8 Marzo," a feminist anthem by the Movimento Femminista Romano: "Ricordatevi di noi/ siamo morte in una fabbrica.... Noi vivremo eternamente/sinchè durerà la lotta" ("Remember us/we died in a factory. ... Our memory will live forever/as long as the struggle will last"). In the musical *Fire!*—which he wrote and directed—Massimiliano Vintaloro reflects on what compelled him to research the tragedy: "When you are born in a city like Prato, in Tuscany, you can't help but talk or hear about factories. It is something that is part of our DNA, of our daily life. And I have been smelling a factory for thirty years, since I am a textile worker." In the Italian memory of Triangle, some details were changed. For example, for a long time, and sometimes even today, the date of the fire was believed to be March 8, 1908. As a result, the fire was considered the reason for International Women's Day. Sicilian feminist historian Emma Baeri draws a compelling connection between the imagined workers of the presumed fire of March 8, 1908—a fire that never happened—and the real workers of the March 25, 1911 Triangle fire. In Italian feminist memory, she says, this encounter of history and imagination counteracts the absence of women from public historical narratives. In the second decade of the twenty-first century, the organization Toponomastica Femminile (Female Toponomastics) launched a large commemorative initiative, which was spearheaded by writer activist Ester Rizzo Licata. It became known that one-third of the workers who died in the fire were southern Italian immigrant women.

A few contemporary political figures have also felt the force of Triangle history. In 2014, the president of the Italian Chamber of Deputies, Laura Boldrini, was moved by Triangle's resonance for Italian women's and immigrant history to visit the site of the factory during her official visit to the United States. At the Brown Building, she laid flowers in green, white, and red (the colors of the Italian flag). In 2019, U.S. presidential candidate Senator Elizabeth Warren chose to speak at Washington Square Park because of its proximity to the Triangle fire site. In June 2020, in the midst of the COVID-19 pandemic, as people took to the streets to protest the killing by police of George Floyd and other Black people, New York governor Andrew Cuomo compared that moment in U.S. history to Triangle: "Mr. Floyd's murder . . . is a metaphor for the systemic racism and injustice that we have seen. And I stand with the protestors in the point that we need meaningful reform. . . . meaningful change . . . only happens when the people get fully-mobilized and informed . . . That was the labor rights reforms after the Triangle Shirtwaist Factory Fire . . ." Before Warren and Cuomo, other political figures—Frances Perkins, Al Smith, and Robert Wagner—understood that the powerful lessons of Triangle have improved and can continue to improve the lives of working people.

In 2010, the Remember the Triangle Fire Coalition spearheaded the creation of a permanent memorial of the fire on the Brown Building. In December 2015, Governor Cuomo earmarked $1.5 million to fund the construction of the memorial. Unions and private individuals funded an endowment for its preservation. The Triangle Memorial project emerged in a moment of intense debate about who and what gets remembered in public spaces. Monuments and memorials speak volumes about values. Left intact after the fire, the Brown Building is a site where people from around the United States and the world come not only to mourn but also to organize. For over a century, except on the day of the annual commemoration, the building has told its story with barely a whisper, a simple plaque installed there by the ILGWU on the fiftieth anniversary. Two other plaques indicate the building's status as a historic landmark. Most people walk by without noticing. The memorial enables the Brown Building to speak powerfully about the people who once worked there, their hopes and dreams, the lives cut short by neglect and a relentless drive for profit. It tells the story of how their deaths galvanized people to collective action, the effects of which remain with us to this day.

That it has taken over a century to build a Triangle memorial is indicative of how little our society values the lives of immigrant working people, particularly women and girls. That it could be built at all is a testament to the enduring power of the Triangle story to inspire people and move them to take action against apparently insurmountable odds. This long overdue tribute to those who died in the fire, and the social justice movements that emerged in the aftermath of their deaths, is New York City's first labor memorial, one of a handful of memorials to women and girls in the city, and one of only a few labor memorials in the United States.

Intimate and Political Essays on the Triangle Fire

In the spirit that animates so much Triangle-inspired political, artistic, and literary work, *Talking to the Girls: Intimate and Political Essays on the Triangle Shirtwaist Factory Fire* is a multivoiced text. As an anthology, it embodies the voices of a large and diverse community that has recognized and acted on its ethical responsibility to the memory of the Triangle workers. *Talking to the Girls* acknowledges the multiplicity and diversity of the work inspired by the Triangle fire at the beginning of the twenty-first century. Many essays included here were born out of reflections on this work. Many of us who are part of this project first met at the annual commemoration, or a panel discussion, a performance, a march, a community meeting, or through reading one another's work. Often, a single encounter has generated lifelong collaboration. The impetus to create a volume of personal essays emerged from these acts of collaboration that define the Triangle community.

A collaborative spirit has sustained every stage and aspect of the making of this book—from choosing anthology as its format, to the in-depth exchanges with our authors as they composed essays that would stand on their own but also be in conversation with one another, to interviewing Kalpona Akter, to our cowriting of the introduction and part of the epilogue. We, the editors, came to this work as feminist scholars and teachers committed to working-class issues and as women with immigrant roots in Italy—Edvige is a first-generation immigrant and Mary Anne is the granddaughter of immigrants. Our interest in the Triangle fire started at different times and in different places: for Edvige, in 1976, when, as an adolescent, she remembered the fire in the first episode of a feminist radio program she hosted in her Sicilian home town and a year later, when she participated in feminist marches on the streets of Catania; for Mary Anne, at home on Long Island, while she listened to stories about her mother's work in a dress factory, and later when she learned about Triangle in middle school in the late 1970s. By the time we started to conceptualize this book in 2015, between the two of us we had accumulated decades of Triangle fire work. Doing this book together is an extension of that work—work we do not do alone, but with those who share our commitment to remembering the women and girls and to affirming that their deaths motivate activism.

Over the years, the two of us have found ourselves at panel discussions, lectures, meetings, marches, and we have organized events together. Edvige has taken the students from her Triangle fire course to the annual commemoration. She has stood with them in front of the Brown Building, listening to Mary Anne speak as president of the Remember the Triangle Fire Coalition. We have walked together to the home addresses of girls killed by the fire and knelt next to our Hofstra University and New Jersey City University students to chalk the names of workers who died in the fire on the sidewalk. We have talked about what makes all of us involved in Triangle a community. This community, we believe, understands that the meaning of history is found in the realization of its continuous relevance in the present and for the future. Grounded in a single historical moment, Triangle activism embraces other moments. It binds all of us committed to social justice across time and place.

While several of our contributors are scholars, we asked them to surrender the scholarly apparatus of academic writing, including endnotes and bibliography (however, we have included at the back of the book reflections by each author on the process and research that shaped their essay, and a general bibliography that includes the sources our authors, and we, have collectively used). Although historical and archival research is not outside the purview of this book, we invited our contributors to be guided by their own visceral relationship to Triangle. Why is Triangle compelling? What propels people to embrace it as a personal cause and devote years, decades, even a lifetime to it?

"Why did *you* gravitate toward the Triangle fire? Why is it important to *your* life? Write a personal essay," we told our contributors. We trusted that the personal essay would serve as an ideal form to explore the combination of intimate and political that permeates Triangle activism, whether it manifests as political action or artistic, literary, or pedagogical work. "Write from the heart," we urged. That only a handful of personal narratives on the Triangle fire—such as those by Suzanne Pred Bass and Katharine Weber, both descendants of Triangle workers—had appeared in print strengthened our belief that the personal essay was the necessary form for our book. We hoped that by remembering and reflecting on their own Triangle stories, contributors would express a transformative and exemplary process of cultural and historical self-awareness. Sometimes that involved grounding their experiences in a cross-generational story.

Our contributors explore their answers to our questions by tracing and reflecting on how their Triangle story came to be. If, to use Vivian Gornick's distinction, the Triangle fire is the "situation" our authors have in common, we asked them to distill, uncover, and tell us *their* Triangle fire stories. They bring to the page their Triangle experiences, which are rooted in a wide range of contexts—the family, the union, the classroom, the archive, place of origin. Often, an author's writing emerges from more than one of these contexts. The essays coalesce around memoiristic moments where commitment to Triangle activism and personal story intersect. These are moments of great insight for the authors and for readers, as they illustrate how history is not indifferent to our actions. Writing can transform our relationship to the past by generating not just new perspectives but new feelings. Memoirist Louise DeSalvo writes, "Language I have learned by writing . . . gives birth to feeling, not the other way around." Memory work, central to Triangle history, makes an author a vulnerable actor, someone who examines their own place in history as one way to bring the past into the present.

In the exploratory spirit of the genre of the personal essay, the essays included here do not purport to be the last word on Triangle activism. Rather, in looking at their encounter with the fire and what prompted them to find a place in their lives for Triangle, these authors offer models for engaging in and reflecting on activism that are applicable to other historic events. We did not conceive *Talking to the Girls* as a collection, but as a conversation. For this reason, we did not include previously published essays. All the essays were written for this book. We asked our contributors to weave their private memories with public memory of Triangle; they have done so in ways that are dramatically different, even as they resonate with one another. These essays traverse different forms of the personal essay: Some are primarily memoiristic; others move back and forth between the memoiristic and the scholarly, the cultural, or the pedagogical. In every case, they are acts of intimate and political memory that show how our present selves are shaped by an encounter with the past.

Cross-generational trauma, activism, cross-cultural alliances and connections, memorialization—through pedagogical work, performance, or monuments—are but a few of the themes our contributors return to again and again to illustrate the lasting relevance of the fire's history. The five parts around which the book is organized—Witnesses, Families, Teachers, Movements, and Memorials—enable the reader to experience the book's key themes in a highly focused manner.

It seems appropriate to begin the book with "Witnesses." In the opening essay, "Another Spring," writer and performer Annie Lanzillotto considers the vulnerability of twenty-first-century Triangle activist artists like herself, who have lost their housing in the boom of gentrification. "The New Deal Began with My Grandmother Frances Perkins," cowritten by Tomlin Perkins Coggeshall and the Reverend Charles Hoffacker, considers the role of Coggeshall's grandmother, Frances Perkins, in Triangle history through the lens of intimate recollections of family life and the meaning of conversion in her political work. In "The Triangle Factory Fire and the City of Two Who

Survived," literary scholar Ellen Gruber Garvey connects yesterday's and today's immigrants. She tells the stories of her great-uncle's father, Abraham Bernstein, a Triangle fire survivor who testified on behalf of the owners, and Sophie Sasslovsky, who was fired for talking to a union organizer before the fire. Sophie's daughter Fran would become a community organizer in Garvey's Manhattan neighborhood. Paola Corso's lyrical essay takes its title from her poem "Girl Talk" and traces the journey of the poet, daughter of a steelworker, from writing about her native Pittsburgh's Golden Triangle to memorializing Triangle women and girls in her poetry.

"Witnesses" is the segue to "Families," though these two categories often overlap. This part includes four essays by authors whose family members had a direct connection to the Triangle Waist Company. In "A Legacy of Grief: In Search of Rosie Weiner," psychologist Suzanne Pred Bass explores the cross-generational impact of the fire on her family by writing of her two great-aunts, both Triangle workers (one died in the fire, while the other survived). In "My Father, Isidore Abramowitz," Martin Abramowitz reflects on the ethical burden of telling the story of his father, a cutter who testified at the trial of the factory owners and might have been responsible for inadvertently starting the fire. In "The Two Roses: A Great-Niece Remembers," social worker and writer Annie Schneiderman Valliere juxtaposes memories of her great-aunt Rose with what she has learned, after her death, about Rose Schnei-derman, heroine of the labor movement, who would inspire Valliere's own activism. Finally, in "Triangle in Two Acts: From Bubbe Mayses to Bangladesh," historian Annelise Orleck traces the ripples of the Triangle fire and its urgent global relevance by reflecting on her relationship to her grandmother, who worked at Triangle, and to Bangladeshi activist Kalpona Akter.

"Teachers" brings together the pedagogical practices of three teachers who have inventively brought Triangle to their classrooms. In "Teaching the Triangle Fire to Middle School Students," Kimberly Schiller reflects on the journey that led a suburban girl from Long Island to become a teacher-activist committed to remembering the workers who died in the city of her dreams. She acknowledges the women—

in her family, at school, and in books—who have inspired the activist journey that has led her to Triangle. In "Remembering the Triangle Fire in California," cultural studies scholar Laura E. Ruberto connects the Triangle fire and the 1948 Los Gatos Canyon plane crash in California, which killed twenty-eight Mexican citizens, all migrant workers. Feminist scholar and writer Jacqueline Ellis explores a tradition of girlhood activism—from ILGWU organizer Clara Lemlich to March for Our Lives leaders Emma González and Naomi Wadler—in "Teaching the Girls: The Triangle Fire as Affective History." She shows how affect serves as an organizing strategy, a rhetorical tool, and a means of resisting exclusive definitions of girlhood.

"Movements" includes essays by two scholars and a union organizer who show all the ways Triangle history is both personal and political. In "Solidarity Forever!" feminist, immigrant rights and labor activist May Chen writes of her role in helping organize the 1982 Chinese garment workers' strike in New York and her involvement in Triangle as a point of connection and solidarity among women garment workers in the ILGWU across ethnic, racial, and historical lines. Literary scholar Michele Fazio's essay, "Remembering Family: Labor Activism and the Triangle Fire," recovers the author's suppressed family history through storytelling and archival records. This history emerged out of the Triangle fire and continued through the formative years of the Italian American labor movement. In "They Were Not There: A Rumination on the Meaning of the Triangle Shirtwaist Fire to Black Garment Workers in Early-Twentieth-Century New York City," Janette Gayle reflects on her own story as a Black immigrant woman and labor historian as she reconstructs the history of Black women from the American South and from the Caribbean who migrated to New York in search of jobs in the garment industry.

"Memorials" considers the creative ways in which Triangle memory is kept alive through performance and commemorative sites and artifacts. In "Chalk and Smoke, Fabric and Thread: Reflections on Feminist Commemoration," art historian Ellen Wiley Todd considers the power of remembrance in women's visual traditions, from mourning practices after the 1911 Triangle fire to commemorative activities for the 2011 centennial. In "And They Returned Home: Italy Remembers the Triangle Fire Women," Ester Rizzo Licata, the driving force behind Toponomastica Femminile's initiative that has led to the naming of public sites in memory of Triangle workers in Italy, recounts her encounters with the memory of the Italian women who died in the fire. She imagines herself as a bridge between Italy and the United States. In "The Fabric of Memory," Richard Joon Yoo, a member of the two-person design team for the Triangle Fire Memorial, traces his journey through the process of creating the memorial and connects that memory work with gathering the traces of immigrant memory in his Korean American family.

Placed at the end of the book, "Listening to Kalpona," based on our 2019 interview with Kalpona Akter, acknowledges the spirit of *Talking to the Girls* as a book conceived as a conversation. It also marks the transnational and contemporary relevance of Triangle to today's workers. Its placement at the close of the book recognizes the global resonance of the Triangle legacy.

Talking to the Girls

Janet Zandy has written that "almost always in the fire poetry, there are the conversations with dead sisters across time, naming their names, reconstituting their faces, and voices." Through the years of work that have led to this book, we have been in these conversations, as have our contributors—privately and collectively. Sisters, mothers, daughters. One hundred and twenty-nine women and girls died in the fire. Provvidenza Panno, the oldest, was forty-three. Sixty-five were teenage girls. Two were only fourteen. In "talking to the girls," we honor the memory of all the 146, but also assert the importance of writing about the fire in a way that places the "girls" at the center of the conversation—girls who should have never been working in a factory, the teenage girls to whom Lanzillotto sings, the girls in Corso's poems who "talk" to their fellow teenage workers in developing countries like Bangladesh, where the fires continue to rage—girls like Anna Altman, Yetta Berger, Essie

Bernstein, Vincenza Billota, Sarah Brenman, Ida Brodsky, Ada Brucks, Laura Brunetti, Josephine Cammarata, Francesca Caputo, Rosina Cirrito, Sarah Cooper, Clara Dockman, Celia Eisenberg, Dora Evans, Yetta Fichtenholtz, Jennie Franco, Rose Friedman, Diana Gerjuoy, Molly Gerstein, Celia Gitlin, Mary Goldstein, Rosie Grasso, Rachel Grossman, Fannie Hollander, Pauline Horowitz, Ida Jukofsky, Ida Kanowitz, Tessie Kaplan, Beckie Kessler, Beckie Koppelman, Bertha Kula, Tillie Kupfershmidt, Annie L'Abbate, Kate Leone, Jennie Levin, Pauline Levine, Rose Liermark, Bettina Maiale, Rosaria Maltese, Rose Mehl, Yetta Meyers, Gaetana Midolo, Annie Miller, Beckie Neubauer, Annie Nicholas, Sadie Nussbaum, Julia Oberstein, Rose Oringer, Annie Pack, Antonietta Pasqualicchio, Jennie Pildescu, Beckie Reines, Sarah Sabasowitz, Gussie Schiffman, Golda Schpunt, Rose Shapiro, Rose Sorkin, Jennie Stein, Jennie Stellino, Isabella Tortorelli, Bessie Viviano, Sarah Weintraub, Bertha Wendroff, Sonia Wisotsky.

Edvige Giunta and Mary Anne Trasciatti
Teaneck, New Jersey, and Long Beach, New York
March 13, 2021

PART ONE

WITNESSES

CHAPTER 1

Another Spring

▼

Annie Rachele Lanzillotto

For Diane Fortuna and her great-aunt Daisy Lopez Fitze,
Triangle worker who jumped from the ninth floor
and survived for two days

My map of Sicily is wounded. Red pox mark the towns where Triangle workers were born, and now marble plaques, reliefs, and street signs bear their names. This map I can fold neatly and tuck into my tote bag, but the lives the map marks, I can never contain neatly inside. My map is a topography of loss and a songline of salient effort. It folds accordion-style into a neat rectangle with a lacquered cover, but once open, presents the skin of the terrain where twenty-four seamstresses and one elevator operator were born, how close to one another, and the contour of the earth around them—the earth that didn't hold up beneath them.

I spread my map out over the dining room table of organizer Ester Rizzo in her hometown, Licata, and asked her to find their birthplaces: Palermo, Marsala, Marineo, Sciacca, Erice, Bisacquino, Cerda, Cerami, Sperlinga, Noto, Mazara del Vallo, Sambuca, Capaci, Licata, Vittoria, Avola, Villafranca Sicula. Ester underlined each name with a black marker, then circled all of them in red. She had diligently researched the Italian Triangle workers, traced their birth certificates, authenticated the spellings of their names, and tracked down their birthplaces one by one. She had binders of all their documents. Like a detective, she'd figured out who were siblings with whom and contacted descendants. Ester and the group Toponomastica Femminile saw to it that plaques were installed in their honor in the towns of their births. She got on the phone with the mayor of each Sicilian town, informed them of the history and significance of the fire, and urged them to take the necessary action to honor these workers. The map's red wounds looked stitched by her hand-drawn black dashes. Ester Rizzo stitched wounds.

Twenty-four Sicilians left this triangular puzzle piece of earth and died at the Triangle factory. In the early 1900s, for them, Sicily held no promise. The 1908 Messina earthquake killed eighty thousand people, with incalculably devastating effects on the area. Nineteen eleven Gotham lifted these twenty-four youth impossibly high. Rescue ladders were not yet tall enough. Nineteen eleven presaged 9/11.

In the summer of 2018, I didn't travel to Sicily with the intention of trekking to towns where the shirtwaist makers were born, but somehow Triangle is always there, calling. Sicily spirals inward, from seacoasts to mountains to the lush lava-fortified earth skirt around the looming Etna and the vast arid lands around Enna—known as the *ombelico*, the belly button, of Sicily—pretty much dead center on the island. In Enna, I had an unexpected and overwhelming feeling for the girls of Triangle. To get to the top of Enna, a steep vertical rise, I'd driven up a rickety approach that jutted out from the mountain, a midair skinny track of hairpin curves held up by concrete stilts. On top of the mountain, I climbed the steps into the cathedral, and, just beyond the nave, found the most curious ladder. The ladder was tall, reaching all the way up to the top cathedral vaults. The ladder was wooden, handmade, each rung a rounded, knotted tree branch fitted tongue and groove into the vertical legs made from trunks of the tallest trees. The ladder had a natural bend, like a spine gradually narrowing to the top. Of all the exquisite art and statuary and marble and fresco and gilt mosaic and carved wooden ceilings, and even a handmade Zimbelstern made of a wheel of brass bells pulled by a rope on a lever, out of all of it, this ladder captivated me most. All I could think was, That's what the girls needed at Triangle—an ancient endless spine of ladder reaching up and up and up and up, high enough, high enough, high enough.

Triangle is always there, calling.

After performing for LGBTQ youth in Palermo in June, I found the Triangle memorial at Palazzina Stella Maris rendered in silver patina bas-relief: a woman's face, like a portrait of the sun. Her expression is one of awe—wide eyes, sunray extensions of long wavy hair, rays tipped with leaves. A sewing machine appendage of her body frames her breasts. I returned to scholar Stefania Taviano's house in Messina, and, from there, wrote to Edvige Giunta in New Jersey: "Can you put me in touch with that Sicilian woman who is getting Triangle plaques installed in the girls' hometowns?" As it turned out, Ester Rizzo was about to unveil the latest plaque in Avola. I drove down the east coast. When I arrived in Avola, it was raining hard, raindrops thick and cool, as if from a faucet. Two villagers stood in the deluge outside their front doors, pushing palmyra-stalk brooms to sweep away the rain from their doorsteps. The last time I'd seen someone sweeping away the rain with a broom was in the Bronx, when I was a child, on a street of Italian immigrants and their descendants. This is the type of act that makes me hunger to be in southern Italy. It resides in the heart, where Triangle resonates. In Avola, in piazza Trieste, an elegant and simple memorial waited to be unveiled: a white shirt with a waist belt stretched over a freestanding plaque, a ring of a dozen perennial flowers not yet in bloom planted around the base.

A funeral was going on in San Giovanni Battista, at the head of the piazza. Men smoked on the church steps, looking down over the piazza as if standing on the bow of a ship, examining the rough sea. They took note of my presence. Mourners with black umbrellas, the women in heels, made their way up the marble steps and into the church. I waited under an awning across the street. The rain stopped and cars pulled up. Down the street, two women and one man got out of a car—a purple umbrella, long, flowing bell-bottom pants, and a flowered shirt. My heart opened at the sight of them. Their energy. Their purpose. I knew instantly these were my people—people who are called, who honor the seamstresses, who speak these names to the next generation, who guard the memory of a handful of young lives. We were linked by a mission to keep their names alive as well as to continue the work for equity, workplace safety, and justice. We were brought together by the workers who had been sacrificed to violent greed. We contemplated: Whose lives get sacrificed and why? What are the rest of us to do about it? We saw how, in the larger context, the workplace problems that Triangle illuminated were just exported to factories in developing nations. These are the figures for Dhaka, Bangladesh, alone: in 2017, 100 killed and 50 injured; in 2013, 1,234 killed and 2,500 injured; in 2012, 117 killed and 200 injured. It's too much. These twenty-four Sicilian girls and women, we could hold in our hearts and minds. We could know all their names.

Triangle felt personal.

We walked toward one another, into big hugs, and introduced ourselves. Ester and her husband, Giovanni "Vanni" Salvio, from Licata, and Vera Parisi from Avola. Without knowing it, we had been working in tandem on opposite sides of the ocean. On the other side of the Atlantic, the Remember the Triangle Fire Coalition in New York City had honored these same girls. Members of Ruth Sergel's *Chalk* project marked their names outside the apartment houses where they lived after immigrating to New York. At the intersection of the streets of their deaths, we called their names and rang bells, while Toponomastica Femminile honored the places of their births.

Forty or so people soon gathered and circled around the *camicetta bianca*. The mayor of Avola, Luca Cannata, wore a ceremonial red-white-and-green sash. The plaque listed the names of the twenty-four Sicilian girls and women who died in the fire and read:

> They left their land with little money in their pockets but a suit-case full of hopes and dreams. This space is dedicated to them and to all the women who have fought with tenacity to better the world. Because memory is a warning to the present. [translation from the Italian]

Ester Rizzo, Mayor Cannata, and others said a few words. Then they clamored for me to speak. I was the New Yorker, the Italian American, from four thousand miles away and, it seemed, from another point in time. I was from the epicenter of the hopes of these young immigrant girls. I was a returning granddaughter of southern Italian teenagers, peasants who had immigrated to New York. I was a member of the Remember the Triangle Fire Coalition. In that moment, at that shirtwaist flag post, I represented the trust that, in America, the seamstresses were remembered and would be properly memorialized. That America didn't forget. That despite our New York fast lifestyles and the constantly changing topography of the city, these young lives would be remembered and honored. I looked around the circle of Sicilians and felt the import of the moment. My mother always told me, "Once you open your mouth, you're fine." So I opened my mouth and riffed about the abject poverty that had driven the girls away from this *paradiso*, in search of work, only work; how they had become New Yorkers in short time—and with courage, staunched the heartbreak of leaving their families and homeland, and staked their fate on the unknown. How they walked the downtown New York City streets, the Village, how in New York we knew each building where they'd lived, and the paths they'd walked to work each day. I spoke of some of the girls, like little Rosie Grasso, who left the hill town of Cerami, who most likely never saw much of Sicily beyond the port from which she left, only to move to a tenement at 174 Thompson Street and to be locked in a factory on Washington Place. Her sixteen years of life and all her potential—ripped away from her.

"We mourn these girls as our children," I said. "These are our daughters."

The word *paradiso* came across my lips a few times, and the word for girls: *ragazze*. I could never get out of my head how very young most of the seamstresses were. When I finished, a classy woman came up to me and said she had goose bumps from my speech. She held out her bare forearm for me to touch. Then she reached into her pocketbook to give me an offering: a *caramella di mandorle d'Avola*, hard candy made from the almonds of the town. I was very moved. I explained to her that I was on a book tour for *Hard Candy*, a memoir I'd written about the last years of my mother's life. The central metaphor of the book was how hard candy helps Italian ladies cope with the bitterness of life. At the book readings, I told her, I'd pass around my mother's favorite pocketbook, filled with hard candy for audience members to reach in

Figure 1.1. Toponomastica Femminile. From left to right, Angela Vecchio, Ester Rizzo, Graziella Di Prima, Annie Lanzillotto. Viale 8 Marzo, Licata, Sicily, 2018. Photographer unknown; photo courtesy of Ester Rizzo.

and take. So when she, filled with emotion, pulled a bag of hard candy out of her pocketbook and handed it to me, it was as if the gods had granted me a golden shield and sword. A Sicilian lady giving me hard candy out of her pocketbook for my journey—the most potent of gestures. I felt blessed and knighted. I cried on the spot.

Ester invited me to Licata, where she brought me to piazza Giacomo Matteotti to see the marble plaque for seamstress Clotilde Terranova, engraved in classic lettering. From there, we went to viale 8 Marzo, where there's a sign, VIALETO CLOTILDE TERRANOVA, and other markers for women who lost their lives to various forms of violence. The peaceful garden and fountain provided a healing place for contemplating the tragic and violent endings of far too many women's lives.

Ester and Vanni drove me a couple of hours northwest from Licata to Villafranca Sicula, where Triangle Factory elevator operator Gaspare Mortillaro was born. As we drove up and down and around hills of fertile fields of grapevines and olive and almond and fig trees, I wished Clotilde and Gaspare could see Sicily now, that their paths could have crossed here instead of at Washington Place and Greene Street. I was jarred by the paradise from which they came. Driving through the verdant fields of Sicilian hills made the sting of Triangle that much more severe for me. We were all as grapes from these vines in this rocky, rich soil.

Ester arranged a visit with Mayor Mimmo Balsamo of Villafranca Sicula inside the town hall. On the wall just inside the entrance is a terracotta bas-relief by *villafranchese* artist Giovanni Smeraldi, dedicated to Gaspare Mortillaro. Featured in the sculpture: hands outstretched, reaching for help away from flames; faces with mouths open in calls for help; fields of grapes beneath the workers; a tall building on the corner, where girls sit at sewing machines; and on top of the building, out of the flames, a dove with wings wide in the sky. I was impressed by the depth of honor with which Mayor Balsamo spoke of Gaspare. Sitting in his office, I felt the gravitas of the moment.

I began to write this essay on April 2, 2018. Looking back to my earliest correspondence with Ruth Sergel, I realized it was exactly ten years ago to the day that about twenty of us voted via email to name our group Remember the Triangle Fire Coalition. There'd been a lively debate about what to call ourselves. No other verbs made it past the first round, but we debated a pantry of nouns: centennial, fire, coalition, commemoration, remembrance, 146, project, committee, memorial, factory, uprising, bread and roses. This was the first group decision I participated in with these activists and organizers and artists united around Triangle. Ruth set the plurality bar high—every voice would be heard as we volleyed toward consensus. Our operative verb became *to remember*. We came to Triangle from different paths, but we all agreed to remember, from our varied disciplines, in our own ways, and to join ranks as rememberers, and to nudge our city to remember and to act upon that memory.

There's something about a perceived link of vulnerabilities that connects me to Triangle. I am not a factory worker, nor am I an immigrant. But I relate to these girls. I began to "chalk" soon after we'd been evicted from our Brooklyn apartment in a rampant wave of gentrification in 2007. My life and the life of my family were vulnerable to the landlord class, which I saw as part of the same money-lusting fabric as the Triangle bosses who had locked the workers in the factory. My landlord's name was Mr. War. One day, Mr. War stopped me and my partner in the hallway and said he'd "give" us six months to vacate the apartment. It was his legal right to do so. We didn't know then that we were living through one of the epic redefinitions of New York City. Neighborhood thoroughfares filled with mom-and-pop businesses would soon be replaced by generic franchises, and prewar buildings would catapult to market rates of millions of dollars. The Park Slope neighborhood where we lived, where my uncle Frank was once an iceman, now hemorrhaged working-class and artist residents. Full-time artists, middle-aged, working-class, and LGBTQ—we were the people who lost our apartments, left our neighborhoods, and scattered to other people's homes, states or countries. We'd held out as long as we could, but one by one, despite our best hopes and strategies, we surrendered. Our community was shredded. Friendships and support systems foundered. I finally understood the cliché—tearing the fabric of society. That's what it felt like—the shearing of a community. Over the years, we'd each ponied up several hundred thousand dollars in rent. We'd paid the ticking meter of time. We'd bought the privilege of living within the city limits, on a dead-end path to losing our homes and each other as neighbors and community members.

If "geography is destiny"—as Napoleon reportedly said—then, in New York City, "real estate is destiny." The Asch Building, at 23–29 Washington Place, erected between 1900 and 1901, one hundred feet wide and about ninety feet deep up Greene Street, ten stories high, was fireproof for its day. The building survived. The granite and limestone held the fire like a pizza oven.

The history of New York City as a home became alive for me in new ways when I began to chalk. The first names Ruth Sergel assigned me were Millie Prato, Rosie Bassino, and Rosie Grasso.

Ninety-three MacDougal Street was new when Millie Prato lived there. Built in 1900, in 2018 it rented for fifty-eight dollars a square foot, or $3,472 per month for a one-bedroom apartment. Realtors boast that it is "in the center of the action . . . less than a five-minute walk to Washington Square Park," a walk Millie Prato knew well—to the factory, where seamstresses earned a dime an hour on twelve-hour shifts. In 1925, the San Remo Café opened on the ground floor of 93 MacDougal, where bohemians and Beats hung out; Gore Vidal famously flirted at the bar with Jack Kerouac. In 2008, I got down on my knees on the sidewalk outside 93 and chalked Millie Prato's name and address and the years of her birth and death. From the sidewalk, I looked up at the facade of the building as a locus for Millie Prato's life, somewhere to place her alive, a doorway she pushed open, the roof over her head, the threshold she stepped through to come home—where she would never return on March 25, 1911. I pictured Millie turning her head, glancing at someone on the street, and saying "*Ciao*" as she walked into the building.

Ninety-seven West Houston, where Rosie Bassino lived, no longer existed in 2008. For Rosie, I walked fastidiously up and down Houston Street to hypothesize where number 97 must have been, between West Broadway and Thompson. I chose a spot to the right of a fancy store whose windows reflected shiny yellow streaks of taxi traffic, chalked her name and dates, shouted "Rosie!" up at the sky over the monolith building that spanned the block, and waited. I imagined Rosie looking both ways, laughing, crossing Houston southward on her way home from her shift.

One hundred and seventy-four Thompson Street was next to a Japanese restaurant in 2008. The kitchen workers routinely sat smoking on the step in front of what had once been Rosie Grasso's front door. I called her name up at the building and down the street. Then I got down on the sidewalk and chalked. Rosie Grasso was always the most vivid in my imagination, partly because of her age—sixteen.

Italo Calvino writes of the "daily massacre of the city." The same downtown that promised Rosie Grasso a place she could try her luck—the mountains of edifices, with doors, if only they opened—exacts a cost, and for Rosie, the price was life itself. The city bears some culpability. Calvino aptly critiqued city life: "There's a guilty way of inhabiting the city; to accept the condition of the ferocious beast to whom we dangle our children to be devoured." The city both saves and slays us. For all that the city has to give, for all the times that urban subculture saves our lives by offering us freedoms we never could have imagined, for all the chances, for work opportunities, for life-changing universities, lifesaving hospitals, for the freedom of anonymity in diverse crowds, for that New York feeling that your life could change just by walking down the street, for all that, a toll is exacted in blood on streets and sidewalks and out the windows of impossibly tall edifices where fire climbs higher into the sky than rescuers. Desperate shards of hope in the moment of jumping—whether from the ninth floor, like Daisy Lopez Fitze, or the 106th floor of the North Tower of the World Trade Center, like "the falling man"—that below, there just might be some giant cushion, or a net strong enough to catch one's body. It is a moment of no choice at all. Open air offers the last hope and nothing to hold on to but city sky in blues and whites, with tidal waves of fire and smoke blasting workers out of windows.

With the progressive legislation that passed in the fire's wake, Triangle workers became martyrs, and their names rallying cries. No legislative progress would have been made without the help, attention, presence, fund-raising, large platforms, bail money put up for strikers, and passion of wealthy, educated women. Society deems some lives dispensable, sacrificeable. The sacrificial class. Lives that are not safeguarded or protected, but massacred by negligence, indifference, distrust, and greed. Cannon fodder. It is only when wealth and privilege came to the aid of sweatshop workers that tragedy and oppression transformed into legislative action and multiple streaks of sociopolitical change.

Just a week after the fire, the plight of the shirtwaist makers was heard at the Metropolitan Opera House, not in the form of an opera, but a meeting that demanded change, hosted by Anne Tracy Morgan, daughter of John Pierpont Morgan and Frances Louise Tracy. Dubbed "the mink brigade" in the press, during the 1909 Uprising these socialite advocates had picketed alongside sweatshop girls. They had donned fur muffs and collars, a visual counterpoint that offered dissuasion against otherwise brutal police action against picketers. *The New York Times* headlined Anne Morgan as saying, "We can't live our own lives without doing something to help them." Although the word *them* stings me as a reinforcement of class divisions, I am a believer in cross-class coalition building, and I appreciate Morgan's underlying sentiment. It is this compulsion that brings many of us to Triangle—this overwhelming unsettledness that something must be done to right the capsized boat.

Cross-class collaboration and intersectionality of movements strengthens coalition building and develops resources and political sway. Uptown women aligned the suffrage movement with the union movement. Alva Vanderbilt Belmont and Fola La Follette, daughter of suffrage leader Belle Case La Follette, joined the cause. Fola La Follette wrote and acted. She was a founding member of Actors' Equity, of which I and others in the coalition are proud members. The link of women, through Triangle, over the course of the past hundred years, fascinates me. I fantasize that we can all be in one room together. For a brief moment, some of us actually were alive at the same time. I was six when La Follette died. It makes me think of those young grade-school kids in the Triangle commemoration crowds I've sung to, the children who come to carry shirtwaists. We gotta talk more with the six-year-olds.

In 2009, one of my favorite high school buddies, Rosie Imperato, returned to live in New York City. I invited her to a coalition meeting. I remember telling Rosie that in the coalition were the best-hearted New Yorkers that I knew: artists, organizers, activists, union workers, descendants of Triangle workers. I remember feeling that it was these girls who brought us all together. They were still sewing, stitching, ruching, winding bobbins, only now it was our lives across a hundred years they linked. In my artist's mind, I heard them singing, and I saw them walking in the Village to and from work. I shared all this with Rosie as we walked into a room on lower Broadway, the city darkening around us. As we entered the room, we saw a dozen or so people sitting around a square table, passing around homemade rugelach baked by Natalie Sosinsky and Italian cookies. It could have been 1911. The faces and names of Triangle workers could have been our own—we had the same faces, the same names as in 1911, when we lost thirteen Rosies, eleven Anns, eight Jennies, six Sarahs, six Marys.

At one pivotal coalition meeting, Ruth Sergel led a go-around, directing us to put ideas on the table for what we wanted to see happen for the centennial memorial. Ruth gave us a directive: Say only ideas you are ready to commit to and work hands-on to make happen. After the go-around, we would break up into working groups to make action plans. I saw shirtwaist kites, silky, rippling in the breeze, installed on the facade of 23–29 Washington Place, upward at angles, and at night, underlit, brighter than the UN. But Ruth's direction harkened me to think pragmatically, to take stock of my own energy and resources, and how much running around I had the health to do. This wasn't a go-around for big ideas, but for commitments and follow-through work. For work, I had to ask myself, What can I commit to do? Sentences, phrases, lyrics, melodies—I could make on my own, even if I was in bed, sick. Writing was a street game. You didn't need fancy clubs or rackets or club memberships, or even a goddamn ball. You just had to do it. What was brightest in my mind were the faces of the hundreds of schoolkids in the crowd at the memorial events. At the ninety-ninth memorial, my band sang a couple of original songs and protest anthems. Ed Vargas, who would become the director of Labor Relations for the New York State Department of Labor, was the annual emcee for the ceremony. He shouted to me to stay out there and keep singing. I looked out over the crowd. Hundreds of schoolchildren wore red firemen's hats. I bandied back and forth with the kids. I wanted the kids to have an inspiring message, not just be traumatized by images of the carnage of the fire. I wanted to uplift the kids. I shouted, "Look up at the building!" I talked about Joe Zito and his heroics, how he saved girls in the elevator. I directed the kids to shout "Thanks, Joe! Thanks, Joe-oh-oh. Thanks, Joe! Thanks, Joe-oh-oh." We chanted this over and over. The kids smiled, focused on a hero. The day after that memorial, I received a message from

Joe Zito's great-granddaughter, Jane Fazio-Villeda, who told me she had been in the crowd with her son Nick, and that of all the years she'd gone to the memorials, no one had ever thanked her grandfather. The focus had always been on the victims, not the survivors. We began a correspondence, in which she shared information and documents about her grandfather's life before and after Triangle. All this flashed in my mind as my turn came in the big group go-around, and of all the ideas in my head, the words that came out of my mouth were, "I commit to sing an unsung hero. I will write a ballad for Joe Zito." A praise song for an Italian American hero. The chorus, I could already sing in my mind:

> Lemme tell you 'bout Joe Zito,
> The kinda man you wanna know.
> Selfless acts of courage were his destiny.
> Elevator Man! Triangle Factory!

And so, when we broke up into working groups, I sat alone, lifted my pen, and turned a clean page in my notebook.

The New York City real estate boom displaced around 30 percent of the coalition's core working group. Many of us were part of one vulnerable group working to remember in the public sphere another fatally vulnerable group: fallen garment workers. We fund-raised and volunteered while our own livelihoods in the city were threatened by the same forces of the hydra of unchecked greed. In *Twenty Years at Hull House*, one of my heroes, Jane Addams, railed against "aesthetic reflection." Yet that's all I really seemed able to do in the movement most of the time: just write the next poem or song or create the next vision. The combination of a compromised immune system from cancer and cancer treatments and the condition of poverty makes it so that I cannot count on breathing or stamina or immunity or cash to get me to meetings and street actions or a job to affect policy, or to run for office, or commit to legwork. But I can write the next piece, come up with the next idea. When Rosie Imperato, who'd joined the coalition board and worked tirelessly, telephoned me and said, "We need a visual" for the Labor Day Parade, I was able to still myself, go deep, meditate, quiet my mind, and let myself

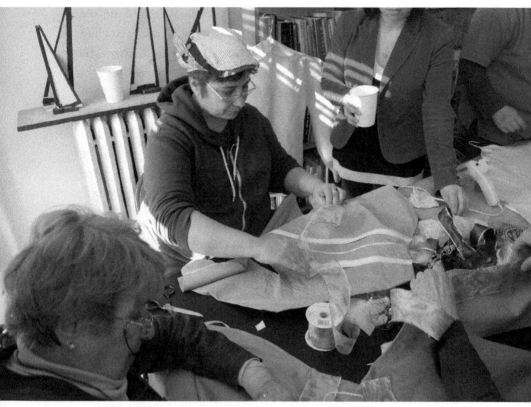

Figure 1.2. Sewing Circle—Annie and her mother, Rachele, sewing shirtwaist kites for the centennial memorial at the home of LuLu LoLo and Dan Evans, 331 E 116th St, New York, NY, 2011. Photo by Roy Campolongo; courtesy of the photographer.

be shaken to the core by some ancestral voice: *Make 146 shirtwaists like kites in the sky.* I called Rosie back and described the concept and vision to her, then sent her an image of a shirtwaist with mutton sleeves. She rendered a bigger than life-size sketch, and a working group of coalition members inspired by the concept got to work on fabricating mock-ups. Step by step, people added to the design and structure to make the shirtwaists fly, and the project organically built around a whole community of over a hundred coalition members gathering for shirtwaist factory days to make all 146. We did everything with our own hands, on the cheap.

We worked at several sites, but our shirtwaist factory with a magical luster of this cross-generational art project resided at artist LuLu LoLo's house, 331 East 116th Street. LuLu dedicated a room in her house to Triangle memorabilia and historic photos, shirtwaists, and props from her play *Soliloquy for a Seamstress*. Her house was our community shrine, museum, and gathering ground. We brought bolts of fabric and notions and trim from Materials for the Arts. LuLu's husband, Dan Evans, gave tours of the Crabapple Chapel in their backyard. Our community had a locus, a home. Creating art for Triangle memorial events was something we could do together. I brought my mother, Rachele, to these sewing and craft days of making the shirtwaist kites. Lace, buttons, bobbins and thread, notions and trim, cross-stitches and running stitches were my mother's vocabulary. Her skill and memory of shirt ruching offered an education for me and other people around the worktable.

Three Hundred Thirty One still stands, but we lost it as our community space. The upkeep was out of reach. We did not rally around the sustainability of housing for the artists among us. Real estate, as it is organized in our urban society, is a cornerstone for community engagement. A loss of real estate created a fissure in our community as we lost our gathering ground. I've fought in recent years to keep a roof over my head, a rent-stabilized lease, protection from so many elements. Doors. Windows. A fire escape. Locks that open. Smoke detectors in two rooms. In the coalition, we weren't fighting for housing for middle-aged female independent artists in New York City, but some of us should have been. I should have been. No one was advocating for us, not even ourselves. Many of the full-time, female, middle-aged, independent working artists in the room would lose our New York City housing within a couple of years of one another. Ruth Sergel would go to the next affordable neighborhood after outer Brooklyn—Berlin. After swaths of Brooklyn were gentrified, after artists moved to Berlin, word was that the next affordable neighborhood was Napoli. Meanwhile in Napoli, there was a squatters housing movement: Magnamecce o Pesone, whose members were being pushed out of their flats by the wave of housing being converted into hotels and Airbnb lodgings. In their rallying cry, I heard the many intonations of ouroburus, the tail devourer. The bodies of the sacrificial class are on the line time and again. Is it possible to eat oneself to sustain one's life?

I was back to sleeping on the floor of my mother's rent-stabilized apartment. The category I checked on government forms was the designation "homeless/staying on couch of family/friends." The 2000 U.S. census estimated "couch-surfers" at more than five million.

I am a mix of the impoverished immigrant roots of the Triangle workers and the educated and socially connected who trellised their plight with political prowess. I am part of a generation of artists who moved back to the very tenement buildings our parents' generation had worked to lift their families out of, a trend that created a generation gap of chagrin. Worse than that was the deep well of shame we felt when we were priced-out from those same tenement buildings. The arc of epidemics, from AIDS to gentrification, resulted in an erasure of LGBTQ lives and underground culture as we knew it. Over the years, the underground would reinvent and pop up elsewhere. The term *pop-up* took on a new meaning. Where the city lost mom-and-pop shops and small bookstores lost their leases, soon a pop-up gay bookstore was created that moved from place to place. Perhaps we will move toward nomadic culture. For now, we clutch onto what housing we have. The immensity of loss and duration of stress drove many LGBTQ working-class artists into mental health crises. For all our efforts in the struggle for survival and LGBTQ civil rights, there was a collective toll on our lives and community that can easily go unnoticed in a city that "prospers."

When I think of Rosie Grasso, I grieve. I can't pass Thompson Street without calling her name. This is true for all the streets I've chalked. Rosie! on Thompson Street; Josephine! on Cornelia; Millie! on MacDougal; Michelina! on Bleecker; Catherine! on Bedford; Rosie! on Houston; Frances! and Bettina! on Sullivan; Ida! on Fourth; Sadie! on Sixth; Daisy! on Charleton. I call for them, as we did in the Bronx of my childhood—standing outside someone's building and shouting the person's name up at the windows, just as our ancestors did in the *paesi* and shtetls where so many of the seamstresses were born.

Getting down on the concrete sidewalk to chalk and lifting a shirt-waist kite at the intersection of Washington and Greene are now New York City spring rituals, acknowledgments of our common hopes and fragility. They are reminders of all things ephemeral: our lives, names, homes, bodies, in relationship with the body of the city. Every spring I see chalkers' hands and knees marked in the pastels of chalk dust and black street grit. On the sidewalks of New York, I see Ash Wednesday churchgoers, foreheads crossed with ashes. I see green-clad revelers walk by and hear Saint Patrick's Day bagpipes. I notice the rise of purple crocuses. These are the signifiers of the last frigid days of winter and the cyclical victory of spring. Green shoots raise their poles, then pink and purple blooming flags pop open above concrete, asphalt, steel, iron, and glass. I chalk. I lift a shirtwaist kite in the sky. I hand one over to a youth who, for the first time, learns the history. This is how I know spring is here.

CHAPTER 2

The New Deal Began with My Grandmother Frances Perkins

▼

Tomlin Perkins Coggeshall
and the Reverend Charles Hoffacker

I remember eating arrowroot biscuits in bed with my grandmother. We were at her family place, The Brick House, in Newcastle, Maine. The house had been a wedding present from her great-grandfather, Edmund Perkins, to his son, Edmund junior and his bride, Cynthia Otis Perkins, in 1837. Until my grandmother died, in 1965, my parents and I made an annual eight-hour drive from New York City to Maine to spend the summer at The Brick House. My grandmother would usually come from Ithaca, New York, where she lived at the time and was a guest professor at the School of Industrial and Labor Relations (ILR) at Cornell University, to spend a few weeks with us.

In the morning, I would often climb in bed with her and we would nibble arrowroot biscuits, which she kept in her room, while we talked about whatever was on my mind. Beatrix Potter books were close at hand. It felt safe and cozy. I was her only grandchild and felt her warm, intelligent, and loving energy flowing in my direction. It was 1959. I was five years old. She was almost eighty.

One morning, I asked her about a cardboard box she kept below a windowsill in her bedroom. I was fascinated by its contents: two strands of rope with multiple wooden crosspieces. Grandma explained, "Oh, that's a rope ladder fire escape we could use in case there is a bad fire in the house and we need a way out." My curiosity piqued, I asked,

Figure 2.1. The upper right window is the one that little Tomlin climbed down to test the ladder at the Perkins Homestead. Photo by Cervin Robinson; courtesy of the Library of Congress, Prints & Photographs Division, Historic American Buildings Survey, HABS ME, 8-NEWC, 2-1.

"Could we try it?" Sensing that I was ready for a new experience, she said that indeed we could.

The windowsills were low in the upstairs of the house, only about eight inches off the floor. The rope ladder was attached to the sill and consisted of a single length of rope looped back upon itself, with each wooden rung connected between the two strands on both sides. The top of the loop was fastened to the sill with a wooden block held in place by three large screws, probably installed by a workman she had hired years back.

Grandma opened the window and together we lowered the rope ladder outside until none of it remained in the box. Attached to the first rung (the last rung to be dropped out the window) were two metal brackets that pushed it away from the house to provide space between the rope ladder and the house so one could grasp the rungs without getting fingers scraped. The ladder reached almost to the ground.

Figure 2.2. Little Tomlin with his maternal
grandmother, Frances Perkins.
Photographer unknown;
photo courtesy of Tomlin Coggeshall.

"May I try it?" I asked.

I'm not sure if she gave me permission or advised against doing
so, or if I decided to go ahead and climb down. I know that she did
not try to stop me. After I reached the ground, I came right back up. I
reported that the ladder had worked perfectly.

Testing out the ladder successfully, as I did that day with my grandmother, gave me a sense of affirmation and preparation that I still call
upon. I've lived a good life, with guidance and support from many, but
I still feel that I received one of my earliest doses of confidence and
belief in myself from my grandmother. She embodied something more
reliable, solid, and dependable than did my parents. My mother, her
daughter, was unpredictable and often had loud arguments with my
father. He was a gentle and intellectual man, an abstract artist, whom I
came to love more and more as he grew older. He stood by my mother
regardless of the emotional turmoil that she often generated.

My mother's personality had many dimensions, but her mostly untreated bipolar disorder was probably at the root of the turmoil in my family life and between my parents that I witnessed as a child. Her father, Paul Wilson, also had bipolar disorder, but in his day, there was no diagnosis and no treatment. Although I inherited it myself and have had very difficult experiences, I am very fortunate, unlike my mother or her father, to live in a time when there is an understanding of the disease and treatment options. Not until the last few years of her life did my mother have access to the supplements and drugs that have alleviated my symptoms. Consequently, my mother self-medicated with alcohol to ease the sometimes overwhelming anxiety that, I now realize, she felt. Often, she would drink into the wee hours of the morning. She would become loud and belligerent. It was difficult to have such an erratic mother, though she was also very loving to me. And I loved her very much. There were lots of good times. She had many wonderful traits, including a brilliant mind and the ability to be the life of a cocktail party with her equally brilliant circle of friends.

As long as she was alive, my grandmother represented a counterpoint to the turbulence that I experienced at home. When I was with my grandmother, there was a steadiness and a clear understanding of what was happening and how things were to be done. I still feel her steadiness and wisdom today, and the sense she gave me not only of the right way to do things but also what might be worth doing. A few years after I climbed down the rope ladder, I learned the reason why that cardboard box was in my grandmother's bedroom. Perhaps related to the talk that must have followed my climb down the rope ladder, my mother told me a story about when she had caused a fire in the lower field on a dry August day. Apparently, Mum was taking a ride on her pony. At one point, she lit a cigarette, not noticing that the field was tinder-dry. Either her discarded match or an ash she flicked from her cigarette set the field on fire. The flames spread quickly. To this day, that field is marked by ditches carved by a neighbor's bulldozer in a hasty but effective effort to make firebreaks. My grandmother must have been very upset at her daughter's carelessness but also thankful for how the neighbor's quick work contained the fire. Only much later in life did I realize why my grandmother was so very cautious about fire. As far as I can remember, my grandmother and I never talked about her work; I guess I was too young in her eyes.

On March 25, 1911, my grandmother was thirty years old, not yet married to my grandfather, and studying for a master's degree at Columbia University. In between her studies, she also worked for her friend and mentor, Florence Kelley, who hired her as the executive secretary of the National Consumers League's New York office. The focus of the Consumer League's work was to expose and oppose the harsh, unregulated, and unsafe working conditions that many Americans endured to manufacture consumer products.

On the afternoon of that March 25, my grandmother was visiting a friend who lived on Washington Square. The guests had just sat down to tea when they heard fire whistles, bells, and shouts. My grandmother rushed over to see what was happening. She saw flames coming out of the ten-story Asch Building, where she knew that hundreds of workers were employed at the Triangle Waist Company on the top three floors. She watched in horror as many young workers died a horrific death.

My grandmother was deeply shaken by what she witnessed. She knew that almost two years earlier the garment workers in that very building had gone on strike and had been rebuffed and persecuted. A week after the fire, she attended a large public meeting at the Metropolitan Opera House, called by a group of leading citizens. Rose Schneiderman, a fiery immigrant trade union leader in her twenties, gave a historic address, speaking passionately about workers maimed and killed due to horrendous sweatshop conditions. My grandmother realized that much more might be required of her than she had imagined before the fire. Making workplaces safer and more humane would call for an intense lifelong commitment on her part. The Triangle Shirtwaist Factory fire became a catalyst for her work to promote widespread social change. Although Franklin Delano Roosevelt would not be elected president until 1932, my grandmother later recognized March 25, 1911, as the day the New Deal began. It also marked an important moment in her conversion to the world. Brought up in the Congregational Church, my grandmother became an Episcopalian in her early adulthood. Her faith guided her career and gave her strength to persevere.

Christianity, Frances Perkins's lifelong faith, is a religion of conversion. In many cases, there is not just one conversion but a series of turnings toward, which include turning toward God, Christ, the church, the sacraments, or the Scriptures. Conversions (and reconversions) can be subtle or dramatic, gradual or sudden. There can also be a conversion toward the world. Here the world is not to be taken as creation or as a society organized against God—as in the old phrase "the world, the flesh, and the devil"—but, rather, a creation beloved by God and suffering because of human sin, a creation that is broken and desperate for repair. Frances Perkins recognized the world as beloved by God. She saw its brokenness and responded through compassionate service that led her to high public office. Witnessing the Triangle fire began for her a new and deeper conversion to the world. In time, her actions, based on and motivated by her experience of the Triangle fire, produced many positive changes, including commonsense safety practices that today we take for granted, among them exit signs, fire drills, fire doors, multiple extinguishers, and workplace waste containers that are emptied daily.

Some politicians talk about their faith because they assume that doing so may win them public support. The U.S. Constitution disallows a religious test for public office. So does my Christian conscience. When it comes to deciding how to vote, I am not concerned with the conversions a candidate may have experienced—with one exception. I would like to know if the candidate has undergone a significant conversion to the world. Such a conversion can happen to people who belong to different religious communities or none at all. What matters to me is whether the candidate deeply recognizes the beauty and brokenness of creation and humanity.

When former president Teddy Roosevelt was asked to chair the Committee on Safety, a privately funded body formed in the wake of the Triangle fire, he suggested that Frances Perkins serve as executive director. She later commented, "The Triangle fire was a torch that lighted up the whole industrial scene." Teddy Roosevelt and my grandmother had been corresponding about social reform issues and she had been investigating and researching fire safety issues for the Consumers League. She had already warned that New York City was loaded with firetraps. After the Triangle fire, her fire-prevention expertise came to be very much in demand. New York State Assembly member and future governor Al Smith served on the Committee on Safety with my grandmother. They became good friends in the process. He would later envision and support social reforms that improved the lives of workingmen and women in New York State. After the Triangle fire, Smith worked with state senator Robert Wagner to establish the Factory Investigating Commission, in which my grandmother came to play a pivotal role. She seized the opportunity to show both the public and politicians the decrepit and dangerous conditions that threatened the safety of workers every day. On one occasion, she took Wagner to an upstate factory where the so-called fire escape required crawling through a tiny hole in the wall that exited to an iron ladder covered with ice and that ended twelve feet above the ground.

The Factory Investigating Commission possessed subpoena power and was designed to propose legislation. Its mandate was expanded to address not only fire hazards but also dangerous chemicals and other safety issues. Countless civic groups, experts, and workers appeared before this investigative body. Commissioners investigated 3,385 workplaces, heard testimony amounting to more than seven thousand pages, and conducted fifty-nine hearings across the state, as documented by the U.S. Department of Labor. Among their legislative accomplishments was a law that limited the workweek to ten hours a day, six days a week. The state laws to which my grandmother contributed still form the basis for New York labor laws and fire codes. They also established a model on which city and state fire codes are based throughout the nation and the world.

In her work with the Factory Investigating Commission and elsewhere, my grandmother demonstrated adherence to several common-sense principles. First, she was willing to get her hands dirty. Not only did she visit and explore grimy industrial sites; she also embraced practical politics, which included working with New York's famous (and sometimes notorious) Tammany Hall. She made alliances for the common good wherever she found willing partners. Second, she had great respect for data. Perhaps it reflected the fact that she had graduated from Mount Holyoke College with a degree in chemistry and physics. After she became FDR's labor secretary, she transformed the Bureau of Labor Statistics into a model of reliability and objectivity. Hard facts could be put to the service of high principles. In addition, she relied on her background in social work—at the dawn of social work as a professional field, she applied the conference method to public problems, such as dangerous workplaces where politicians and social workers needed to cooperate. Stephen Paul Miller explored this subject in *The New Deal as a Triumph of Social Work: Frances Perkins and the Confluence of Early Twentieth Century Social Work with Mid-Twentieth Century Politics and Government.*

Frances Perkins promoted better working conditions through a method then considered novel: large public meetings and conferences. Her initial successes led to additional legislative victories in such areas as minimum wage, workers' compensation, women's suffrage, and government reorganization. In these fields, New York State set examples for the nation. As they worked together from 1928 to 1932, Frances Perkins and then New York State governor Franklin Roosevelt were, perhaps unknowingly, paving the way for the federal New Deal.

When I was a schoolboy in New York City, I participated in fire drills as a matter of course. It was essential, we were told, to practice vacating a building quickly in the event of fire. These drills were fun: They always came as a surprise, bringing to a halt whatever we were doing so that we could scramble outside to be counted. I didn't know then that my grandmother had had a hand in these exercises, since she worked closely with the National Fire Prevention Association (NFPA) to institute better safety requirements for workplaces—which must have affected schools, as well.

Witnessing the Triangle fire was a pivotal event in my grandmother's life. So was another event that took place in New York City more than twenty years after the fire, and after my grandmother had already served in the administrations of New York governors Al Smith and Franklin Roosevelt. On a cold night in February 1933, Frances Perkins met with Franklin Roosevelt at his residence on East Sixty-fifth Street. He would be inaugurated as president of the United States the next month, and he wanted my grandmother to serve as secretary of labor. If she accepted, she would be the first woman to serve as a member of a presidential cabinet. She arrived at the Roosevelt home with a hastily written list of what she wanted to accomplish if she were to become labor secretary. If she was going to Washington, she wanted to get something done. During their meeting, she brought up each item: a forty-hour workweek; minimum wage; workers' compensation; unemployment compensation; a federal ban on child labor; direct federal aid to states for unemployment relief; old-age pension (which would come to be known as Social Security); a revitalized public employment service; and national health insurance. Her list of proposed programs was nothing less than a restructuring of American society and economy in the midst of the national crisis we call the Great Depression. Roosevelt said he would not oppose her working on the items on her list and so, with the regrettable exception of health insurance, all the points on my grandmother's list were realized through New Deal legislation. Although most of these programs met with thunderous opposition and continue to be resisted—to some extent—the New Deal happened and changed America forever. Countless people helped bring it about, but I believe my grandmother's biographer, Kirstin Downey, was correct when she titled her book *The Woman Behind the New Deal.*

The family home in Newcastle, Maine, still bears witness to my grandmother's caution regarding fires and her universal concern for people. Boxes of sand for putting out fires remain at the base of the cellar stairs as well as in the barn. Signs that read PLEASE DO NOT SMOKE IN ANY PART OF THIS BUILDING, F. PERKINS remain posted on inside walls of sheds and the barn for all to see. This house, now known as the Frances Perkins Homestead, was designated a National Historic Landmark in 2014. In January 2020, it was purchased by the Frances Perkins Center.

Founded in 2008, and also located in Newcastle, Maine, the Frances Perkins Center honors my grandmother's legacy by furthering her commitment to the principle that government should provide all the people under its jurisdiction with the best-possible life. It also preserves the family home that shaped her character as a place to further her work focused on social justice and economic security for all. The Frances Perkins Center convenes leaders and future leaders in labor, public policy, and related fields to generate creative solutions to today's social and economic problems. It also teaches students of all ages about a remarkable woman whose work continues to better the lives of ordinary Americans. In addition, the Frances Perkins Center bestows annual awards to honor people whose work for social justice and economic security exemplifies the spirit of my grandmother. I am delighted whenever one of these awards is bestowed, for each of them honors someone who is carrying my grandmother's work into the twenty-first century.

The past twenty years have seen a resurgence of interest in my grandmother's life, her faith, and her work, beginning with Downey's biography, published in 2009. In the same year, she was honored as a public servant and prophetic witness by being given an annual feast day (May 13) on the Episcopal Church's calendar of saints. A prayer for that day describes her as someone who "sought to build a society in which all may live in health and decency." Frances Perkins is likely not the only saintly grandmother. Other saintly grandmothers, most of them not widely known, may be helping to hold together our troubled world in ways we barely understand. I am grateful that my grandmother's saintliness has been officially recognized by her church, which is also my church. Lectures that she gave in 1948 at St. Thomas Church in New York City are the basis of the first book devoted to her faith, *Tread the City's Streets Again: Frances Perkins Shares Her Theology*, by Donn Mitchell, published in 2019.

A high point of interest in Frances Perkins was presidential candidate Elizabeth Warren's speech before a crowd in Washington Square Park, adjacent to the site of the Triangle fire, on September 16, 2019. This speech celebrated how my grandmother worked for big structural change out of her deep belief that government, if run effectively, can greatly improve people's lives. It was delivered from a specially commissioned podium that artisans in Brooklyn, New York, had crafted out of wood from the barn at the Frances Perkins Homestead. I felt deeply moved as I stood there that night and listened to Senator Warren recount my grandmother's story to a vast, cheering crowd:

> While the women of the trade unions kept pushing from the outside, Frances pushed from the inside. She understood that these women died because of the greed of their bosses and the corruption of elected officials.
>
> So she went up to Albany, ready to fight. . . .
>
> So, what did one woman—one very persistent woman—backed by millions of people across this country get done? Social Security. Unemployment insurance. Abolition of child labor. Minimum wage. The right to join a union. Even the very existence of the weekend. Big, structural change. One woman, and millions of people to back her up.
>
> The tragic story of the Triangle Factory fire is a story about power.
>
> A story of what happens when the rich and the powerful take control of government and use it to increase their own profits while they stick it to working people.
>
> But what happened in the aftermath of the fire is a different story about power—our power, about what's possible when we all fight together as one.

What happened in the aftermath of the Triangle fire was an important chapter in my grandmother's life and the story of millions of working people in our country—a story about the United States of America at our best.

My grandmother died in 1965. She is buried in Newcastle, the place on Earth that she most considered home. Beyond the Frances Perkins Center and Homestead and her nearby grave site, there is another memorial to her in Newcastle that bears testimony to who she was—and is. At St. Andrew's Episcopal Church, an icon of Frances Perkins is on permanent display. This colorful sacred image is not a conventional

Figure 2.3. Saint Frances Perkins icon at St. Andrew's Church, Newcastle, Maine. Icon by Suzanne Schleck. Photo by Tomlin Coggeshall; courtesy of the photographer.

portrait. Rather, through the principles of traditional iconography, it bears witness to her current life in God. The icon depicts my grandmother in glory, wearing clothing of her time and her signature tricorn hat, holding an open scroll. On the scroll appears a statement she wrote to her friend Justice Felix Frankfurter after she retired from government, in which she explained her vocation as secretary of labor: "I came to Washington to work for God, FDR, and the millions of forgotten, plain, common workingmen."

It is an extraordinary experience for me to gaze upon this holy icon and recall the days when my grandmother and I shared arrowroot biscuits, safe and snug in bed together, prepared to escape a fire, however unlikely, thanks to her experience from the Triangle fire and wisdom from her New England upbringing, most of it passed on to her from her grandmother Cynthis Otis Perkins.

My work on the formation of the Frances Perkins Center has been a journey of discovery and teamwork. I've been able to use many skills that I have acquired during my varied career. I like to think that some of my grandmother's social skills needed to build consensus and momentum might have been expressed through me. I am honored to have worked with so many people to build an organization that, in my grandmother's name, works for social justice and economic security for all. I expect to be involved with the Frances Perkins Center for the foreseeable future, but I have other passions and interests that I intend to pursue, as well. These include climate-change management, accelerating the transition to hydrogen as fuel for electric vehicles, stock market reform, and the reintroduction of improved forms of nuclear power as part of the clean energy mix, to name a few. In everything I do, I feel my grandmother encouraging me, helping me make good decisions, and, at times, showing me the best way forward.

CHAPTER 3

The Triangle Factory Fire
and the City of Two Who Survived

▼

Ellen Gruber Garvey

New York City could have plaques on every building to explain our history and memories. In this apartment an immigrant family of eight cooked and slept in three rooms and sewed buttonholes all day. That Lower East Side condo building used to house the *Jewish Daily Forward*. The building just off Washington Square used to house the Triangle Waist Company. This street is where thousands marched in 1911 to mourn the dead of the Triangle fire, and decades later, for better housing and to protect immigrants.

The Asch Building (now the Brown Building) does have a plaque and will soon have a monument—cloth panels cast in steel that will form a long ribbon down the building. I contributed five pieces of fabric to those panels, including one for my great-uncle Sam's father, Abraham Bernstein, who escaped the fire, and another for my friend Frances Goldin's mother, Sophie Sasslovsky, who luckily lost her job at Triangle two weeks before the fire for talking to a union organizer.

Abraham's piece is embroidered table linen, blotched by spilled wine, as if it had been used at a family dinner. Abraham valued his family ties over loyalty to other workers at the Triangle Factory—or to the truth, I've discovered.

On Sophie's piece I stamped a parading chain of sewing machines. After Sophie came to the United States from Tsarist Russia when she

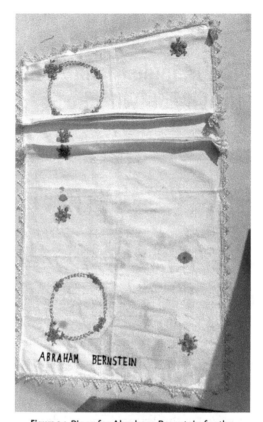

Figure 3.1. Piece for Abraham Bernstein for the Triangle Fire Memorial. This pleated piece represents Sam's work as a tucker. The Collective Ribbon, March 17, 2019, Fashion Institute of Technology, New York, NY. Photo by Ellen Gruber Garvey; courtesy of the photographer.

was about sixteen, she helped seventeen family members immigrate to the United States, bringing first those who could sew best and earn money to bring the others. Sewn to the piece are likely the only lacy purple panties in the memorial, embroidered with the words *safety* and *freedom* in honor of her ninety-five-year-old daughter, Frances Goldin, a lifelong housing activist.

I started digging into my family's involvement in the Triangle factory after I moved to Lewis Street on the Lower East Side a few years ago. Many Triangle workers once lived in my new neighborhood. Many

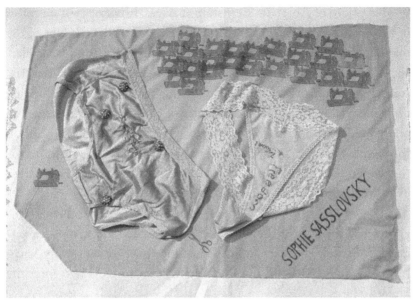

Figure 3.2. Piece for Sophie Sasslovsky for the Triangle Fire Memorial, decorated with rubber-stamped sewing machines. The Collective Ribbon, Fashion Institute of Technology, New York, NY, March 17, 2019. Photo by Richard Joon Yoo; courtesy of the Collective Ribbon Archive.

of their houses would have been demolished in city planner Robert Moses's 1959 urban renewal schemes, but Frances Goldin and her friends founded a group that saved the neighborhood from demolition. Across Manhattan, Jane Jacobs organized to save Washington Square Park from the same plans. Photos of Fran agitating in different parts of New York City hang in her apartment—picketing greedy landlords, running for state legislature alongside W. E. B. Du Bois on Vito Marcantonio's American Labor Party ticket, marching against gentrification, and cheering on the LGBT Pride March. Her mother, Sophie, retreated to safety in Queens, but she passed along her Triangle story, and Fran enlarged and deepened her own life by fighting against the powerful, hand in hand with her neighbors and community. Fran's work ties the world of the Triangle fire and older labor and leftist movements to current progressive battles and the streets of the Lower East Side. All her marches ought to have worn grooves into the streets of Lower Manhattan.

No photo of Abraham Bernstein survives. His story left no traces in the neighborhood, but his testimony marked the transcript of the manslaughter trial of the Triangle owners, Max Blanck and Isaac Harris. My great-uncle Sam—Abraham's son—also appears in the trial transcript. Abraham's distressing story emerges in census and shipping data, the trial record, and oral histories of workers. He was a recently arrived older sewing machine operator who must have gotten his job through his relatives in management at Triangle, and then testified for the owners. Abraham compromised with the powerful to protect his own small corner of the universe.

These older immigrant stories echo in the lives of today's immigrants and the attacks they face: They are bullied, imprisoned, separated from their children, and deported for no worse subterfuges than those my own and Fran's immigrant ancestors employed to enter the United States.

Juxtapositions

As a cultural historian, I study the ways ordinary people took control of information and put it to their own uses. I love that the nineteenth-century newspaper readers' scrapbooks I've researched are not preoccupied with family memorabilia and family photos. Each stretches outward, revealing how its maker read and understood events in the world. Reading them, I learned to notice the language of juxtaposition. Newspaper articles and fragments acquire meaning through proximity or omission. Juxtapositions can lead to new insights or connections. This is the case with my own and Fran's families' ship manifests and census records, and the transcript of the trial of the Triangle owners, who were married to Abraham's relatives.

The Triangle fire can seem a starkly gendered drama: callous male bosses and better-off male workers versus poor young women. One of the high-paid male cutters probably started the fire when his discarded cigarette butt ignited thin pattern paper and bins of fabric waste. A few stories bridge the gender divide: Joe Zito, the heroic elevator operator, rode up and down, rescuing workers until the cable gave way under the weight of people climbing on the elevator car; the factory manager, known to be mean, and "a dog," rescued people from the fire.

Men sewed, too. Abraham Bernstein sat at a sewing machine on the ninth floor and escaped by elevator. In one interview, Zito complained that "several men too . . . crowded their way into the car in spite of the girls." Abraham must have been among those men. No one in my family suggested that there had been anything wrong in his saving his own life. Who cared about chivalry, the sweetening on patriarchy, in a factory where women were underpaid, sexually harassed, and exploited? And what were the priorities when workers were desperate to earn enough to get their families out of perilous Europe? Half a year after the fire, Abraham could afford to bring over more relatives from Ukraine.

I was a teenager when my great-uncle Sam Bernstein told me that his father had escaped the fire. On March 25, 1911, Sam had run over from the nearby sweatshop where he sewed, and he had seen corpses on the sidewalk—one of them that of a cousin. Someone had cut off the dead man's finger, and taken his diamond ring. My older cousin Peter also remembered his grandpa Sam's story of the missing ring, and that Abraham was related to the owners. That was it for family Triangle conversation. Digging in records has turned up more.

My great-uncle Sam died in 1976. Frail and thin, he outlived his wife and first cousin, my ample, exuberant great-aunt, Anna Gruber Bernstein, by a decade and a half. Sam went from sewing to cutting to pattern making, though not at Triangle. He belonged to the ILGWU, which helped build Hillman Housing where, coincidentally, I now live. When I was a kid, the women in my family carried plastic rain bonnets in ILGWU cases in their purses—union swag. They unpacked homemade potato kugel and gefilte fish from shopping bags emblazoned JUDY BOND ON STRIKE: DON'T BUY JUDY BOND BLOUSES! Sam sang in the union chorus. I should have been proud of this, but I could not bear his quavery tenor at every family event as he sang "Is this the little girl I carried?" from *Fiddler on the Roof*. The synthetic Broadway schmaltz replaced stories about his real-life experience in the small Ukrainian town of Sossov, from which he had emigrated when he was fifteen. He tried to keep the culture alive in other ways. He once offered me the enormous sum of a dollar to taste gefilte fish. It looked revolting—pinkish, with fish jelly clinging to it. I refused. Now I love it.

Uncle Sam showed me how he went to fashion shows and sketched the new outfits to figure out how to make patterns from them. He gave me a dress from his workplace. It was matronly, with layers of floaty yellow chiffon, not something I would ever wear. Yet I kept it in my closet for a while out of a sense of obligation, the family connection to the garment trade, and the fascination for an object he had helped make.

Frances and Sophie

Sophie Sasslovsky was a forelady (sometimes her daughter Fran said "floor lady") at Triangle. But a boss spotted her talking to a union organizer in the stairwell and discharged her. Fran said Sophie had the forelady job because of her sewing skills. Foreladies, one survivor testified at the trial, went up and down the stairs and in and out of the doors throughout their workday. They had more mobility in the shop than the girls and women who sat at the long tables of sewing machines, enough mobility to be in the stairwell and talk to the organizer. Would she have run into Abraham, who testified he was in the stairwell?

Had Sophie not been saved, and Fran not been born, the Lower East Side would look very different from the way it does today. So would the literary landscape. When Fran, who was a literary agent as well as an activist, enthusiastically represented a manuscript about an Arizona miners' strike but couldn't find a publisher for it, its author, Barbara Kingsolver, mentioned that she had written a novel. *The Bean Trees* became a bestseller and launched Kingsolver's career. Fran created chains of connection. She traveled regularly to visit her client Mumia Abu-Jamal on death row near Pittsburgh. You might get pulled in to buy the chocolate she took to Mumia's supporters who put her up on those visits, or into picking up cucumbers at another friend's house for the tea with delicate sandwiches she served when Adrienne Rich came to the agency's office.

After I rummaged in the dry, eye-straining census and birth and death records, I asked Fran to check whether I'd found the right Sophie Sasslovsky. When I read the bare bureaucratic record to Fran, she wept at the mention of her siblings, all now dead. Fran's daughter told me that Sophie was talking with the union organizer because he was a good-looking fella, and she was sweet on him.

Since the 1970s, Fran has attended the gay pride parade in New York, carrying a sparkly sign that says I ADORE MY LESBIAN DAUGHTERS: KEEP THEM SAFE. Sophie's daughter, too, believes it's important to take risks for sex and love. She has two lesbian daughters, but whoever goes to the march with her can be her lesbian daughter for the day. People rush up to hug her. They weep, wishing they had a mother who would take such public pride in them. For years, she would offer to call their estranged parents to tell them what a wonderful child they had. Lately, Fran, her hair a radiant purple, sits in her wheelchair on the sidewalk, holding her sign as marchers parade by.

Fran never worked in a clothing factory, but she knew how to sew and darn. I can show you a couple of sweater elbows she elegantly took care of for me and my wife, stitching the torn edges together. After she helped stop Robert Moses from demolishing much of the Lower East Side, Fran went on to fight for affordable housing in that neighborhood. She kept her hands busy at the city's Board of Estimate meetings, stitching away at her mending pile of lacy bras and underpants. It distracted and discomfited the powerful men in the room, so they couldn't pay full attention to wheeling and dealing. She insisted on interjecting her ordinary life, her body, into a world where no one was supposed to think about bodies and their need for safe working conditions and good housing. The two lacy panties embroidered with the words *safety* and *freedom* that are part of the piece I made for Sophie thus commemorate Fran, too.

The neighborhood where I moved embraced new waves of immigrants and migrants from the Caribbean, Mexico, and China. When her housing group celebrated victories, Fran made blintzes while others unpacked homemade pernil and rice and beans from shopping bags emblazoned SAVE THE LOWER EAST SIDE. Fran danced salsa and merengue. I haven't always appreciated Fran's push to link everyone in chains of connection. Being sent across town to borrow a coffeepot for the party and check in on another neighbor along the way made me impatient. Couldn't we just buy another coffeepot? But now I'm part of a community, a new family, connected through the coffeepot, the chocolate, the cucumbers.

Digging into Family

In the papers that I inherited and schlepped from one apartment to another, without reading them until I moved to Lewis Street, I found notes from my great-aunt Anna, who married Sam and became Abraham's daughter-in-law. She died in 1961, in her sixties. A carbon copy of a letter by her sister celebrates Anna's care for the children she took in and praises her kind heart. Nothing in these papers about Sam or Abraham or the Triangle Factory. None of the family trees that people occasionally started and stuffed into the folders includes the people I want to know about. Cousin Carl Sagan once convened older family members at his home to fill out a genealogical chart. My mother was horrified to find that her brother had written in my then partner as my spouse. My mother did not adore her lesbian daughter.

Anna's younger sister Clara died at ninety, the last one standing. My sister and I used to try to get her to teach us some Yiddish, but she proudly, implausibly, claimed to have forgotten it all. My mother would dredge up a few phrases from childhood: *Er macht sich nisht gornisht visendik*, "He makes himself unknowing." It feels different from "He pretends not to know." I have learned that at the trial of the Triangle owners, Abraham made himself unknowing.

Why did Abraham Bernstein work at Triangle? Moishe, his eldest child, came to New York from Sossov in Ukraine in 1904, at around age sixteen. He changed his name to Morris. In 1908, Morris paid for the steerage ticket of his brother Schulim, who soon became Sam. Sam recalled the grueling time at sea as one month, though the records show it was ten days. According to other papers, and what he told the family, Sam was fifteen, but he told the steamship company he was seventeen and a journeyman tailor. When Morris paid for forty-seven-year-old Abraham's ticket, Abraham traveled the same route, on the same ship. He arrived in New York on April 3, 1910, in steerage, or "between decks," as the Hamburg steamship line indicates.

Abraham's arrival was sandwiched between the February 1910 end of the garment industry strike led by Triangle workers, which was savagely resisted by the Triangle owners, and the fire. He landed just in time to be included when the 1910 census taker knocked on the door of their Avenue C apartment. Sam, Morris, and Morris's wife, Tillie, told the census taker that they could speak English. Abraham could not. He did not find work until at least two weeks after he arrived. He was listed as a baker on the ship manifest but as a silk weaver on the 1910 census. In his late forties, perhaps he could not break into the baking business in New York, and was unwilling to go to nearby Paterson, New Jersey, to work in its silk-weaving mills, I speculate, piecing together a narrative from the records' fragments. Abraham's son Morris appeared as a locksmith on the ship manifest, but in New York he soon turned to work in ladies' waists, and by 1910 was an operator in that line. Sam also found work in ladies' waists.

I often meet immigrants now who were highly skilled and educated in their own countries—chemists, architects, pharmacists, teachers. But in the United States, they drive cabs or wash dishes or clean houses. Maybe Morris's locksmithing and Abraham's baking or silk weaving were skills that they had to abandon.

Before the fire, many immigrants considered the Triangle Waist Company a desirable, modern step up from piecework in a cramped tenement apartment. One fire victim, Yetta Goldstein, left her job at the Paterson silk mills to work at Triangle because she could make an additional dollar a week to send to her bedridden mother in Warsaw. Abraham might have been relieved to find a job at Triangle. Although he would have been an observant Jew back in Sossov, after being out of work in New York, a job at the Triangle Factory that entailed working on Saturdays seemed worth it.

It was likely his cousin, manager Samuel Bernstein, who got Abraham the job. There were many Bernsteins at Triangle. Witnesses at the trial of the owners explained family connections. The names double in on one another. Max Blanck was married to Bertha Bernstein Blanck. Her brothers were Samuel Bernstein, the manager, and Jacob, who died in the fire. They were Abraham's cousins, as were at least five other Bernsteins, and others with different last names.

Such a common name makes for a confusion of Bernsteins. Great-Uncle Sam and Great-Aunt Anna Bernstein lived in an apartment on the Grand Concourse in the Bronx, a neighborhood where many Jewish immigrants from the Lower East Side moved—including others named Sam Bernstein. They once received an invitation to a wedding of a couple they didn't know. Sam would have nothing to do with it, but why miss a wedding? Anna burst in on the Orthodox groom's all-male gathering table to congratulate him, and then ate and danced all evening, at least as she told it. Maybe the Sam Bernstein who didn't get his invitation was one of the Bernsteins in the factory.

Before she married Sam, Great-Aunt Anna traveled from Sassov along the same route as Abraham and her future husband. She arrived in the United States with her mother and two younger sisters on April 3, 1913, in second class. I found them in the immigrant arrival records, about to move in with their father and brothers on the Lower East Side. I was dumbstruck when I read they moved to Lewis Street, in a building long demolished. The address was exactly where I live now. I stared yearningly into the screen, hoping it would reveal more, and learned for the first time how young my always elderly great-aunts were when they arrived: Anna seventeen, Clara fifteen, and their younger sister seven. The faces of the young Gruber sisters who traveled to reunite with family blur together with those of the young Triangle victims and of today's immigrant children separated from their families and caged at the border.

The Trial

For decades, Sam teased his wife, Anna, for having immigrated in pricey, comfortable second class, not steerage, as he and his brother and father had traveled. The difference mattered.

Although it had taken Morris four years to scrape together the money to buy Sam a steerage ticket, and another two to get one for Abraham, Abraham needed only a year and a half to amass the money for three second-class tickets for his wife, Celia, and two cousins, who arrived in October 1911. Abraham's statement at the December 1911 manslaughter trial of Blanck and Harris makes me wonder if his testimony helped pay for the tickets. Shortly after the fire, in his deposition to the district attorney, Abraham said the Washington Street door was locked at quitting time. But at the trial, he changed his story.

The trial record offers shocking accounts of how quickly 146 people lost their lives—their panic, desperation, and heroism. It is also a record of prosecutor Charles S. Bostwick's attempts to get the story of the horrors out, and of defense lawyer Max Steuer's mostly successful tactics of blocking witnesses from describing events in ways the jury could hear or believe. The narrowly defined case turned on whether the Washington Place door was locked, specifically at quitting time, and whether the owners locked it themselves or knew it was locked that day. Abraham Bernstein was one of the few workers who testified for the bosses. Although many Triangle workers spoke little English, the defense lawyer repeatedly objected to letting the prosecution witnesses speak through interpreters and forced them to listen to questions and testify in their second (or sometimes fifth) language. He hoped that they would be less clear, and that their accents would stir the jury's prejudices in favor of the owners. But defense witnesses had interpreters if they needed them. Abraham spoke through an interpreter. Throughout, *er hat gemakht zikh nisht gornisht visendik*, he made himself unknowing.

The accumulated trial testimony shows the women bunched together at their long tables, too cramped to leave their rows. Abraham testified that he worked on the ninth floor, at the end of the first table next to the Washington Place elevators. David Von Drehle describes the chaos of the brief time after the fire started, when it was still possible to get out—the crowd pushing from the elevators to the locked door, or to the windows in the choking smoke and flames. "People survived thanks to . . . a seat assignment near an exit, or by following the right mad rush in one direction or another. . . . They survived by acting a bit more quickly, or boldly, or brutally. But the truth is that most people working on the ninth floor that day did not survive at all."

Abraham's testimony is confused and disturbing. The owners' lawyer seems to have chosen him to humanize the owners, to testify that workers had free access to the Washington Place staircase, where the locked door blocked workers from escaping, and to create the impression of a relaxed, humane atmosphere in the factory. Steuer prompted him to remember going to the tenth floor to see Max Blanck:

A. My boy didn't feel well and I went up to Mr. Blanck to ask him to send me a doctor.

Q. How did you know that your boy was not feeling well that day?

A. They telephoned to me in the shop that I should come home, he didn't feel well.

Q. Did you go up through that door any other time or was that the only time?

A. When I was eating my dinner, after I had my dinner sometimes I used to go down and smoke a cigar.

Q. Did you go down through the Washington Place door?

A. No, with the elevator. . . .

Q. I want to know whether you ever used the Washington Place door or stairway door going up stairs or down stairs any other time except that once that you told us about?

A. Well I say that I did go, when I was sitting right by the door, I used to go down stairs sometimes and smoke a cigar.

Steuer reframed this testimony in his summation: "Now Bernstein said that during the lunch hour he would go out of the Washington Place door and sit on the stone steps and there smoke." Steuer slyly slipped in the notion that the workers had a lunch *hour*—rather than eating hurriedly in the cramped space of their machines, as later oral histories related. Abraham's cigar smoking both backed up the owners' claim that rule-abiding workers did not smoke on the factory floor and distanced him from the burning cigarette that caused the fire. His assertion that there was free movement to the Washington Place staircase during the day was a red herring, since the real issue was whether the door was locked at quitting time, funneling the workers to the Greene Street exit to have their purses inspected.

Prosecutor Bostwick asked more about Abraham's use of the Washington Street stairs.

> A. I said already that I did go when my boy didn't feel well I went up to Mr. Blank to ask him to send me a doctor.

And then later, "I went to tell Mr. Blank that he felt better,—the boy."

The boy, this boy whose welfare the slaughtering bosses were so concerned about, must have been my great-uncle Sam, Abraham's youngest son in the United States, seventeen or eighteen years old by this point. Did he know he appeared in his father's testimony? Did he even know his father testified?

As Bostwick tried to get at whether doors were locked, Abraham made claims about free access and agency. "In summer the doors . . . used to be open. . . . I myself closed that door because from the draught I had caught a cold in the shoulder." In his version of Triangle, workers opened and closed doors at will to take care of their health and comfort. But survivor Lillian Weiner testified that manager Samuel Bernstein had forbidden her to open a window.

Bostwick read back the far more damning statement that Abraham had given just after the fire when he saw him in the DA's office: "I did not remember there was a way to go down on Washington Place side by the stairway there."

> A. No, I didn't say that.

> Q. Do you remember saying to me: "That you didn't see any of the girls trying to go through the Washington Street door; I was awfully excited"?

> A. I say it now that I didn't see any; I didn't take notice.

Q. Did you state to me that that door was— "I knew there was a Washington Place door, that door was always locked."?

A. Oh, no.

Abraham made himself unknowing.

Bostwick showed that Abraham changed his testimony from what he had told him earlier at the DA's office.

The owners withheld the workers' last pay after the fire, forcing them to go to the office for it. There, Leon Stein found, the bosses offered some workers money to testify for the defense at the December 1911 trial. Did Abraham take it? Is that why his wife could travel from Sassov in October 1911 in second class rather than steerage? Maybe he just wanted to bring his wife over quickly, to have her at their dining table, too. He still worked in ladies' waists by the 1915 state census, but in 1920 he reported working as a watchman. Did he continue at Triangle and take over the job of pawing through the workers' purses, looking for shirtwaists? And how did he have the wherewithal to become a "merchant," as he called himself in his 1926 naturalization papers? Was he just making himself unknowing to pay a debt, if only of gratitude, to his Bernstein relatives and connections who probably secured him the job at Triangle? How beholden was he?

Jacob Bernstein, brother of manager Samuel Bernstein and of the owner's wife, Bertha Bernstein Blanck, and therefore Abraham's cousin, died in the fire. Jacob appears in Triangle worker Kate Alterman's harrowing account of frantic workers trying to escape the ninth-floor flames. She testified of "Bernstein, the manager's brother, going around like a wild cat on the windows, and he was chasing his head out of the window and pulled himself back. He wanted to jump, I suppose, but he was afraid. And then I saw the flames covering him." Steuer made Alterman repeat her statement three times, in English, and when she used the same phrasing each time, he'd won his sneaky, sneering game: She must have memorized it; she must have been coached. The jury could ignore her. A piece I made for Jacob for the Triangle Memorial has a picture of a wildcat.

The Map and the Lower East Side

Ruth Sergel's *Chalk* project map shows that nearly all the Triangle victims lived on the Lower East Side. Google Maps turns them into a group of faceless paper dolls standing in clusters, with the front ones protecting those in back. I stretch the map and watch the paper dolls move apart as they leave the factory and head home. Some lived closer to the factory. Their homes are now part of exorbitantly valuable real estate near New York University. Lofts like the Triangle Factory space were originally for storage, not meant for large numbers of workers. The open floor plans allowed fire to spread quickly. As manufacturing left New York in the 1970s and 1980s, these spaces became artists' lofts. There should be a plaque for the first artist's loft. Soon, the well-off discovered loft living and the old factory spaces became condos, where new owners showed off the history of industrial use. The oil stains on strong oak floors and the now-polished gouges where heavy machinery had rested could be featured in design magazines.

Other Triangle victims lived farther east, on streets that would have been demolished by Robert Moses's urban renewal in the 1950s if Frances Goldin and her friends had not stopped him.

A *New York Evening World* headline the week of the fire called the neighborhood "a mourning zone created by the factory fire." Anyone who lived there would have seen the horror of repeated funeral processions leaving from their neighbors' homes. An editor at the *Forward* wrote the day after the fire, "The streets of the East Side are filled with tears. People are rushing around crazed, haggard, their eyes bulging— running around, wringing their hands, trying to begin telling the tale of what they saw and not being able to." Then on April 5, the silent memorial demonstration with the bodies of the unidentified wound through the Lower East Side in dreary rain to the Triangle site. The crowd, estimated at 75,000 in the English-language press and half a million in the Yiddish press, converged with marchers from the morgue uptown to stretch for forty blocks. The East Side group started next to the office of the *Forward*. The crowd silently marched past the houses of the dead and broke into sobs and screams when they passed near the factory.

The *Forward* reported: "Leading the procession was a large black wagon filled with flowers that were later sent to grace the graves of the deceased. Then came the 1,200 surviving workers of the Triangle shop, all wearing black. The men wore black bands on their hats and sleeves." Did Sophie Sasslovsky join the larger procession, or march with the survivors, holding the hands of her former coworkers in the cold rain? The grooves this march could have worn in the pavement would have been streaked with ashes.

Abraham must have marched with them, in a black armband and hatband. Was he in shock from the horror-soaked experience of escaping the fire? Only a few days later, he talked of his experience to the DA. But the *Forward*'s account of the December trial placed him as "one of a large number of other witnesses . . . called on Harris's behalf, almost all of them relatives or people put forward by the bosses." Yet Abraham's wife, who sailed to New York shortly before the trial, and his sons would not have known that he testified unless he told them. The *Forward* got his name wrong, referring to him as H. Bernstein.

Remnants

The garment workers' unions built the 807 apartments of Hillman Housing, where I live now. A plaque praises labor leader Sidney Hillman. Most of the tenements of the area were replaced by high-rises.

Union activists fought for fire safety in the factories. Housing activists continue to fight for fire safety in residential buildings. The same kinds of connivers who had kept factories unsafe for years continued their backroom deals to stop residential fire safety measures. Before he officially entered politics, Donald Trump, for example, successfully lobbied against and blocked a measure that would have required his luxury towers to be retrofitted with sprinklers. In 2018, a Trump Tower tenant died in a fire that would have been prevented if the law Trump fought against had passed, *Curbed New York* reported. There's a giant gold Trump Tower sign there but no plaque for the burned tenant.

Essie Bernstein, maybe another relative, lived on Essex Street; Jennie Levin lived nearby, on Delancey. Both died at nineteen. Essie and Jennie might have met at 175 Delancey Street to walk together to Triangle. That building now does have a plaque: It is the Frances Goldin Senior Citizen Apartments, part of a huge new development. Fran fought to ensure that more of that development's housing is affordable. The building's name honors her lifetime of work to save the Lower East Side. Most of the residents are Chinese and Latinx immigrants; some worked in later-generation clothing sweatshops in the 1970s and 1980s. I made a piece for the Triangle memorial to honor the Asian immigrant displaced garment workers who now survive by collecting deposit cans from the streets. Other victims lived near the former *Forward* building. Beckie Koppelman, age sixteen, lived at 191 Madison Street, at the corner of Rutgers Street. The address turns up on an old envelope in my files: My father lived there in the 1940s, after he got home from World War II.

My mother's ancestors stayed on the Lower East Side for some time. What did it mean to kindhearted Great-Aunt Anna that her future father-in-law testified for the bosses who were responsible for the horrific fire? Did Anna even know about the fire? What do immigrants know of the events that preceded their arrival in a new land?

Abraham died in 1940. I doubt that my leftist, union-supporting mother knew his history. She relished bringing out defamatory tidbits about people's misdeeds in quarrels. She would surely have worked up a feud from the story of Abraham's testifying for the bosses. But would she even have been aware of the fire when Abraham was alive? It was hardly referred to in English-language publications outside of fire insurance and engineering circles for decades, if a search of digitized periodicals and Google Books is reliable. It appeared in a 1938 Federal Theatre radio play, and in a 1940 drama starring Yiddish stage actress Molly Picon, in which an immigrant family on Broome Street loses a daughter to the fire. Even if Picon's play brought the fire to my mother's attention, Abraham died two months after the play closed. How likely was it that my mother saw the play and asked Abraham about it? Did Uncle Sam, who strove to keep heritage alive, seek out any of this history? The Triangle fire's fiftieth anniversary, in 1961, awakened public attention, as did Leon Stein's 1962 book, *The Triangle*

Fire. The historical record existed on some other plane from the lives of my family members.

If I were to sew a memorial piece for manager Samuel Bernstein, who continued to work for Blanck and Harris after the fire, should I show him covering his ears? How did he feel, hearing his brother's desperation to live mocked at the trial, the repetition of Kate Alterman's account of Jacob's attempt to escape used to trivialize the lives lost to the fire? Maybe he wasn't at the trial that day. Samuel, who was in charge of hiring and firing, would have been the one who fired Sophie for talking to a union organizer. And though I cringe at being associated with him for roles he played at Triangle, this act by my cousin, manager Samuel Bernstein, may have unintentionally saved the life of Frances Goldin's mother, Sophie Sasslovsky.

Immigrants Then and Now

Sophie Sasslovsky, the eldest child in her family, came from Russia in 1906. She was sixteen. She and her sister brought the rest of a large family over. At least two siblings used different names on the ship manifest, for reasons now lost. Fran's niece, who saw Sophie Sasslovsky every Shabbos, remembered hearing that Sophie chose the relatives to bring over from Russia in order of who sewed better, so they could earn more and bring over the others faster. Fran's family preserved its story of caretaking and community. Getting family out of Europe was urgent, and chivalry or deference to age was not the issue.

That would have been true in my family, too. My relatives and those around them never spoke of being refugees. They slid into the story of economic opportunity in the golden land. Those still in Sossov depended on the money sent home. But their leave-taking was sandwiched between pogroms, the 1932 famine in Ukraine, and looming World War II. The last hundreds of remaining Jews of Sossov were murdered between July 1941 and July 1943. Jews leaving Ukraine did what they could to get to the United States, as do people now fleeing Honduras, Guatemala, Syria, Mexico, Haiti, Afghanistan, and so many other places where it is difficult to survive.

The Triangle trial took place at the Tweed Courthouse. Two blocks uptown is the Federal Courthouse, where Immigration and Customs Enforcement (ICE) holds check-ins and hearings, and snatches immigrants into detention. Activists from the New Sanctuary Coalition (NSC), an immigrant rights group I volunteer with, accompany people to hearings to make sure judges and guards know that immigrants have friends and community. Their stories echo my family's. Every week, the NSC silently circles the building in their Jericho Walk, which ends in a tremendous shout. The walls are still standing, but perhaps the walkers have worn faint grooves into the sidewalk.

When many Americans now smugly claim their ancestors entered the United States legally, unlike those who sneak in without papers today, I want to ask them about those lies and subterfuges along the way that allowed them a safe haven, like Uncle Sam's claim to be older on the steamship records than in his other papers, or Abraham's fluctuating statements about his occupation. If they'd done that now, ICE might be at their door, ready to detain them in a for-profit prison. If Sophie, Morris, Sam, and my grandfather arrived on their own as fifteen-, sixteen-, and seventeen-year-olds now, they would be held in detention center tents in Texas, instead of beginning the chain of rescuing the rest of their families. If Sophie's siblings had used their own names, would they have been allowed into the country? If they came now under another name and later acknowledged it, would they be deported?

Dig back far enough and many more of us used subterfuges. Many of us are refugees.

Postscript: Frances Goldin died in May 2020, age ninety-five, at home, after I wrote this essay. Because of the COVID-19 pandemic, she was with only her home health aide, and not surrounded by family and friends, as she would have been at any other time. Tributes have appeared in print, and at a May 2020 gathering, where more stories were shared. She left an apartment full of memorabilia of her activism. Some of it will be available to researchers at New York University's Tamiment Library. My wife and I took her I ADORE MY LESBIAN DAUGHTERS sign to the Lesbian Herstory Archives for their collection.

CHAPTER 4

Girl Talk

Paola Corso

1.

Triangle Girls I call them.
Some barely in their teens when they
    perished in the fire.
Some mothers.
Some sisters.
All of them. Daughters.
And the Triangle Girls say to the Chinese
    girls, the Indonesian girls,
the Vietnamese, the Taiwanese.
To Bangladeshi girls, Mexican girls, Costa
    Rican and Puerto Rican.
Girls. Girls.
To the Dominican girls, Honduran,
    Armenian and Nicaraguan.
To the Brazilian girls, Haitian girls, the
    United States of American immigrant.
Girls. Girls working in sweatshops around
    the world one hundred years later.

But before hearing the voices of Triangle factory workers in Lower Manhattan and what they might say about dangerous working conditions in the garment industry today, I heard boy talk in another triangle—my native Pittsburgh.

2.

Pittsburgh's triangle is a coming together of three rivers, what we call the Golden Triangle. And like my grandmother made the sign of the cross when she spotted a church, so do I when I pass this sacred confluence. In the name of the Allegheny, and of the Monongahela, and of the Holy Ohio. Amen.

Pittsburgh's triangle is class, ethnicity, and gender. In my family, that was steelworker, Italian, and male. Both my Calabrian father and grandfather were crane operators at a steel mill. Both died of cancer in the sootiest of industrial cities.

The boy talk I heard: stories about working lives. The boy talk I heard: studies that say steel workers and cancer go together. Though my father was able to move on from the mill, my grandfather operated a crane above a coal-fired furnace for forty-seven years before he retired. He died of leukemia, the type of cancer that crane operators were prone to get.

More boy talk: Pittsburgh's triangle is a football helmet with a decal in gold, red, and blue to signify how steel was made—iron ore fired up and cooled down. The men in my family made steel. I wrote poetry about them. My raw material: oral histories, interview notes, hundreds of pages of findings, union documents, and worker testimonies. It was a cleansing where the personal becomes visible through a lens that encompasses social reform—the creation of government air pollution regulations in the steel industry.

I struggled to find another triangle for female family members that unified their gender and ethnicity, their work. My Sicilian grandmother had a job in a mirror plant for a short time before she joined her sister to help with their uncle's fruit business. My mother was a hospital clerk. My sister worked a few factory jobs, from rubber plant to optical equipment assembly. I worked in a laundry and department store.

Our working lives were so diverse that it was difficult to find common ground as I had with my grandfather and father.

As much as I wanted to write about them, I didn't want to portray their work as anecdotal or peripheral. I thought too much of their strength, their courage, and their determination. I wanted them to be front and center of social reform, to demand a reader's attention. Their work should be viewed as a powerful collective effort in an industry as mammoth as steel was for men.

Where to find another triangle?

3.

What I remember: I'm fourteen, sitting at a sewing machine—the same age as Kate Leone and Rosaria Maltese, the youngest Triangle Shirtwaist Factory workers to die in the fire. I'm in a classroom, not a sweatshop.

I'm better with a hammer and nails than a needle and thread, but I'm here because girls aren't allowed to take shop. We take home ec. We learn to sew and cook. We learn to stitch our own aprons and three-corner scarves to wear when we hard-boil eggs and bake snickerdoodles.

I learn the parts of the machine—all thirty of them. The bobbin holds the thread inside the machine. My teacher points to hers and asks us to find the bobbin on our machines. That would be easy enough, except there's a bobbin case and a bobbin winder spindle and bobbin winder tension, and now I'm confused.

Some sewing machine parts, like a feed dog, make us girls giggle. I wonder why the piece that moves the fabric along as we sew is called a "dog." It doesn't look like one. Is it because it works like a dog? I don't have time to figure this out because we are supposed to find the feed dog and control knob that raises and lowers it—I guess to make the dog bigger or smaller.

Then my teacher says it's not the size of the dog, but the thickness of the fabric. She passes around different kinds to touch—corduroy, silk, velvet, wool, and fabric so sheer that you see right through it. Now we understand why we have to control our dog.

We're fourteen-year-old girls. We sew for forty-seven minutes, not eleven or twelve hours. We're allowed to get up from our machines to go the bathroom, to leave as soon as the bell rings or when there's a fire drill.

We open the door and walk out.

4.

We learn more parts of the sewing machine. Like the gas pedal in a car, a knee or foot control revving up the engine can cause an accident if we're not careful. The harder we press, the faster the machine sews, the less control we have. Our teacher says not to hurry. There's no quota to meet. As if she'd give us a ticket for speeding.

We move on to the needle—needle plate, needle clamp, needle control knob—as we learn how to thread it. More rules:

Pull your hair back so it doesn't get caught in moving parts.

Avoid wearing loose-fitting sleeves, sweaters, jewelry, ties and ribbons when operating the machine.

Always wear protective eyewear in the event a needle or pin breaks and the sharp point flies in your face.

Always keep your head above the sewing machine.

Always use both hands to raise and lower the machine head.

Never operate a machine without proper lighting.

Never look away from your sewing machine for any reason.

Never pull your chair forward while operating the machine.

Never talk to your neighbor while she's operating her machine.

Never sew over straight pins.

Keep your feet off the treadle when setting or threading the needle.

Keep your fingers away from the path of the needle. Put them on the cloth on either side of the needle.

Report immediately a machine that doesn't operate properly or has broken parts.

Report accidents or injuries immediately.

The teacher quizzes us on the parts of the machine and our safety rules. Whoever passes gets to practice sewing on a piece of scrap.

5.

I'm looking down at a triangle of fabric, lime green, with bright pink flowers. My teacher instructs us to place it under the needle so there's exactly five-eighths of an inch seam between stitches and the edge. I line it up just right. That's because there's a piece of tape on the throat plate to help stitch straight for girls like me who are better with a hammer and nails than a needle and thread.

I put my foot on the pedal, but I'm afraid to press down. What if a loose hair from my ponytail gets caught? What if the light goes out while I'm sewing? Or I forget and lean forward in my chair? What if I sew my finger instead of the fabric and the needle gets caught in my nail and I bleed to death before my teacher gets to her first-aid kit?

At fourteen, I'm too young to drive a car, too young to sew on a machine.

My hands sweat as I hold the fabric on both sides of the needle. I wipe them on my skirt and get back in position. I'm ready for the gas. I press down lightly. The needle doesn't move. Harder. The engine starts to make a grinding noise, but the needle still doesn't budge. Harder—until it bobs up and down and picks up speed.

I sew one side of my triangle scarf. Turn one corner. A second side. I try hard not to blink as I turn the next corner but take it too wide, sewing too close to the edge. I stop dead, lift the presser foot, and tug at my fabric to line it up again. This time, I use the hand wheel to move the needle up and down, slowly. I stop halfway on the last side so I have enough room to reach in with my hands and turn the two pieces right side out. One side is wrong. I spend the rest of class with a seam ripper, tearing apart my three-corner scarf.

I want to quit this triangle.

6.

What I remember: I'm sitting at a sewing machine, stitching a pair of slacks and matching blazer, not a shirtwaist. I don't even know what a shirtwaist is.

I'm better with a needle and thread now than I am with a hammer and nails because I've been sewing for almost four years. In Mrs. Sousa's class, we're learning to make coats and quilts, sophisticated clothes with pleats and welt pockets, lining and top stitching, collars and belts and buttonholes. Matching purses.

We don't use *Simplicity* patterns anymore because they're too easy. We like the *McCall's, Butterick,* and *Vogue* ones. Some of us don't use a pattern. We design our own clothes like Mrs. Sousa. It makes us feel creative, choosing the style and fabric, buttons, buckles, and trim. We wear our works of art.

We'll sew our prom gowns in the fall, raincoats in the spring, bathing suits and sun hats for summer, dresses for our high school graduation. Even the clatter of our sewing machines in high gear isn't as loud as our girl chatter about our latest creations.

My mother thinks I've become such a good seamstress that I could start my own business after high school and sew for other people, like Mrs. Iannuzzi does. One Christmas, Mom paid her to make matching red corduroy jumpers for me, my sister, and my cousin. But I don't think I'd enjoy sewing the same article of clothing over and over again for other people.

My sister didn't go to college and she works in a dentist's office. I'm glad that my father wants me to become the first female in the family to get a degree. My girlfriends are going for economics, chemistry, nursing, and nutrition. I'm not so good at those. When I ask my father, he says he has something in mind for me. He wants me to be a home economics teacher and show others how to sew.

I'm seventeen, I sew, but I want a different future for myself.

Sarah Brenman was seventeen and she sewed. Laura Brunetti, Josephine Cammarata, Francesca Caputo, Celia Eisenberg, and Molly Gerstein. They were seventeen and they sewed. Israel Rosen, Sarah

Sabasowitz, Rosie Shapiro, Isabella Tortorelli, Sarah Weintraub, Sonia Wisotsky. Did these Triangle workers ever dream they could get a high school diploma or go to college?

I'm trying to sew far away from that three-corner scarf and a career in home ec, and yet it seems as though I'm in reverse, backstitching to that very same triangle.

7.

When I go to college, the Singer machine stays at home. Even when I come back for breaks, I don't want to sit in a chair and watch a needle bob up and down. If I have to gas a pedal, I want it to be in a car. My wardrobe consists of blue jeans and flannel shirts. There is nothing I need or want to sew.

I take an Introduction to Sociology course and become enthralled with my professor's lectures on social order, social problems, social acceptance, social change. C. Wright Mills's *The Sociological Imagination* teaches me to be aware of the relationship between the personal and the social.

I begin college at a state school outside Pittsburgh, with plans to become a home economics teacher, but transfer to a private college in Boston to major in sociology. My father is disappointed. I have abandoned a practical degree at an affordable college close to home in a field I had experience in for a "worthless" degree at an expensive college thirteen hours away, with no promise of earning a living for myself. And he uses his pension to pay for my education.

Like the Triangle workers, my father was an immigrant. He crossed the ocean in steerage and passed through Ellis Island, a guinea wop who flunked his first grade of school because he couldn't speak English, then managed to graduate from high school and get a job in a steel mill, where he operated a crane, like his father.

He escaped his fire. He quit the mill, served in World War II, and went to college on the G.I. Bill. Eventually, he showed his teachers he could spell and write his name when he became the school business administrator who signed their paychecks.

With a name like Mariano Procopio Corso, my father was determined to prove he was an honest Italian man with no Mafia ties.
When my mother called him once to bring home a postage stamp
from the school district office so she could mail a letter, he asked her,
"Are the girls sick?"

"No," she replied.

"Is the car running?"

"Yes," she said.

He told her to go out and buy the stamp herself. He would not
take office supplies for personal use.

I paid for my own graduate school education in community organizing and nonprofit administration by becoming a resident of California, where I attended a state college for nominal tuition. Yet that didn't
change how my father felt about my academic choices—this degree,
or another I earned in creative writing at a New York City university a
few years later. Not long after I graduated, I became pregnant.

8.

I wear bedraggled clothes that don't match, half-zippered, buttoned
wrong, inside out. My hair is a disheveled braid. I've got a six-pound,
eight-ounce newborn in my arms and a nursing pillow fastened around
my waist like a tutu. I put my son down on a makeshift changing table
and leave a hand on his stomach so he doesn't roll. I grab a cloth diaper
from the clean pile and fumble to fold it into a triangle with my free
hand but end up with more than three sides. I position him squarely
in the middle to regain a sense of precision.

I've been a writer for many years and a mother for a few weeks. I'm
good at crafting prose and not so good at caring for newborns. I don't
have time to do them both and do them well. I stop writing prose and
turn to poetry. When I return to teaching the following semester, I ride
the subway forty-five minutes each way to the university and write. I
read the Poetry in Motion posters and I write. I watch women knitting,
teens break-dancing, and I write. I watch office workers completing *The
New York Times* crossword puzzle, and I write. I hear Chinese fiddles

and steel drums, doo-wop and mariachi. I write. Phone conversations, batteries for sale, Gospel readings, and pleas for small change. I write about Pittsburgh, about what I know—my father's and grandfather's working lives in the steel industry.

Dad isn't flattered that I interview him. He isn't impressed that I have the same work ethic and determination that got him from the steel mill to the business office. He asks me when I'm going to stop living like a pauper. Put down the pen and get to work.

My father died before a Pittsburgh newspaper reviewer wrote "You can take Paola Corso out of Pittsburgh, but you can't take Pittsburgh out of Paola Corso." My first book, *Death by Renaissance*, has been published. The poems are about my father, his dying mill town and how to revive it.

He died before Janet Zandy called my poems "poetry of witness," before I read her work about hands and physical labor, women and cultural work, poetry and the Triangle Shirtwaist Factory fire. I learned about garment workers who were mostly Italian and Jewish women and girls. This combination of class, ethnicity, and gender in a major industry was the New York equivalent of my family's work life in Pittsburgh as Calabrian male steel workers.

I had found another Triangle.

I want to say to my father, I'm sewing again, Dad.

9.

Triangle Girls, some barely in their teens, some mothers, some sisters, all of them daughters. But I don't make the connection between their personal lives and a larger social context until I come across a story. It goes like this:

A woman sits down to tea with a friend in Washington Square Park, when they hear a disturbance outside. Fire engines. Screams. They lift up their skirts and run toward it to see women and girls high up in a building, jumping out the window to their deaths on the sidewalk below, coming down with so much speed and force that they break through fire department nets.

That woman was Frances Perkins. Perkins, who became secretary of labor under President Franklin D. Roosevelt and a major force behind workplace reform, said witnessing the Triangle fire was in heart and in mind "a never to-be-forgotten reminder of why I had to spend my life fighting conditions that could permit such a tragedy."

Perkins inspires me. When I finish the first section of *Once I Was Told the Air Was Not for Breathing*, which features steelworkers and toxic coal-fired furnaces in Pittsburgh's Golden Triangle, I begin to draft a second section on the Triangle fire. How to write about the shirtwaist factory tragedy one hundred years later and recapture the urgency, the emotional impact Frances Perkins experienced as an eyewitness? How to portray these women not just as victims of sweatshop conditions and a collective symbol of injustice, but as mothers, daughters, sisters? What if readers can learn about their personal lives through the way family members recognized them at the morgue?

I write "Identified":

> Sophie Salemi
> by the stitched knee of her stocking mama
>   darned the day before
> Julia Rosen
> the hair braids her daughter Esther fixed
>   for her that morning
> Kate Leone
> by a blue skirt she wore to Randall's Island
>   hospital to visit her son
> Jennie Levin
> the baby's sock found tucked in the heel of
>   her shoe.

I've never worked in a garment factory, but I've patched the knees of my son's grass-stained pants. I've never worked in a garment factory, but I've French-braided my sister's hair for special occasions. I've visited a sick child in the hospital. I've been a working mother who leaves her newborn at home. I've never worked in a garment factory, but I recognize these acts of love.

Piecing together their last moments with family members into lines of a poem was an act of sewing in itself. Each defining detail is distinct, and yet the poem becomes a seamless representation of many day-to-day lives, the lives of working-class immigrant women in New York City in 1911.

10.

The day I chalk "March 25, 1911" on the blackboard to prepare for my English as a Second Language Conversation Club lesson is the day a student arrives to class early. She puts an apple on my desk and tells me she found a job in Chinatown and will no longer be able to attend school.

My poem "Of My Eye" was born from this exchange and my reaction to the news:

> You found a job. Doing what?
> Seamstress. She smiles,
> takes the chalk from my hand
> and draws pattern pieces. Tell me
> about the dresses you sew,
> how many pleats, how many cents
> how many hours, how many times
> will I look through thick bangs
> fringing your eyes and wonder
> how many floors, how many
> escapes, how many doors
> will be locked.

My student is a Chinese immigrant, a young mother, a sweatshop worker. I worry for her safety:

> Of my eye, the apple
> shaped as your heart
> Mei Lu, womanmotherstudent
> learning English, the words

> to say your teacher can't
> take a bite, hear the crisp,
> smell its sweetness break the air
> between us when I think
> of clenching my fist, to keep you safe,
>   to keep you
> all safe, not bolts of fabric.

I keep the apple in my pocket during the centennial march for the Triangle fire in New York City. I'm with Italian and Italian American women from the Malia Collective. We carry 146 blouses with sashes bearing the names of those who perished, who sat at the sewing table—as my student now sits. We hold them high:

> Shirtwaists raised to the sky,
> their delicate sleeves float the wind
> down Broadway—every life
> borrowed, every life returned.

A history lesson for my ESL class coincided with my student's personal experience one hundred years later. It inspired me to write "Of My Eye." I wasn't just conveying what I read in the page of a history book about deplorable sweatshop conditions. I saw them as my student chalked pattern pieces she sews for a few cents each before she hugged me and said good-bye. In that embrace, a Triangle worker of the past was embodied by a young garment worker of today. I held on to them both.

Again, I am a poet seamstress, this time cobbling two time periods in my writing. I have come to see the words I choose and how I stitch them together as a conscious act to take up the profession my father chose for me—one I now choose for myself.

11.

The voices I hear: snatches of conversation with friends marching beside me at the centennial commemoration, microphoned voices of government officials and politicians, union organizers and workers, voices of activists, poets, and musicians.

The voices I hear: sewing machines humming, my home economics teacher saying I have to sew another triangle scarf, my mother saying I should be a seamstress, my father saying I should go to college, teach others how to sew.

The voices I hear: Mei Lu saying I won't be her teacher anymore.

The voices I hear: Triangle Girls talking to Mei Lu in New York's Chinatown. Triangle Girls reaching out, making an international appeal, tapping the shoulders of every woman and every girl working under sweatshop conditions to get their attention. Voices loud and clear:

> And the Triangle Girls say to the Chinese
>   girls, the Indonesian girls,
> the Vietnamese, the Taiwanese.
> Girls. Girls.
> To the Bangladeshi girls, Mexican girls,
>   Costa Rican and Puerto Rican.
> Girls. Girls.
> To the Dominican girls, Honduran girls,
>   Armenian and Nicaraguan.
> To the Brazilian girls, Haitian girls, the
>   United States of American immigrant.
> Girls. Girls.

The Triangle Girls are listening and talking to Merina in Bangladesh. She works fourteen hours a day, six days a week, with her sisters. Merina makes the equivalent of about sixteen dollars a week. And if a worker demands higher wages, she is slapped back to her sewing machine.

Merina works in the Rana Plaza garment factory, a factory built up to the sun, a factory with cracks, a factory the owner says will last a hundred years. Workers refuse to go in, afraid the factory will fall.

The manager threatens to withhold their pay if they don't get to work.

Not long after, the earth in Bangladesh quakes. Eight floors collapse. In seconds, a heap of slab and iron. Merina, her face inches from a collapsed concrete ceiling, is trapped for three days and can barely move. She recalls hearing moans and cries for help at first, until, after three days, there is silence. She tries to keep herself up, afraid that if she falls asleep, she will never wake up. In time, stench from rotting bodies fills the air around her. Another worker, Roksana, says the building collapses in "the blink of an eye." A few hours later, she wakes up in rubble.

"There was a girl's dead body underneath me…the blood from her ears and nose was all over my back and face. It soaked my back completely," she says.

As they hear the sound of screaming sirens, village fathers run the distance to find their daughters through a maze of dusty lanes, passing by blacksmiths at work and the smoke from their brick kilns. Survivors slide down bolts of fabric to the ground, where they're moved, relay-style, into wheelchairs and stretchers to the hospital.

Laboni, 21, left arm amputated

Rikta, 27, right arm amputated

Pakhi, 25, both legs amputated

Rescuers hammer through walls and shimmy down shafts with hacksaws to free trapped survivors who suck the sweat on their clothes to stay alive. Didar Hossain goes into the ruins numerous times to help dozens of workers. He finds some are alive but partially trapped in the rubble.

"Please brother, don't leave me, get me out—even if you have to cut off my hand," a girl pleads with him. Hossain uses a knife and some anesthetic to amputate her hand.

"She was screaming and I was screaming too, and I cried when I saw her crying. I felt really bad, but there was no other way," he says.

After the amputation, Hossain ties her arm to her body before they begin to crawl toward the light.

"This is how we got out," he explains.

Others are buried deep in rubble or suffocate to death from smoke inhalation.

And the Triangle Girls say, Girls. Eleven hundred and thirty-four more Dead.

There's Reshma, who wants someone to hear her in a crescent hole, someone to take her out from seventeen days of darkness after the Rana Plaza collapse, sipping on drips of rainwater, rationing biscuits she bought before work because she was too rushed to make lunch. She hits wreckage with sticks and rods until the sound of her tapping is heard after a bulldozer clears rubble.

She's lifted onto a stretcher and hooked to oxygen, the pink scarf she wore to work more than two weeks ago still wrapped around her neck as families of victims and crippled survivors owed back pay and compensation pull their children out of school to work. Western retailers offer sympathy. Police fire rubber bullets at protesters.

And the Triangle Girls say to the Bangladeshi girls, Mexican girls, Costa Rican and Puerto Rican.

> To the Chinese girls, the Indonesian,
>   the Vietnamese, the Taiwanese.
> Girls. Girls.
> To the Dominican girls, Honduran girls,
>   Armenian and Nicaraguan.
> To the Brazilian girls, Haitian girls, the
>   United States of American immigrant.
> Girls. Girls.

Working in sweatshops around the world one hundred years later. To family members and loved ones, organizers and activists, teachers and students, writers and artists, I hear them say:

> Let our fire light your way.
> Let our fire flame your passion.
> Let it spark from your lips these words: *Noi ricordiamo.*
>   *Ich gedenk. Wŏmen jìdé. Chúng tôi nhớ. Menk' hishum*
>   *yenk'. Nou sonje. Kita ingat. Nou sonje. Recordem.*
>   *Nosotros recordamos.*

We remember.

12.

I'm sitting at a long table with a threaded needle in one hand and fabric pinched between my fingers in the other, ready to stitch a piece of my Sicilian grandmother's pillowcase onto an unrolled bolt of material the length of the table. I've been sewing my words into poems about the Triangle fire for some time now, but I haven't sewn with cloth in years.

I'm shaping my grandmother's pillowcase into a triangle and stitching it next to pieces of fabric of different textures, shapes, and colors. They are all part of a 320-foot Collective Ribbon that will become the texture for a future Triangle Fire Memorial. I join women with Italian and Jewish backgrounds, Asian, Hispanic, and African backgrounds who bring a special piece of fabric to sew onto the ribbon at the Fashion Institute of Technology.

While I sew and later give a poetry reading, I don a cotton smock that my Sicilian grandmother wore in the fruit store where she labored for nearly fifty years. I tell the audience a little bit about her—that she was one of nine children, that she quit school after the fifth grade to work, and that I can see she wasn't much of a seamstress as she darned the smock to stitch up ripped pockets and tears in the thin fabric. If you look closely, I say, you'll see her stitches are coarse, uneven, and hurried. But she had reinforcements. At the neckline, a holy medal of Mary with a prayer, "Our Lady of Mercy Pray for Us," and by the zipper, a safety pin. In case.

As I read, women sew. They occasionally glance up but mostly keep their heads down. Their eyes are focused on the task at hand. To sew and sew in memory of the Triangle workers. I can almost hear the clip of their scissors cutting and shaping, thimble tapping needle. Hear the pull of thread through fabric. I hear whispers and pins dropping. On this day, the act of sewing is sacred.

As I sew, others take turns reading their poems and performing their music, singing their songs. I hold the third corner of my Nonna's triangle cloth in place and stitch with a double-threaded needle.

This is the triangle I am meant to sew. A triangle layered with all the ones before it that have shaped me—Pittsburgh's golden confluence

Figure 4.1. Paola Corso holding her grandmother's darned smock.
The Collective Ribbon, March 17, 2019, Fashion Institute of Technology,
New York, NY. Photographer unknown; photo courtesy of Paola Corso.

of three rivers; of class, ethnicity, and gender; a lime green and pink-flowered triangle head scarf from home economics class; a newborn's diaper I learn to fold into three corners as a new mother. A triangle of poetry, history, and community.

I imagine the day when we'll all look up to the memorial at the former Triangle factory site and see the Collective Ribbon we've sewn cast in steel, see a light that shines above on the names of each of the 146 workers who perished in the fire, see our own reflection in the light joining them.

Sewn together in our presence, in our memory.

PART TWO

FAMILIES

CHAPTER 5

A Legacy of Grief
In Search of Rosie Weiner

▼

Suzanne Pred Bass

When I was a child, the shriek of fire engines in the night rattled my bones until the sounds faded away down Gun Hill Road. It was in the large two-bedroom, ground-floor apartment at 3508 King's College Place in the North Bronx that I first saw grief and fear in my grandmother's eyes and in my mother's eyes. That's where I learned about the fire that had killed my great-aunt Rosie some forty years earlier. Katie, Rosie's younger sister, had survived.

We lived on the ground floor because my mother wanted us to be able to go in and out of the building easily. It made little sense, since there was an elevator. Now I think her choice had to do with her deep anxiety about fires. There were about forty apartments in the six-floor building, and kids ran up and down and in and out. The building was on the same block as PS 94, my elementary school. Although the school was close to where we lived, my mother rarely managed to get us there on time. The Reservoir Oval Park was a few blocks away, as was Van Cortlandt Park.

My parents still lived at 3508 King's College Place when I started attending Antioch College. In the early 1960s, when the ILGWU apartments for union people were completed, they moved there. A union affiliation was the ticket to getting one of those apartments. My father was in the teachers' union, though it was Katie's husband, Philip

Lubliner, who helped my parents secure the apartment. Uncle Phil was president of the Pocketbook, Leather Goods and Independent Novelties Workers' Union (this union is sometimes listed under different names).

My maternal grandmother, Minnie Weiner Rashkin, lived around the corner from us, on Putnam Place. We saw her often. My mother depended on her mother, more than I could understand as a child. They spoke Yiddish all the time.

A fussy eater, I only liked plain food. Grandma Minnie would boil carrots and potatoes just for me. I remember the smell and taste of her sweet yeasty bread with raisins. Occasionally, she cooked a family meal at her small one-room apartment, where her youngest son, Henry, also lived until he got married. I think Uncle Henry slept on a foldout bed in the hallway. Grandma must have slept on a couch.

Although Grandma Minnie spent much time at our house, when my mother was offered an office job at PS 94 and asked her if she would take care of us, Grandma Minnie refused. My grandmother might have felt it was too much to care for three kids; but probably she thought my mother shouldn't have worked outside the home. Minnie had been raised by a single mother, my great-grandmother Sarah, who had come to New York City from Russia with her eight children in 1902. Sarah's husband never joined them. Sarah never became a U.S. citizen. Instead, Minnie wanted to become a citizen. I might have helped her prepare for the test, though it was my brother Ralph who helped her the most. Eventually, Minnie became a citizen, proud to have learned to write in English and to know enough U.S. history to pass her citizenship exam.

Minnie was in her late fifties when I was a child. I always thought she looked much older than her age. Short, chubby, broad features, old-fashioned clothes, drab oxford shoes that laced—they might have had a heel. She died in the early 1950s, while my parents were traveling in Europe. The family informed my father, but not my mother, as they were all concerned about her reaction. Only when she got home did she find out. The shock must have reminded her of the death of her father, Samuel Rashkin. While walking on the street, he had fallen down suddenly and died. He was in his early fifties. A policeman saw my mother on the street and told her that her father had just died. My mother's family life was riddled with sudden, dramatic losses and narrow escapes.

Four decades before Minnie's death, her sister Rosie had died behind a locked door at the Triangle Waist Company. Their sister Katie had survived by grabbing the cable of the last elevator down from the ninth floor. I grew up learning about seventeen-year-old Katie's courage and quick thinking. She told the story of her extraordinary escape from the fire when she testified at the trial of Triangle factory owners Max Blanck and Isaac Harris. Katie had worked at Triangle cutting lace for five months. She was in the dressing room, putting her hat and coat on, when she heard people cry fire. She ran to the Washington Place side of the factory to look for Rosie, then back toward Greene Street, looking for her sister near the dressing rooms. She never found her. In her testimony at the trial, she recounted those moments with remarkable lucidity:

> I went back again from the Greene Street side towards the Washington Place passenger elevator, I knocked at the door and thought the elevator would come up, I seen he didn't come, and the smoke was coming very thick, he was not up—he didn't come up—and I was choking with smoke, I couldn't stand it no more, I went to the windows and put my face out to get some air, and I called down—I cried "Fire" downstairs, and people were looking up. Then people pushed me towards the windows and I went away from the windows back again towards the elevator. Suddenly he come up, and there was a whole lot of girls and they rushed there and I was pushed back. Then I seen the flames were coming up from the Greene Street entrance toward Washington Place; I went back to the door.

Unable to contain her tears, Katie demonstrated how the door behind which her sister died was locked:

> I turned the knob this way and that way [indicating] I pushed it towards myself and I couldn't open it, then I pushed it inward and it wouldn't go. I then cried out, "The door is locked."

. . .

Then the elevator was not far down yet—it was, I think, between the eighth and ninth floor—and I landed—I don't remember—on top of the girls' heads or on top of the elevator, until I got down to the street. My face was facing down and my feet extending out and as I was going down my feet were hurting me, my ankles were hurting on the doors and I cried, "Girls, my feet are being—"

While Katie's testimony offered an incredible account of her survival, it also implicitly conveyed the devastating fact of her sister's death in the fire. The first time I read Katie's testimony on Cornell's Kheel Center website, I cried. I heard the voice of the seventeen-year-old immigrant, my mother's adored aunt, the girl who would become my great-aunt.

Katie must have married Philip Lubliner not long after the fire. He lived on Eighth Street, across from Katie and Rosie's building. When I was a child, I visited Katie at her house on Cortelyou Road in Brooklyn. So many people in the family lived in apartments. Aunt Katie had a house, a cocker spaniel named Corkie, and she was warm and expansive. Occasionally, she would visit us, or we would see her at weddings and bar mitzvahs. When she moved from Brooklyn to Miami, Florida, she gave my mother her Limoges candlesticks and her china set so that my mother would have something that had belonged to her. Sometimes she would come up to New York and stay with my mother at Penn South. My mother was thrilled to have her.

Because my grandmother died when I was only seven, Aunt Katie was the only relative on my mother's side left from that generation. To have known Katie, a vibrant, gutsy woman, was a gift to a girl with almost no women figures as heroic role models. Yet when I was asked in school to write about the woman I most admired, I drew a blank. Most of my peers chose their mothers. At a loss, I summoned three names: Marian Anderson, Helen Keller, and Eleanor Roosevelt. I wish I could have named Clara Lemlich or Frances Perkins. I wish I could have named my great-aunt Katie Weiner. In the end, I think I chose Eleanor Roosevelt.

Figure 5.1. Weiner family at holiday table. Katie Weiner Lubliner
and Phil Lubliner at the head of the table; Minnie, bottom left.
Photographer unknown; photo courtesy of Suzanne Pred Bass.

Katie saved her life by willing herself to walk away from a doorway
that wouldn't open and head instead toward an overcrowded elevator
on its last trip down to safety. She might not have made it, except for
her friend Annie Sprinsock, who, according to some accounts, grabbed
Katie by the arm and held her above her head while the elevator de-
scended. Katie was seventeen. She survived the fire. She lived. She
remembered. Rosie's age is another story. It's as elusive as the beloved
ghost who has inhabited my family through four generations. When I
asked Katie about the fire, she told me how she had grabbed the cable
and come down the last elevator. But she did not mention Rosie. Ever.
My mother was the one who told me, much, much later, that as a young
child, she had gone with her mother to identify Rosie's body.

Picture this four-year-old girl at the makeshift morgue at the Char-
ities Pier. The howling. The wailing. The charred remains. She hears.
She sees. She will remember.

That was all my mother told me. She didn't say anything else about
Rosie. And I didn't ask. Nobody in my family talked about Rosie.

Like her siblings who traveled with their mother to America at the turn of the century, Rosie was born in Russia, in the shtetl Zhitomer. My great-grandmother's birth name was Zlotta, but after she arrived in the United States, she became Sarah. Rosie's name on the ship manifest is Ruchel. Did she change her name to fit her new American life? Did some anti-Semitic, anti-immigrant officer make the change? I do not know, any more than I know her age.

The ship manifest of her journey from Russia to New York in 1902 says she was fourteen. Thus she would have been twenty-three in 1911 —that's the age on her cemetery tombstone. However, the union report, issued after a heart-wrenching visit to her family, says she was nineteen. The victims' list published by the Kheel Center indicates that she was twenty. In his book about the Triangle fire, Leon Stein says she was seventeen.

Rosie was seventeen, nineteen, twenty, twenty-three—perhaps none of the above. There's no birth certificate, and so I waver between trust in other records and loyalty to a family tradition of women who often chopped some years off their birth dates. My own mother led me to believe that she was eleven years younger than my father. After she died, I found her birth certificate and learned she was only seven years younger. I feel the pull of a generation of women who desired to be thought of as younger.

I ponder what age best suits the mournful, unspoken family story that is Rosie's story, a death story more than a life story. Only nineteen. Nineteen screams the unbearable injustice of her death. Just a teenager. Not yet twenty. Only nineteen. But twenty-three would give her a little more life. In the end, I settle for the presumed accuracy of the historical record. She is twenty-three that morning of March 25 when she leaves home for work. She will always be twenty-three.

I struggle to extract the pieces of Rosie's story, buried as they are underneath layers of torn family memories and official records that disclose only partial truths. As I peel each layer, I look for the impossible evidence of never-recorded facts.

Assembling the puzzle that was Rosie's lost life, I formulate questions, hypothesize answers, make and remake choices. Nothing sticks.

But there are things I have learned about the barely two decades that Rosie lived.

She was engaged. According to the Union Relief Report for the Ladies' Waist and Dressmakers' Union No. 25 of the ILGWU, her fiancé lived with her, her mother, and Rosie's siblings David and Katie. The union report says Rosie's mother wanted him to leave the apartment after the fire. From the same union report, I learned that over the years Rosie had saved four hundred dollars from her then eight-dollar-a-week salary to purchase a farm in the country. It is hard to imagine how she managed to save such a sum. Is that figure incorrectly recorded, as well? Rosie didn't get to the farm she painstakingly saved to buy. After her death, her mother insisted the money go toward a tombstone, not a farm: IN MEMORY OF MY BELOVED DAUGHTER AND OUR DEAR SISTER.

No farm. No wedding. No children. No chance to see the world move forward with cars, airplanes, talking movies, television. No chance to rejoice in the labor union victories for workers' safety in the aftermath of the fire.

Her descendants lost so much, too. We never knew her.

My mother told me that Rosie's mother, my great-grandmother Sarah, never recovered from Rosie's death. She went to live on a farm that her son David bought in Brainard, New York, probably in 1912. There she died of stomach cancer less than three years after Rosie's death. My mother also told me about Rosie and Katie's older sister Esther, who died when she was run over by a trolley. I didn't know, until the historian Michael Hirsch told me, that Esther died in 1903, on March 25, the day of Rosie's death. According to her death certificate, Esther was nineteen years old. My mother told her story sadly but matter-of-factly. She could talk about this death, which happened three years before she was born. It also held a lesson—about the dangers of crossing streets. And a trolley accident did not carry the horrific details of death in a raging factory fire.

On the eighth anniversary of Esther's death, March 25, 1911, my great-grandmother must have been home, grieving the daughter she had lost eight years earlier. A *yahrzeit* memorial candle must have burned in her home. In a matter of hours, another daughter would be dead, consumed by fire at the Triangle Waist Company.

Rosie's heart must have been heavy while she walked to work that day. She would have remembered Esther well, since she was about fifteen in 1903. In the minutes in which she could still move in the midst of the fire and smoke, she must have thought of her mother, who had already lost a daughter, and of saving Katie.

Grandma Minnie saved my life twice. When I was eighteen months, she noticed my "green pallor" and discovered that I had drunk some benzine from a can I had found on the floor. I was rushed to Montefiore Hospital, a few blocks away, where the doctor told my mother, before pumping my stomach, "Say good-bye to your little girl." When I was about four, she disagreed with a doctor who had diagnosed me with trench mouth. As it turns out, Dr. Zeif had hearing problems and had missed the double pneumonia that was rumbling in my chest. No more girls were to die untimely deaths on Minnie Weiner Rashkin's watch.

I see a line of women in my family walking with Rosie, talking to her, grieving for her, trying to stop the flow of senseless tragedies. All the women in my family, and perhaps especially Rosie and Katie, were *farbrente meydlekh*, wonderful fiery girls. Among the many nicknames my mother had for me, "Suzie *brente*" was one of my favorites because I knew she meant I had a special spark. My mother encouraged creativity in me and my two older brothers. And zaniness, too. She yearned for us to have lives that were less troubled than hers, but she could not escape the trauma that haunted her and her mother. We inhaled it, too. She carried Rosie's story in her insistence that we champion the underdog and rebel against oppression. She taught us that to cross a picket line was to betray all workers.

After the acquittal of Blanck and Harris, my great-uncle David had the foresight to find the back door the two had men exited from to avoid the furious mob assembled in front of the courthouse and the courage to confront them: "Murderers! Not guilty? Not guilty? Where is the justice? We will get you yet."

According to news reports, he then collapsed. But David could not tell his son Melvin or his grandson Don about the fire. It was only in 2011 that my cousin Don realized his connection to this history. He called me to ask for information about Minnie, Rosie, and Katie. It was in that conversation that he first learned about the Triangle fire and what had happened to Rosie and Katie.

Our grandparents and our parents believed they were protecting us by not talking about the fire and the family's terrible loss. My delayed grief encompasses the weight of Rosie's death for everyone in the family. I sit at my computer, fingers tapping the keyboard, searching for the key that will connect my life to Rosie's life. I take Rosie's hand, feel its warmth, and reassure her that I still think about her, all she lost, all that her family lost. I type, "I am the great-niece of two Triangle workers: Rosie Weiner, who died in the fire, and her younger sister, Katie Weiner, who survived." This is who I am.

The Triangle fire has forever marked my family. I seek to understand the connection between how I have lived my life and Rosie's life and death. I have struggled and stumbled, celebrated and despaired. I have tried to claim my link to Rosie—and Katie: sit-ins and "ban the bomb" demonstrations in the fifties and sixties, the petition against the graduation loyalty oath that drew threats from my high school principal, rallies against wars in Vietnam and Iraq, rallies for abortion rights, the Women's March, and Save the Planet protests. Activism has been my best anchor.

As a union member, Rosie must have been part of the Uprising of the 20,000. Perhaps fifteen-year-old Katie, who would marry a future union president, was part of the strike, too. In 2018, my daughter, Rosie's great-great-niece, was arrested for civil disobedience in the Senate halls for protesting at the confirmation hearings for the Supreme Court nominee Brett Kavanaugh. The urgency to better the world through protest and activism is central to my daughters and niece and nephews' generation—the dying planet, the plight of immigrants, the scourge of HIV/AIDS, women's struggles. Now my grandsons, seven and ten years old, know about the terribly unfair working conditions that led to the Triangle fire and understand what happened to Rosie and Katie.

Figure 5.2. Great-Aunt Rosie Weiner, ca 1910–1911.
Photographer unknown; photo courtesy of Suzanne Pred Bass.

In my living room there is a bookcase, eight feet long and almost four feet high. A photo of Rosie that my mother had stands dead center on top of that bookcase. She keeps me company. She looks shy, perhaps self-conscious, but also determined and proud. There is a slight smile on her closed lips. She wears a broad-brimmed hat and a suit with velvet cuffs and a velvet collar. There are small, beautiful buttons on her almost mid-calf shoes. She carries a large handbag with a metal clasp. I notice the awkward elegance in her bearing. Her arm rests on a chair and she shows off what looks like an engagement ring. Her full mouth and wide-set eyes call out to me. Remember me. Hold on to me. And I do.

People want to know about Rosie. Her photo, enlarged to poster size, graces every Triangle fire commemoration and the Remember the Triangle Fire Coalition's website. Every year, high school and college students and media people make inquiries to me about her. She is thought about, written about, talked about. She is in documentaries. Her name will be on the Triangle Fire Memorial.

My life radiates with an awareness of workers' rights and struggles. I have carried the stories of my great-aunts, passed down from one generation to the next, a legacy of loss and grief. But knowledge, too. While chalking for Rosie on March 25, 2019, as I do every year, I met someone who lived in her building at 119 St. Marks Place (in her time, 119 East Eighth Street). The building is a stone's throw from Tompkins Square Park and a short walk to the site of the Triangle Factory. I imagine Rosie walked to and from the factory with other young workers who lived nearby. The man who now lives in the building tells me all the apartments in this five- story tenement have two small bedrooms.

I look up at the front of the building and notice bas-reliefs with women's heads. They look like goddesses. I wonder whether Rosie looked up at those images from the very spot where I stand, whether she appreciated them as much as I do today, over a century later. I like to think she did.

CHAPTER 6

My Father, Isidore Abramowitz

▼

Martin Abramowitz

Some of the Triangle girls may have known my father, Isidore Abramowitz, although they worked on separate floors. They may have made small talk or even flirted with him as they waited for the elevator.

Isidore survived the Triangle fire.

He may also have started it.

Why am I telling this story? Friends gently ask if I really want to do this. My frail ninety-year-old brother fears for "our father's good name." Our father's experience in the fire has been partially documented, and suspicion already cast and mercifully forgotten. Why revive it now? The obvious answer is that I have a few fragments to add to the story, and the tragedy that was the Triangle fire demands to be known and remembered in as much detail as we can bring to it. We owe it to the girls and to the seventeen men who perished with them.

Even as I inch into print, I know there's deeper stuff at work. This story and a few earlier fragments of childhood memories are all I have left of my father. I am certain that the fire was a central moment in his life. How could it not have been? Thinking about him and the fire has both enabled and forced me to try to understand the mystery of this man's life; it's been a way, however neurotically and unsuccessfully, to have my father back.

It's a rainy Brooklyn morning in mid-March 1947. I am not yet seven. My sixteen-year-old brother is walking me to school, which he has never done before. He knows, although I do not, that our father has just died.

If we spoke at all, even at the classroom handoff, I have forgotten it. I remember the expanding circles in the puddles as we crossed the street. We must have arrived on the late side, since it took a minute or two to find a hook for my raincoat and a place for my boots in the walk-in sliding-door closet at the back of the classroom. The tangle of damp jackets offered momentary refuge. I remember glare and noise and strangeness and being alone as I joined the class. That's all I will remember from that day and many days beyond it: no funeral, no weeping mother, no visitors at home, no words or hugs of consolation, no acknowledgment of loss and emptiness, no one saying, "This is very sad, but we will take care of you."

"You remember when you saw Daddy in the hospital?" asks my mother. "Now he's in Florida to get better."

Yes, I do remember seeing him in the hospital, but barely.

I stand in the middle of a large, bright, white room. That's as far as I can go. Someone points me to look at a doorway across the room. He's propped on one arm, waves with the other. His face is thin and stubbly. He smiles. Then we are on the street, and someone points to a window way above us.

"Wave. That's Daddy."

All I see is somebody's upper body and a moving arm. I wave.

Sometime in my young adulthood (in the early 1960s), my mother mentioned that my father had been working at the Triangle Waist Company in 1911 (he was eighteen at the time) and had been lucky enough to be out of the building on a delivery when the fire broke out.

This nugget of family history surfaced in the middle of a general conversation about our family's identification with the labor movement. I was at that time a dues-paying and on-strike member of District Council 37 of AFSCME, the American Federation of State, County and Municipal Employees, on strike against New York City's Department of Welfare. My father was what my mother called a "charter" member of the ILGWU ("He knew David Dubinsky"). My mother, who sewed store labels on men's ties, had paid her dues to the other main union in the garment industry, "the Amalgamated."

I felt proud that my father had been an "extra" in this historically significant, terrible drama. I might have wondered then whether he had carried any "survivor guilt." I remember thinking that my very existence and those of my children and all who will come after them to the end of time were a direct result of the fact that he was "not there." I often think of that.

What I didn't think about until I was well into my sixties, long after my mother had passed, was that she had done it again: She had told me "another story" about my father. To protect me, she had told me that my father had not died; to protect him, she had made him a delivery boy nowhere near the fire.

But in 2003, I learned that at the time of the fire, he *was* there, inside the factory. Browsing in a bookstore, among the new titles, I spotted David Von Drehle's *Triangle: The Fire That Changed America*. I had read Leon Stein's book in my early twenties and had searched for a mention of my father, only to be disappointed to find none. Now, looking at the cover of Von Drehle's book, I wondered whether I wanted to go through that search again. Nevertheless, I checked the index and there he was: Abramowitz, Isidore, pages 118–19. I decided to buy the book, if only to confirm the family story and document my father's incredible luck at being out of the building. I didn't wait to take it home to find out.

On my feet, at the "New Titles" table, I read that Isidore Abramowitz was not a delivery boy, but an eighth-floor cutter who was in the building when the fire started. The fire, I read, had started in a bucket of trimmings closest to his workstation; he was the first to notice it, and tried to put it out before fleeing—and surviving. Here is Von Drehle:

Abramowitz was taking his coat and hat from a nearby peg when he noticed the fire in his scrap bin. Perhaps the cutter had been sneaking a smoke . . . Or maybe it was another cutter—they were a close-knit group and liked to stand around talking together. Or maybe it was a cutter's assistant. At any rate, the fire marshal would later conclude that someone tossed a match or cigarette butt into Abramowitz's scrap bin before it was completely extinguished.

I try to remember what I felt as I read and reread this, still on my feet, in that bookstore. The best I can recall is a mix of shock, anguish, excitement, and, I admit it now, some strange gladness that at least now I knew something more about my father. I even felt a perverse pride that he had made a difference, if in this terrible way, and would be remembered. I would have a story to tell.

Soon after reading Von Drehle's book, I started researching the census and the trial. Van Drehle's account was based on the previously long-lost transcript of the trial, so the transcript (now online at Cornell's Kheel Center) was my next stop. Would it tell me anything about this Abramowitz that would help me know if this cutter was my father? Would it tell me how old he was or where he was born?

My computer was down, so I used my cell phone to go online. I can't remember where I sat—some place public, where other people texted and emailed. The pages came into view. As I started scrolling, I felt as if my father were alive and we were texting.

Monday afternoon, December 11, 1911. Ten pages of testimony, give-and-take; seventy-six questions to him, mostly to establish how the work floor was laid out, who was where, where the fire broke out, and who did what. This Isidore made a point of being deferential, particularly when questioned by the judge: a lot of yes and no questions; the answer was always "Yes, sir" or "No, sir." Many more mentions of *sir* than in the responses of the six witnesses who had testified before him that day.

Several of those earlier witnesses had testified in Yiddish, and the English-speaking witness who took the stand just before Isidore had to be urged to speak loudly enough so the jury could hear him. Isidore testified in English and, apparently, in a voice that carried.

At one point, the judge asked, "As soon as you saw the fire, what did you do?"

The transcript reads "No answer."

I see him breaking down at this point, though not crying. My heart breaks for him. Impossible to know whether he actually broke down, but it's at least suggestive that the judge did not pursue the question. Rather, the prosecutor picked up the questioning, asked a few less potentially loaded questions, then circled back with a rephrase: "What was the first thing you did when you saw the fire?"

"I spilled a pail of water on it."

This story was so at variance with my mother's version. In the days, weeks, and months to come, I struggled to process it. Was there any way my mother might have been telling the truth on this one? Could there have been another Isidore Abramowitz working at the Triangle while my father was making deliveries? No way to know; the payroll records were destroyed in the fire.

So maybe there was another Isidore Abramowitz, a cutter. Cutters were the elite workers in the garment industry. But how likely was it that my father would have reached that position at age eighteen?

As I write this, I have just unrolled, not for the first time, a wide and barely readable copy of a page of the U.S. Census of 1910, the year before the fire. One hundred and sixty Orchard Street. There he is, seventeen-year-old Israel Abramowitz (over the years, he was Israel, Isidore, Izzy; my mother called him Irving). Born in Romania. Arrived in the United States at age nine. He lived with his mother, grandmother, younger brother David, and two slightly older girl boarders, Tillie Koffler and Beckie Weiss. Occupation: "cutter at shirtwaist company."

One more piece of evidence: My brother, still worried about our father's good name, tells me, "Daddy was there. He told me, when I was a teenager, that he saw the fire break out and left the building."

My father was a cutter and he was in the building at the time of the fire, and *an* Isidore Abramowitz testified to his centrality to what happened as the workday ended. Still, how crazy is it to think what the destroyed payroll records couldn't prove—that maybe there was another Isidore Abramowitz? Would press reports of his testimony reveal more? Did *that* Isidore Abramowitz limp to the stand with a clubfoot, as my father would have? Was he beyond his teen years, as my father was not? Was his voice heavily accented? Was he bearded? Wearing a skullcap? Then it would not have been *him*.

I went online again. Nothing in *The New York Times* or the index of the *Forward*. But there were other New York dailies, other Yiddish papers. This would take scholarship and deep diving. I decided to let it go and try to examine my motives. I thought about possible outcomes. Finding nothing would prove nothing. Finding him as an eighteen-year-old living on Orchard Street or walking with a limp would remove all doubt. So would learning that Isidore was an older man—not my father.

I realized that I'd rather not know, and that I was afraid of the possibility that it was not him, that this story I have been carrying and telling for years has been a myth—like the myth of his not dying, and that I know even less about him than I thought. I need this story.

And there is still a question about my mother's version of the story. It's possible that she was telling it as she herself had heard it from my father when they "courted" almost twenty years later. But I'm hoping and am inclined to believe that he shared with his life partner the truth as he understood it—and as he carried it all those years.

The question about what and how he told my mother is huge and leads me to wonder about my father's inner life. Did he carry this terrible memory alone, or did he find solace in sharing? Important as that question is for me, though, for almost twenty years, it feels as if there has hardly been a day when I have not been asking myself other questions, all of them without answer, all of them attempts to get closer to this man I barely remember.

What did he think or know about what happened? Could he have known whether it was his ash or match that caused the fire? How guilty did he feel in his heart? Did he stay on the street as the factory burned and the girls leaped to their deaths? What did he say at home? What was he feeling during the tremendous public outpouring of mourning? How much private comfort could he take in the fact that public outrage was directed not at whoever's match or ash it was, but at the fact that the doors had been locked and the workers trapped inside? What did he feel when he testified at the trial of Blanck and Harris?

Figure 6.1. A prosperous time. Isidore Abramowtiz with his intended, late 1920s. Photographer unknown; photo courtesy of Martin Abramowitz.

Was he dreading being identified as the direct cause of the fire? And later, did he realize that the fire led to improvements in the working lives of millions of people? Most of all: How did he live for thirty-six years with the memory of 146 deaths? How much forgetting was he able to do to keep going?

All I know is that he did keep going.

My brother tells me that in 1920 Isidore was arrested by the fledgling FBI in a roundup of suspected anarchists that came to be known as the Palmer Raids. I've made two Freedom of Information requests to the FBI and the National Archives. The files, if they exist, are beyond my reach. Had he been radicalized by the Triangle experience? Or was he simply in the wrong place (like a union hall) at the wrong time? Could he have made that story up?

A few photos from the late 1920s show him as an American immigrant success story, in a suit and a fashionably broad necktie, cigar in hand, looking pleased with himself and his intended (my mother), at a time when he was presiding over his own men's clothing manufacturing company. The company and his investments disappeared with the Depression. My mother told me that she had been worried about the impact of my father's losses on his emotional stability. He had told her, "I'm not going to jump off a building."

Did he flashback to memories of the Triangle girls leaping to their deaths?

He, my mother, and my brother doubled up in an apartment with my mother's sister and her family until things improved. In 1940, when I was born, he was working steadily as a cutter, and the family was in its own one-bedroom apartment in Brighton Beach, Brooklyn.

There is one photo of him, probably from the late 1930s, taken from across a garment factory worktable. At the center of the picture, a man stands proud and erect behind the table. He is tall, broad-shouldered, well-suited, discreetly neck-tied, and smiles. His left hand rests lightly on the table; his right holds something, perhaps a tool. The photo is about this man. My father, a head shorter, stands to the man's right, off at the edge of the frame. His open coat jacket shows a broad tie from an earlier day. He looks into the camera as if he has just wandered into the picture. He is a walk-by in someone else's story—diminished, a bystander. I ache for him.

Another photo. It's 1941. Outdoors, against a brick wall, he holds me, a frowning toddler, in his right arm. His huge right hand (a cutter's hand) secures me at my knees. He is almost completely bald. His suspendered pants ride high against an extended belly. He smiles off center, not at me nor at the camera. In his late forties, he is an old man. The cracks of time in the photo seem thematically right.

That's the last photo. Pneumonia in the winter of 1946. Heart disease was the immediate killer in March 1947. He was not yet fifty-four.

I have long considered the loss of my father when I was seven, and my mother's attempt to conceal that loss, as the formative experience of my life. Although I, too, have "kept going" and made my way in the

Figure 6.2. Isidore Abramowitz, late 1930s.
Photographer unknown; photo courtesy of Martin Abramowitz.

Figure 6.3. Isidore Abramowitz with Martin
Abramowitz, 1941. Photographer unknown;
photo courtesy of Martin Abramowitz.

world, I am deeply aware of the ways in which I and the people closest to me have paid a price for my becoming fatherless at seven. Wondering about my father's life has been a major theme in my life, even before I began to put the Triangle fire pieces together.

How did Isidore's family get from Iaşi, Romania, to the port of Le Havre? What was it like for nine-year-old Isidore to be fatherless in a strange-tongued metropolis? What did he know about his father? Who were Tillie Koffler and Beckie Weiss, those two apparently unrelated boarders his own age? Could there have been some sexual encounter on Orchard Street? Did my father have any meaningful connection with a woman before he sent some mutual relative as an emissary to his twentysomething future wife, twelve years younger? The story goes that at the time she was washing the floor and suggested he show up in person. In 1947, when he became ill, did he know he was dying and would leave his two sons—one still so young—fatherless, as he had been when his father died?

My Triangle speculations—that is, after all, what they are—have deepened my questioning, and, I think, my empathy and pity for this man. Yet I remain conscious of the fact that what I imagine to have been my father's guilt, anguish, and attempts to forget pale in significance before the 146 deaths and the ultimate responsibility of Blanck and Harris. At times, I have felt egoistic and disproportionate in my focus on my father, and even questioned my motives in telling this story. But it's the story I have been given.

I began telling the story privately to family and friends while conducting the modest research that led me to uncover few but important fragments of the story of my father's place in the Triangle fire. Now I tell that story wherever I can, to whomever I can. I try to use it to help commemorate those who died. As a board member of the Remember the Triangle Fire Coalition, I want to see the names of the workers and their stories as part of a memorial at the building that was their death place. I may not know whether it was my father who caused the fire, or what feelings he carried with him for the rest of his life, but I feel a responsibility to the memory of the workers.

I'm at a window way above the street, on the ninth floor of 23–29 Washington Place, at the Greene Street corner. It's a late March morning, and the organizers of the annual commemoration ceremony are beginning to set things up. The fire truck is in place but has not yet extended its ladder to the sixth floor, as far as it could uselessly reach in 1911.

The facade of the building is basically still the one the girls saw as they came to work, but they would not recognize the interior space. This is now a university building, with dropped ceilings, so brightly lit that, as I exit the elevator, my eyes feel the glare bouncing off the IKEA-style student workstations. I am here to honor the memory of the Triangle workers. But the room is too different. I am not moved.

The window is in a glass-walled conference room. I force myself to stare down, until I feel them—standing there, fire and smoke behind them, some alone, some holding hands. Are they thinking they just might survive if they jump? Or do they know they are lost?

Those poor girls, those poor girls.

I cry. I cry for them. I cry for my father. And for myself.

CHAPTER 7

The Two Roses
A Great-Niece Remembers

▼

Annie Schneiderman Valliere

Origins

Rose was eight years old when she left for America with her mother and two younger brothers. It was 1890. Her father, Samuel, had left months earlier. They left Sawin, the town where she was born, in the geographic area that is now Poland but between 1815 and 1917 was also part of the Russian Empire. They slipped through borders without passports because Jews were not allowed to leave the Russian Empire. How Rose's mother, Dora, escaped from Europe and came to America with three small children was the first family story that her grandson, Herb Schneiderman, my father, told me. I still hold the image of Dora hiding the youngest, Charles, under her shawl so that his chatter would not be heard by the guards as she and the children slipped through the Polish-German border.

I was in college when I first read *All for One*, Rose's 1967 memoir, and learned many details about her early life and her activism. In her book, she described the family's harrowing escape and other experiences of her childhood in Poland and later in the United States. She also wrote of her father, who directed biblical plays for a traveling troupe. From him, she inherited the ability to hold an audience captive. But it was from her mother that Rose inherited courage and determination.

It was Dora who stood up to the Russian government when Samuel was conscripted into the army. Russian law required that Jews enter the military between the ages of twelve and twenty-five, and serve for twenty-five years. Non-Jews, however, were not called to serve until they were between eighteen and forty-three. This law was meant to "de-Jewify" Jewish young men. Sons who were the only male children were exempt from compulsory military service. Samuel was an only son. But when a wealthy Jewish family purchased Samuel's exemption so that their own son would not be drafted, he was called to serve. Dora, pregnant with Rose, hired a carriage to take her to the next town. She went to the Russian army office and successfully pleaded her case to the head officer.

In the United States, Rose's family first lived in a one-bedroom tenement apartment on New York's Lower East Side. They shared an outhouse with several families. Two years after their arrival, Rose's father died, leaving the family destitute. Rose was devastated. She wrote about her father: "Like Mother, he was not demonstrative, but he shared his love of books with us, reading to us a great deal and helping me with my lessons." A month after her father died, Rose's sister, Jane, was born. Dora, urged by a Jewish welfare organization, temporarily placed Harry and Charles in an orphanage. Ten-year-old Rose left school to become Jane's caretaker while her mother took a job lining capes. Dora's sister, Rebecca, and her husband came to the United States soon after, and Rebecca took over the care of Jane during the day. Because she wanted Rose to resume her education, Dora placed her temporarily in the Hebrew Guardian Society Orphanage. Most of the orphanage matrons were strict and used physical punishment. One of Rose's worst memories was having her beautiful red hair—the red hair that would one day become part of her fiery image—cut off within hours of arriving at the orphanage. Among her few cherished memories at the orphanage was singing: "One thing made the week endurable for me. On Friday night and Saturday morning, when we gathered in the synagogue, we sang hymns. I loved singing and let myself go. Even today I can sing 'Ain Kelohanu' ["There Is None Like Our God"] and feel a real thrill."

Figure 7.1. "Rose Schneiderman, girl strike leader."
Rose Schneiderman making cap linings at the Hein & Fox cap factory
the same year she helped lead the cap makers' citywide strike of
1905. Photographer unknown; Rose Schneiderman Photo Collection,
Tamiment Library and the Robert F. Wagner Labor Archives; photo
courtesy of New York University.

A year after Rose had gone to stay at the orphanage, Dora brought
her back home, planning to send her to school. But Dora lost her job
and thirteen-year-old Rose had to leave school once again and work to
support her family. After working as a department store check girl, she
took a job in a cap factory for better wages. She discovered that factory

work meant long hours, low wages, unsafe and unsanitary conditions, sexual harassment, and other forms of maltreatment. This discovery transformed the immigrant girl into a labor activist.

Rose understood that her mother had saved her father from a life of servitude to the Russian government and years of separation from the family. She also understood that her father had taken great risks to escape from Poland and that her mother had demonstrated remarkable courage and initiative to escape with her children and join her husband across the ocean. She embraced her parents' resolve and built upon it tenfold, living her life in the pursuit of liberty. She became Rose Schneiderman, heroine of the labor movement. With her famous speech after the Triangle fire, the tiny redheaded Jewish immigrant inspired the audience at the Metropolitan Opera House and the community at large. She remains an important figure in the international labor movement.

For a long time, however, I knew nothing about Rose's landmark work in labor, her contribution to the suffrage movement, and her activism in other human rights movements. I did not even know about her speech at the Metropolitan Opera House. I was a little girl and she was my beloved little aunt Rose. Only after her death did I begin to ask questions about her. In 1991, I started to research her life. Eventually, my dedication to Aunt Rose led me to share her story with others. The knowledge and understanding of Rose as a labor activist that I acquired later in my life has reframed my memories of my aunt, so that when I return to those childhood memories where I find Aunt Rose, the historical figure enters the room, as well.

Rose, the Labor Activist

Even before her rousing Triangle fire speech, Rose was a force in New York's labor movement. In 1903, when she was twenty-one, Rose and her friend Bessie Braut helped organize the first women's local of the Jewish Socialist United Cloth Hat and Cap Makers' Union. By 1904, the local had swelled from the original twenty-five to a couple hundred members. At a time when women did not serve in union leadership positions, Rose was elected to the New York City Central Labor Union.

In the following year, she helped lead a citywide cap makers' strike. Her talent and audacity caught the attention of members of the New York branch of the National Women's Trade Union League (NWTUL), a cross-class alliance that advocated for women workers in New York. In 1906, Rose was elected vice president of the organization and continued her role as the Lower East Side organizer. She spoke on street corners and in front of factories in New York, at mass meetings of box and cigar makers. She spoke to factory owners and shop managers on the floor of factory buildings, and to senators on the floor of the New York State Capitol. She spoke to garment workers at Faneuil Hall, in Boston, and to college students at Radcliffe and Mount Holyoke. And she spoke at the National Woman Suffrage Association Convention in Washington, D.C., a mass suffrage meeting at Carnegie Hall, and even a suffrage rally at a graveyard across from Vassar College.

In September 1909, as the Lower East Side organizer and a vice president of the New York Women's Trade Union League, Rose assisted the workers at the Triangle Waist Company and the Leiserson Company in their strikes. These strikes helped mobilize the shirtwaist workers to demand a general strike, which became the 1909 Uprising of the 20,000.

Rose worked side by side with her friends Clara Lemlich and Pauline Newman. Clara was working at Leiserson and Pauline was a former Triangle worker. Both were ILGWU organizers. All three were firebrands. Rose and her fellow members of the NYWTUL and the ILGWU helped the strikers of the Triangle Waist Company and thousands of other shirtwaist workers keep up their fight for fourteen weeks.

On November 25, 1910, a fire broke out in a factory in Newark, New Jersey, killing twenty-five women and girls. I am sure Rose was affected by the fire. She had experienced a fire in the cap factory where she worked in her early years. She had been lucky that the fire had occurred at night. No lives were lost then. Rose and the NYWTUL had fought to get factories to follow the minimal safety laws on the books, but the fire in Newark made them realize how unaware workers were of the safety laws that existed to protect them. It wasn't enough to try to get the factory owners to change. It was necessary to empower the workers. Rose and members of the NYWTUL spoke from atop ladders they set up on street corners at the end of the workday. They urged workers to come forward to the committee investigating safety issues in factories, led by Leonora O'Reilly, who shared the NYWTUL vice presidency with Rose. It took the Triangle Factory fire, however, to get better fire safety and worker protections onto the floor of the New York Senate and finally into the national consciousness.

The day after the Triangle fire, Rose and a group of NYWTUL members pounded the pavement on the Lower East Side, looking for the survivors, the wounded, and the family members of the dead. Leon Stein quotes Rose: "We went into the East Side to look for our people. . . . Our workers in the Women's Trade Union League took the volunteers from the Red Cross and together we went to find those who in this moment of great sorrow had become oblivious to their own needs." Rose knew just where to look:

> We found them. You could find them by the flowers of mourning nailed to the tenements. You could find them by the wailing in the streets of relatives and friends gathered for funerals. But sometimes you climbed floor after floor up an old tenement, went down a long, dark hall, knocked on the door and after it was opened found them sitting there—a father and his children or an old mother who had lost her daughter, sitting there silent and crushed.

Four days later, Pauline Newman asked Rose to speak at a memorial for the victims at the Labor Lyceum in Philadelphia. Prior to the memorial, Pauline wrote to Rose: "Take care Rose dear, and do not break down." It would not be Rose's last appearance at a Triangle fire commemoration.

On April 2, 1911, Rose spoke at the Metropolitan Opera House. She would later thank *The New York Times* for "preserving her words," because her speech was, as usual, not scripted. "She stood silently for a moment and then began to speak hardly above a whisper," *The New York Times* reported. But she held the packed house of mourners and protestors spellbound:

I would be a traitor to these poor burned bodies if I came here to talk good fellowship. We have tried you good people of the public and we have found you wanting.

The old Inquisition had its rack and its thumbscrews and its instruments of torture with iron teeth. We know what these things are today; the iron teeth are our necessities, the thumb-screws are the high-powered and swift machinery close to which we must work, and the rack is here in the firetrap structures that will destroy us the minute they catch on fire.

Rose's speech would become a reminder of the horrors of working conditions in the Progressive Era.

On Wednesday, April 5, 1911, Rose accompanied the funeral carriages of the seven unidentified victims of the fire. *The New York Times* described her lagging behind at the edge of the procession, dripping wet under the rain, and nearly collapsing. NYWTUL President Mary Dreier and Secretary Helen Marot took her by the arms. In her memoir, Rose wrote: "[W]e of the WTUL marched in the procession with other trade-union men and women, all of us filled with anguish and regret that we had never been able to organize the Triangle workers. But in our grief and anger we, who were dedicated to the task of awakening the community to the plight of working women, would not remain silent."

The Triangle fire would stay with Rose. Fifty years later, she attended the first large commemoration with Pauline Newman, Frances Perkins, Eleanor Roosevelt, David Dubinsky (former president of the ILGWU), New York Fire Department officials, and survivors. Through Rose's legacy, I, too, have developed a strong connection to the Triangle fire. In March of 2011, my husband and I drove from Maine to New York for the centennial of the fire. While we were still on the highway, I received a call from my friend Eliza Walton. She told me that the governor of Maine, Paul LePage, had removed the labor history mural from the Maine Department of Labor. The painting depicted the history of Maine labor and included Frances Perkins and Rose, national figures who had shaped Maine's labor history. The names of the conference

Figure 7.2. The fiftieth anniversary of the Triangle Shirtwaist Factory fire. From left to right (between fire department officials): Pauline Newman, Frances Perkins, Rose Schneiderman, and David Dubinsky. The photo was taken in front of the Brown Building on March 25, 1961. Photographer unknown; Rose Schneiderman Photo Collection, Tamiment Library and the Robert F. Wagner Labor Archives; photo courtesy of New York University.

rooms, including those of Frances Perkins and Rose Schneiderman, had been removed, as well. I could not get past the irony of the governor's actions on the eve of the centennial of the Triangle fire.

On the day of the commemoration, my husband and I stood in front of the Brown Building with students, teachers, union and community activists, New Yorkers, and people from around the world. There were many descendants of Triangle workers. Later that evening, I took my aunt Florence, one of Rose's nieces, then in her eighties, to the Great Hall at Cooper Union. There, performers and speakers evoked the memory of the fire. Aunt Florence and I were asked to stand, along with members of Clara Lemlich's family. When performer LuLu LoLo reenacted Aunt Rose's Metropolitan Opera House speech, I saw before my eyes twenty-eight-year-old Rose, auburn hair in a braid, just tall enough to peer above the podium.

Aunt Rose

My childhood memories of Aunt Rose are few but vivid, a series of fragments from my own memory and from conversations with family members I have questioned again and again to learn more about her.

Rose was small, even compared to other elderly adults in the family. My grandfather and grandmother, Harry and Tilly Schneiderman, were four feet, eleven inches tall; my father, Herb Schneiderman, was a towering five feet, one and a half inches. Rose, at her tallest, was four feet, six inches. She was small even by my child standards. When she greeted us at her apartment door, she was always dressed in her best: a blue dress with a cinch at the waist, sheer stockings, and chunky black heels, reminiscent of her style during the late 1930s and 1940s, when she would still speak at union meetings and served on the National Recovery Administration's Labor Advisory Board in Washington, D.C., or as the secretary of the New York Department of Labor.

Her voice sounded like no one else's in the family. Over time, some of our older relatives had developed New York accents and others developed American Jewish accents. I have heard several audio recordings of Rose's best friend, Pauline Newman; she had an American Jewish accent. They had all left Eastern Europe as children. Yet Rose's voice was marked by a Mid-Atlantic accent. In an interview done by the Oral History Research Office of Columbia University, Frances Perkins remembered Rose's Triangle fire speech: Rose "spoke good English. She was a Jewish girl from the East Side, many of whom didn't in those days speak good English, but she did." Rose had developed an accent like that of Mary Dreier, Eleanor Roosevelt, and the other elite women with whom she worked closely. But behind the accent, she remained connected to her Jewish immigrant origins and family.

I have sought to connect the brave activist I knew only indirectly and the great-aunt I visited at her apartment on the fourteenth floor of the Gramercy House on Manhattan's East Side. Rose lived with and supported her mother until the latter died, in 1938, and so did not have her own home until she was fifty-five, when she moved into her apartment in Gramercy Park. This is where I would visit her. I can't recall many visits, but I remember looking forward to them.

The front door opened into a kitchenette/dining area. There was a little dining table on the left side and, across from it, louvered doors opened on the kitchen cabinets, stove, refrigerator, and sink area. A formal silver tea service sat on the table. In recent years, I saw the set at my cousin David's home. I read the inscription on the platter. It was a gift from the Women's Trade Union League to honor the work Rose had done for the organization. It was in the dining area that I remember hugging her soft, tiny body. She wore her lipstick a bit above her thin lips. Red lipstick would be smudged on my cheek.

In the living room, two blue high-backed upholstered chairs were placed across from each other. Rose and I would sit on the blue chairs, our legs dangling above the floor. A bookshelf covered the entire wall between her bedroom and the living area. Aunt Rose loved books: classics, poetry, politics, history. Aunt Florence told me that "Aunt Rose loved to give books and she always gave you what you wanted and gave beautiful editions." When Rose went into the nursing home, she asked her nieces and nephews to take the books we wanted before they were donated. I was passionate about poetry and so chose books by Anne Moore and Robert Frost. My older sister, Rachel, went home with *The Romance of Leonardo Da Vinci*, by Dmitry Merezhkovsky. My father chose *Carl Sandburg*, by Harry Golden, and my mother chose *On My Own*, inscribed by Eleanor Roosevelt to Rose. When she retired from the NYWTUL position in 1949, Rose told *The New York Times*, "There are so many books to read and plays to see."

On one visit—I must have been about ten—Rose gave Rachel and me the reel-to-reel tape recorder and the tapes on which she had recorded her memoir. She recorded her book on tape because severe arthritis in her hands prevented her from writing. Our family did not recognize the importance of the recordings. Rachel and I and other relatives taped radio shows and family singing on them. It is our luck that one of those tapes still has ten minutes of Rose's voice, in which she talks about her life in Poland. What joy I felt when I found this scrap of memory. Today, I share these rare minutes when I talk about Aunt Rose at public events.

Rose walked everywhere—until she couldn't. She insisted on maintaining her independence and remaining in her apartment despite difficulties with sight, memory, and balance. Her stubbornness drove her to fight the hard human rights battles but sometimes prevented her from changing course when it would have been prudent, especially as she grew old and frail. In 1967, she slipped in her bathtub. She remained there, naked, for three days. The superintendent and her nephew, David, found her. She had pneumonia. She was moved to a nursing facility while awaiting a single room at the Jewish Home and Hospital for the Aged on West 106th Street, on the Upper West Side of Manhattan, where my grandparents were already living. As strong-willed as ever, but with little money, she insisted on a single room because of all she had done for workingwomen. Eventually, the nursing home granted her request.

My father and aunts have described Rose as a woman with no tact. Often, her nieces were the recipients of her criticism and advice. Lisa Kleiner, another great-niece, told me that her mother admired and feared Rose, who would voice strong opinions on how she should raise her children. Rose wanted girls and women to stand up for themselves. She had spent many years instructing, urging, organizing, and mentoring women. She must have felt very passionate about putting those same efforts into the girls and women of our family. In her Triangle fire speech and all her speeches, Rose never minced words: "I would be a traitor to those poor burned bodies if I were to come here and talk good fellowship." She never minced words with us, either. She believed that she would have been a traitor to our family if she had been anything but truthful and direct. Whether they were workers, senators, or family members, Rose didn't suffer fools.

I found her both adorable and intimidating. When the Jewish Home gave her a ninetieth birthday party in April 1972, she said to my father, "Why do they want to give me a birthday party? I don't need a party." Once, I tried to give her cookies I had made and brought from our home in Washington, D.C. She looked up at me from the wheelchair with her steely, deep-set gray-blue eyes bulging from behind her thick glasses and said, "I don't want these cookies. Give them to someone else on the floor." I was eleven. I felt that chilled feeling I would get when my father or mother yelled at me. Rose did not know how to talk to children. I believe she thought she was helping raise strong and independent girls.

Although we saw Rose only three or four times a year, she wrote letters to Rachel and supported her activities and interests. In one letter, dated February 1960, she tells Rachel how important it is for girls to succeed in math and how important languages are: "I am surprised that you have made such fine progress in school and are learning fractions. I hope you like arithmetic because it is important in one's life and if we want to travel to foreign countries to be able to speak [with whom] we meet, also it is important if we want to go to college. . . . So keep up the good work darling." Rachel, who was older and had developed a closer relationship with Aunt Rose than I, told me that Rose did not impart stories of her life as much as she talked of the values of independence, strength, the need for education, and the value of reading.

The Two Roses

After I gave a talk at the Maine State Museum about Rose's life, in honor of the U.S. suffrage centennial, a woman in her fifties, Elizabeth Balsam Hart, approached me with great enthusiasm and told me that her mother, Judith Mabel, had been a waitress at a resort in the Catskills in the summers between 1942 and 1946. During one of these summers, she had met Rose. Rose had spent time taking walks with Elizabeth's mother during work breaks. She became a role model and urged her to be a strong and independent woman. I was surprised to hear of my aunt's having gone to a Jewish resort in the Catskills. I thought she probably vacationed there with friends, though she must have felt more comfortable with the staff than participating in the recreational activities for the patrons. Hart told me that her mother would often speak about Rose and the importance of being an independent and strong woman.

Near death, she had said, "It matters that you know how important Rose was to me."

I have always regretted missing Aunt Rose's funeral. I was a summer babysitter on the coast of Maine when my parents called to tell me she had died. At the time, it didn't seem so important to attend the funeral. Aunt Rose's funeral was held at the Riverside Memorial Chapel in Manhattan. My father told me that about ten family members attended, together with David Dubinsky and Pauline Newman. Pauline had remained her closest friend. The three had been intimately involved with Triangle history, before and after the fire. It was the dawn of the second wave of the women's movement. Although there were tributes in *The New York Times* afterward, the obituary and announcement were placed in the *New York Daily News*, perhaps because it was more affordable—but it drew only a few mourners to the memorial service.

Rose did not tell stories about the Triangle fire. I wish she had, or that I had had the knowledge and foresight to ask. When I was eighteen, after reading about Rose in women's history books, I started to feel her power as if it were flowing through my veins. It got me started on the path to learn more about Aunt Rose. I needed to do further research on the depth and breadth of her involvement in Triangle and her lifelong activism. Rose was in my thoughts as I studied to become a social worker, as I considered becoming a community organizer, and when I tuned up my guitar to sing labor and political songs across Maine. Later, I abandoned the idea of becoming a community organizer, although I continued to be involved in grassroots politics and to sing at union rallies and labor conferences. In the late 1970s, I was asked to sing at an Amalgamated Clothing and Textile Workers Union rally in Biddeford, Maine. I remember walking up and down a church aisle, singing labor songs with the union garment workers who were seated in the church pews on each side of the aisle. In that moment, I felt the power of Rose's labor activism and her love of singing.

After working with adolescents and survivors of domestic abuse, I became a psychotherapist and, later, a middle school social worker. I was in my early twenties when I began to think about writing a book about Aunt Rose, but it was not until I got married, became mother to two stepdaughters, and within a year had a baby girl that I began the project.

I want to tell Rose's story, describe her, rough edges and all. I have racked my memory, have had conversations with family members and other people who knew her, have interviewed scholars and authors, and read books, documents, and letters from libraries across the United States. Rose is always on my mind, sometimes as my little elderly aunt, but more often as the auburn-haired, tiny, bold activist I have come to know. Both are close to my heart.

Aunt Rose's connection to the Triangle fire has bound me to sharing its legacy. In the 1990s, the University of Southern Maine asked me to perform the role of my aunt, reading her Triangle fire speech in a production of *We Were There,* created by Bev Grant and Flo Stern. The Triangle Shirtwaist Factory fire also matters to my children. My son, Louis, wrote a short story for his high school English class in which workers died in a factory fire. My stepdaughter Bethany Roderer and her then husband came to hear me sing labor songs at an American Federation of Labor event in Washington, D.C., on the anniversary of the Triangle fire. My daughter, Rose, has told me that "being a relative of Aunt Rose has been a source of pride."

Rose devoted most of her time to her friends and her work. For the most part, she kept her work and personal life separate from the family. In her memoir, she wrote that she learned to keep secrets and hold other people's confidences, "and never, never tell one friend what another friend said." Many years ago, my father told me that Rose never had boyfriends in the early years because she was embarrassed by her poverty. Many family members thought she was too busy to have romantic relationships. Unbeknownst to our family, Rose was involved with Maud Swartz, an executive of the NYWTUL, from 1914 to Maud's death, in 1937. My reading of her memoir, letters that her friends kept, and the works of Gary Endelman and Annelise Orleck led me to think that Rose and Maud had a long-term partnership in life and work, although they never lived together. Perhaps only Rose and Maud, and maybe their close friends, will ever know the full nature of their relationship. I learned from Orleck and Endelman that, when she

Figure 7.3. Rose with family members at Harry and Tilly Schneiderman's fiftieth anniversary celebration, before the singing began. Rose is seated, second from the right. Annie, age eleven, is sixth from the right, standing. The photo was taken in the dining room atop Butler Hall, Columbia University, New York, 1967. Photographer Emerich C. Gross; photo courtesy of Annie Schneiderman Valliere.

was writing her memoir, Rose took great pains to hide any personal feelings and the intimate nature of her relationships, as well as those of her friends. She also hid the internal politics and struggles within the WTUL, the organization that was so important to her. She was not open even with old friends.

Rose was inordinately protective of her personal life. This does not surprise me. The need to look respectable followed her all her life. This need, as Orleck suggests in her book, came not only from Rose's early personality development but also from dealing with the responses to her socialist and left politics over the years: She was investigated by the New York legislature between 1919 and 1920; she was called the "Rose of Anarchy," a name that followed her in the 1920s and 1930s; in 1938, she garnered the attention of the newly formed House Committee on Un-American Activities (HUAC). Finally, Rose endured the second Red Scare from the late 1940s through the 1950s. When she began to write her book in the 1950s, Rose was likely concerned about publicly sharing anything about her sexuality or the sexuality of her friends.

Speaking to a crowd in Ohio during a suffrage rally in 1912, Rose said, "What the woman who labors wants is the right to live, not simply exist. . . . The worker must have bread, but she must have roses, too. . . ." In her memoir, Rose writes that her sister, Jane, would play the piano while she and her brothers would sing. "I had a pretty good voice, not strong but true, and Harry and Charles and I had grand times singing our heads off." At my grandparents' fiftieth anniversary, the main activity, besides eating, was singing. Our whole Schneiderman extended family sang—and Aunt Rose was in the thick of it. I spent my childhood singing at home with my father, hearing Grandpa Harry sing, performing musical skits with cousins. Later, as a young adult, I performed folk songs that my grandfather, great-uncle, and great-aunt probably sang at the piano, and labor songs that Aunt Rose would have sung. These days, at the end of my presentations about Rose's life and the Triangle fire, I sing—for Rose.

CHAPTER 8

Triangle in Two Acts
From Bubbe Mayses to Bangladesh

Annelise Orleck

My Grandmother, Kalpona, and the Fire:
Last Time, This Time, and Next Time

In the early 1970s, Brighton Beach was not yet Little Odessa—the epicenter of Soviet Jewish immigration to New York. It was a neighborhood of retired garment workers, almost all of them Eastern European Jewish immigrants who had arrived between the 1920s and the 1970s. Many of my neighbors bore the scars of traumatic memories. They also wore with pride their memories of triumphant labor uprisings in "the shops." "The ILG," as they called the International Ladies Garment Workers Union, included numerous retiree groups active in Brighton. Thousands of "Amalgamated" retirees lived there, too, in the Warbasse Houses built by the Amalgamated Clothing Workers Union in the early 1960s on the border of Brighton and Coney Island.

As these white-haired men and women gathered in the vest-pocket parks or on the Brighton Beach Boardwalk, they told of their long-ago struggles. Survivors of the Russian Revolution of 1905, Warsaw ghetto fighters, and survivors of Auschwitz and the Stalinist purges invoked their dead right alongside their living. Stories of the Triangle fire jostled for place among these memories in that narrow neighborhood of Art

Deco buildings, wooden walkways, and sand. As told on those warm nights by the cardplayers and chess players and mandolin players and aging political firebrands, the story of the Triangle fire was an origins myth, a cathartic tragedy of the bad old days: *That's how we built the labor movement. That's how we got to the point where we are now, where you can go to work without having to put your life on the line.*

I grew up with those Triangle stories and, even closer to home, the tales told by my grandmother Lena, who worked there as a girl. Often her stories were parables of deep friendship and loss. Lena had bonded powerfully with her Triangle coworkers as they grew to womanhood in that most famous of shops. She had comic tales. But many of her tales were tragic: young women searching for birth control (leather diaphragms were sold quietly by one of "the girls"); friends seeking safe means to abort their ninth or maybe their tenth child, whom they could not afford to feed.

Lena's reminiscences of danger and disaster ran through my mind as I listened to the songs of struggle and survival that rang out in my neighborhood—in Yiddish, English, sometimes Italian—in the senior centers, on the streets, on the boardwalk. I often smelled traces of fire while walking by the sea. It drifted up into my nostrils from dark singed wooden boards, charred by campfires lit by homeless women and men who slept on the sand. The smell of burned wood, leftover food, and wet clothing marked this outpost on the edge of a city that, in an act of desperation as it faced bankruptcy, had released hundreds of nonviolent mentally ill men and women from public hospitals and asylums. Many landed on the sands of Brighton Beach. But the lingering scent of fire also stirred memories for my grandmother and her friends, of lessons that Lena wanted me never to forget. She and other garment union retirees believed that we had come far from those days, thanks to the rise of powerful unions, thanks to Franklin Roosevelt and Frances Perkins, and to state and federal labor laws. Over the years, this history became a comforting myth.

I am a historian whose work is grounded in activism. Since my first years in graduate school, I have devoted myself to studying the history of workers' movements, connecting the workers of yesterday and those of today. Being the granddaughter of Lena has shaped my work, as has my encounter and friendship with Bangladeshi garment union leader Kalpona Akter. Since we first met, Kalpona and I have stayed in touch. I have seen her again and again, interviewed her, listened to her stories, and kept her life as a point of reference for my work on the early twenty-first-century global uprising against poverty wages.

As the second decade of the twenty-first century dawned and the centennial of the Triangle fire approached, I began to understand that the memory of the fire evoked something much more recent than 1911. It cast a spotlight on the realities of a new global garment industry in which factories burned and workers regularly died. In terms of worker safety, union rights, and living wages, the globalization of the garment trade since the 1980s had taken the world backward at least one hundred years. Hundreds of thousands of women garment workers, I learned, were fighting the same battles that my grandmother and her militant young friends had fought—this time in Bangladesh, Cambodia, Myanmar, Ethiopia. The fires this time were as devastating, as avoidable, as much the products of greed and the dehumanization of women garment workers as the Triangle fire.

On the evening of the Triangle centennial, I stood on a line of hundreds slowly filing into the Great Hall in the basement of New York's Cooper Union. As I reached the front of the line, a union friend introduced me to Kalpona Akter, perhaps the best-known leader of the twenty-first-century garment workers' movement. Thanks to global pressure, Kalpona and her fellow activist Babu Akter had been freed from prison so that they could travel to New York for this event. They had brought with them purple T-shirts with white line drawings of Triangle workers standing side by side with twenty-first-century Bangladeshi clothing makers. In bold, above the drawings, were the words **Not One More Fire.** When Kalpona climbed onto the stage of the Great Hall to address the audience, her eyes swept the room and she stood silent for a moment. Then she said, quietly, words I have never forgotten: "In Bangladesh, it is not 2011. It is 1911."

Lena

My grandmother Lena entered the shops when she was nine and worked at Triangle from 1900 to 1907, the year she had her first child. When her kids were older, she went back to garment work, sewing buttonholes in assorted union shops for decades. She would never work in a nonunion shop, she told me fiercely. She never did.

Lena was single for more than sixty years after her husband's death at thirty-two. Her philandering husband, a raincoat and umbrella salesman, died when my father was two, his older brother seven, his sister eight. Lena had to feed three kids all through the years, until they grew to an age when they could work. She made their clothes on her old sewing machine, which she kept in the front room of the house where she lived when I was young.

She wore not one but two wedding rings. One ring was for her long-dead wandering rogue of a husband, so it was clear that her three children were "legitimate." She was a single mother for most of her parenting life and—well, you know—people talked, people whispered. The other ring, worn on her right hand, was for her best friend, who had died at twenty-nine while trying to self-abort what would have been her tenth child. Two wedding rings—because someone always asked. And she was always ready to tell. She had a look that said, I dare you!

Lena would arch a sharply pointed eyebrow when she sensed that I might be growing skeptical about whatever story she was telling. She'd pause, the moment extending into deep, intentional silence. After a bit, she'd state, slowly and forcefully, "That's the way the story went" or "That's the way it was." Glaring, she silently challenged me to challenge her. Lena, edgy and sarcastic, smart and scary.

My grandmother was eighty when I was born. I was fifteen and she was ninety-five when she died in my uncle's house at the edge of Brooklyn, by the sea. There was a common thread to all our interactions: I was very young and she was very old and unrepentantly intense and insistent that she really did remember all the stories she told me about her long-ago youth and the days of her militance.

Rashe Leah Lieberman was her full name. She was raised on Henry Street, in the heart of the Lower East Side. She had emigrated as a toddler (with her parents) from Kharkov, a violence-prone city in Ukraine that was home to many Jews. The pogroms were bad after 1881, her parents told her, and Eta (my great-grandmother) had relatives in New York. So they took their babies and left.

I was with my daughter and a friend of hers when we happened on Lena's Henry Street house on the day of the Triangle centennial. The girls had volunteered to participate in Ruth Sergel's pop-up annual *Chalk* memorial. They were assigned a house on the block of Henry Street where my grandmother and her parents had once rented an apartment. My father and his brother and sister lived there when they were little. During the 1980s and 1990s, there was a Chinese-owned garment factory in the building. On March 25, 2011, a stream of Chinese families gingerly stepped over the pastel name and dates that my daughter and her friend were chalking. Some stopped to talk to us—of then and now.

Then: Rashe Leah went to work sewing in New York's ready-to-wear clothing industry when she was just nine years old. By her teens, she was, with her two older brothers, responsible for keeping her family fed and clothed. Her father, Herschel, was a caretaker in one of the Henry Street synagogues. He smiles from faded photographs hanging on my stairway, dapper in a straw hat, glasses, and a light, well-combed beard. He leans on a long broom, which he used to sweep the street in front of the shul. That was his job. Lena's mother, Eta, was a pious woman who spoke only Yiddish until, on her deathbed, she shocked her grandchildren by rambling loudly and fervently in perfect English. Eta never worked outside the home, but she took in, fed, and washed for boarders who helped pay the rent. Determined to donate to the upkeep of "poor orphans," Eta fasted one or two days a week and deposited the money she would have spent on food into a metal *pishke* (coin box) she kept nailed to the kitchen wall. "That's how the story went," her daughter told me half a century later.

Boarders and caretaker work notwithstanding, my great-grandparents never had any money, Lena would tell me. They depended on what she and her brothers earned in the "rag trade." The family moved around often because, in those days, landlords would give you a free month's rent, or sometimes more, when you first moved in. Eta would look for the window signs: APARTMENTS TO LET—FREE FOR THE FIRST MONTH OR TWO OR THREE. And the family would move. But only "up or down the block." Henry Street was home and they stayed there for years, until they moved to Williamsburg, then East New York, then Prospect Park.

As a teenage worker, my grandmother desperately wanted to be someone other than Rashe Leah. She adopted the "American" name Lena, maybe right around the time she was lucky enough to land a job at the ultramodern Triangle Waist Company soon after it opened. Maybe it was 1900. Maybe 1902. The ceilings were high and the windows were large. The ads described the building as "fireproof." And in a sense, it was. The building still stands. Even after the fire, you could only see dark smudges on its exterior. Fireproof—on the outside.

Lena was in her twenties when she started at Triangle. Single, olive-skinned, and dark-eyed, she sported at her temples distinctive white wings, which shone on a head of slick black hair. Her fiery eyes, deep voice, razorlike sarcasm, and refusal to suffer fools made her memorable. But, she often said, she was just one among thousands of young immigrant girls and women sewing, sewing, sewing.

My grandmother Lena talked of Triangle not as a tragedy but as her place of work, a community of friends, a starting point for the rest of her life. She worked there as a young woman—before marriage and children—and then again later. She carried her memories of Triangle into garment shops where she worked long after the fire. For forty years, she sewed buttonholes, tiny stitches all along the outlines of the little cuts in the fabric—reinforcing, strengthening, remembering.

She was already a seasoned rabble-rouser by the time she took the Triangle job. Lena claimed to have led her first strike at seventeen. She had been working in a small shop, in a crowded, congested room heated with a coal stove, the air black and thick. The foreman was "handsy." It infuriated Lena. Not so much for herself, because she had no trouble "punching a man who thought he could be fresh," she told me. But it angered her that the foreman was always running his hands across the bodies of "the quiet girls," the ones he knew would not fight back.

One day, Lena let him have it, publicly, loudly. And she was fired.

"Are you coming with me?" she shouted to the other workers. Her friends looked up—Fannia, Elena, Rose.

"Why not?"

There were a million reasons why not, most of all that no one had money to spare. No one could afford to be fired.

These teenagers, rebellious though they might have been at heart, had to return to their parents later that night. And their mothers were waiting, hands out, for their pay. If a girl had nothing to hand over, the family would be short on food that week. Still, angry and tired of being pawed, they rose, or so the story went, following Lena out the door. It was her first strike. It might have been 1905.

She told the story proudly, patting her abundant lap, nodding her head, and smiling. She never told me how it ended. But she insisted that it really happened: "That's the way it went. We walked out. We didn't let them have their way with us. Not then. Not ever again."

It was the dawn of the electric sewing machine era and production speeds had doubled in just a few years. The girls were feeling worn, Lena recalled: "Stretched right about to breaking. All the time. All the time."

Lena found channels for her rage and her fiery energy in anarchist street meetings, where she claimed to have heard the greatest of all rabble-rousers, Emma Goldman, Red Emma, rile up a crowd. "The way she spoke, the way she spoke," my grandmother mused. "She made us feel ready to do anything." Emma Goldman became a mentor, according to Lena. The young girl learned from the older immigrant's brilliant, diamond-hard romantic, hopeful vision of change.

"It makes sense, right?" she'd say in that provocative way. "People could all be free if there was no property, no fences."

Did she really know Emma Goldman? Did she hear her speak? Follow her lead? I have no idea. But why not? "That's the way the story went."

Figure 8.1. Rasha Leah "Lena" Orleck in her Brooklyn backyard.
Photographers unknown; composite photo courtesy of Annelise Orleck.

I had a hard time imagining Lena talking to others that way, thinking that way, and could not envision her as the wiry little girl who had started to work in garment shops. At sixty-five, she sat down in an overstuffed chair and rose rarely after that. When I knew her, she seemed part of that chair, her fingers tapping impatiently on the upholstered arms.

It seemed to me, when I was a child, that Grandma Lena stood up only once a week—on Friday nights, when she roasted chickens for the Sabbath. Somewhere along the way, she had become religious. Her sons were fiercely antireligious, contemptuously referring to rabbis as "beards," by which they meant people who only performed piety. Not the real thing. Not truly spiritual men. But "everyone respected Lena," my mother used to say admiringly about her mother-in-law. "Respected her a lot. And feared her." So neither my father nor my uncle Joe ever mocked her for keeping the Sabbath in those last years. I see her standing there, legs spread wide, a ladle in her hand. She leans over the stove, stirs something, forcefully, militantly, like she did everything else, this incongruous *balabusta*—master of her house. Over the years, Lena must have stood that way a million times—stirring a cast-iron pot with a wooden spoon.

Lena's daughter, my aunt Ruth, who also worked in garment shops from the time she was fourteen, keeping account books for a baby cap company, says her mother told her that she had marched down Fifth Avenue in suffrage parades. Lena had told Ruth about Inez Milholland, one of the founders of New York's Heterodoxy Club, who rode a white horse at the head of the parades, her long hair flowing down her back, in a bodysuit meant to make her look like the naked Lady Godiva.

"It was a long time ago," Ruth said. "Who knows? But I think it's true."

By the time of the Triangle fire, my grandmother was married and had two children, a boy and a girl. She and her husband, Julius, had moved to Providence, Rhode Island, where his family was, and then to Old Orchard Beach, Maine, where they sold umbrellas and raincoats in the summer. Tired of living so far from her family, my grandmother eventually moved back in with her parents on Henry Street. That's one explanation of why she moved to New York.

The better story: Lena found out that my grandfather was having an affair with a woman who sold raincoats and galoshes, so she pretended to leave town, then planned to catch him with his lover. As the story goes, Lena marched into the woman's store—nine-year-old son and ten-year-old daughter beside her, baby in arms—and pulled her husband out.

The way my aunt Ruth (the ten-year-old) remembered it, the storekeeper, my grandfather's girlfriend, had shouted a Yiddish curse as sheepish Julius was dragged out by furious Lena. It was something on the order of "If I can't have you, no one will." At least, that's the way the story went. Julius died six months later.

Lena did a brief stint trying to run a candy store in Williamsburg, Brooklyn. She taught her children to hide under the counter on

Saturday nights, when nearby bars closed. Crowds of drunken fighters spilled onto the street, and bottles sometimes came smashing through windows. Before too long, Lena moved back in again with her parents on Henry Street and, for the ensuing decades, sewed buttonholes to earn her living. The work had its benefits, she liked to say. She learned fluent Italian because most of her coworkers spoke only that. For years, she worked next to Rudy Giuliani's grandmother, she said, and "even his own grandmother found the kid whiny." Or so the story went. Most important to her, these were union jobs. And so when she turned sixty-five, Lena could retire for good because she had a pension. That's when she sat down. She felt she had earned it. And we all did, too.

Kalpona

Kalpona Akter was born almost a century after Lena. Like Lena, she began sewing clothes for an exploding global fashion market when she was a child. Twelve-year-old Kalpona and her ten-year-old brother sometimes worked twenty-hour shifts for weeks on end. They slept on the floor where they sewed until the order was complete, then were allowed to go home for a while.

Kalpona labored in Dhaka's twentieth-century sweatshops until her late teens, when she was blacklisted for union organizing. Since that time, it has been all she does—she organizes, gives speeches, travels the world to tell the stories of life in today's global rag trade. She has entered still-smoldering factory ruins to find labels or invoices that could prove which global corporation had paid to have clothes made there. A lot of what she does, she told me in 2016, when we spoke for hours at the World Social Forum in Montreal, is to help workers figure out who they really work for—in order to help them seek repairs, reparations, some fleeting measure of accountability from the titans of today's cheap, disposable shirts and skirts and jeans and sneakers.

I had first met Kalpona five years earlier at the Triangle Fire Centennial Commemoration in New York City in 2011. By that time, she had accumulated years of tireless travel around the world to help twenty-first-century consumers of fashion see the brutal truth—that Triangle is not a distant historical event that changed everything. To come to the event, Kalpona had been released from Dhaka's notorious nineteenth-century Central Jail, where she had been chained under a desk for seven days. She had been charged with murder. The charges were fake, she told me when we spoke after the event, but she faced a life sentence, or possibly even a death sentence. She had been arrested with fellow organizer Aminul Islam, a close friend with whom Kalpona traveled and organized for years. The charges were later dropped. But in 2012, Islam was kidnapped, tortured, and murdered. To this day, no one has been charged. Kalpona is still shaken by his murder. She believes that it was ordered from above and carried out by police. Every morning, she has to steel herself, Kalpona reflected when we saw each other in Burlington, Vermont, in 2019. When she leaves the apartment where she lives with her mother and brother (also a union organizer), Kalpona wonders if she will see them again.

The night we first met, at Cooper Union on March 25, 2011, Kalpona spoke for her fellow garment workers. But it wasn't only garment workers who filled Cooper Union's Great Hall that night. There were many kinds of workers: taxi drivers and catfish processors, coal miners and garment workers—those who do some of the twenty-first century's most dangerous jobs. It seemed so fitting that the Great Hall was where they told their stories, where New York City high school students read their poetry about the fire, where children's and union retiree choruses sang. In that same columned auditorium, Clara Lemlich had roused the crowd to declare a general strike, Frederick Douglass had argued against slavery, and Oglala Lakota chief Red Cloud had told shocked crowds how the U.S. military was slaughtering his people. On the night of the centennial, Clara Lemlich's eighty-six-year-old daughter, Rita Margules, sat in the front row as then thirty-five-year-old Akter mounted the stairs to the stage.

Those who entered the auditorium had been given newsprint programs with images of Kalpona and Clara under the words "I have something to say." "Those words say a lot," Kalpona said of the words

Clara had spoken 102 years earlier. After she had finished telling stories of fire and loss, of oppression and resistance and the slow pace of change, Kalpona came down the stairs, walked around the front of the stage, and knelt beside the tiny, wizened old woman in the first row, sitting with her own daughter and grandson. Kalpona took Rita's hand and whispered to her, "Your mother is also our mother." Clara inspired Dhaka's workers to fight to improve working conditions in twenty-first-century Bangladesh, just as she had in New York in the years just before and after Triangle. From my seat in the Great Hall, I cried as I watched. When she told me this story years later, Kalpona cried, too.

I have asked Kalpona more than once how she goes forward, knowing that she could die any day. "You can't live if you're always worrying about dying," she says with a faint trace of impatience. Then she admits, "When I start my morning, I can't tell my mom with certainty that I will come back home." Home is a Dhaka apartment that she shares with her mother, her brother, and nephews and nieces. "I never walk in the city alone," she says. "I always have comrades with me." Yet she insists that she doesn't fear dying. At least she is not afraid for herself. She worries about her family. It wears on her to think of the pain her death would cause them. She feels a need to protect them, especially the little ones, her beloved nephews and nieces, whom she hopes to see grow up in a better world.

Some Bangladeshi activists have criticized the landmark 2013 Accord on Fire and Building Safety in Bangladesh, which Akter helped to craft and has worked tirelessly to publicize so that more and more corporations sign on. It is now in its second iteration, reauthorized after the first agreement expired in 2018. Younger activists insist that the agreement is not worker-centered enough, not union-friendly enough, that it offers Western donors too easy a fix. They believe that all the international focus on Kalpona's role in shaping the accord obscures the work of other leaders and thousands of grassroots activists.

In many different settings where these points are raised, I have seen Kalpona pull herself up and reply forcefully, "This is what matters. Before the accord, two hundred or more workers a year died in

Bangladesh making clothes. In 2017, four years after the accord, none died. Zero." She forms her fingers into a circle. "Zero."

In 2017, the first time Kalpona visited me in Vermont, where I live, we sat on a summer camp dock on Lake Fairlee, empty before the season. "I love the quiet," she said, gazing at the light riffling wind on the water. "It is never quiet in Dhaka. There is no place to go to be quiet." She seemed weary. I told her I worried that she does not prioritize taking care of her health. She travels too much, works too hard, lives with too much daily stress. But she cannot stop. She is haunted by the flames, by the memories of holding back mothers straining to run into still-burning buildings to try to find their trapped children.

The second time Kalpona visited Vermont, she was working. She had been invited to speak at the conference of the Food Chain Workers Alliance in Burlington that brought together Walmart workers, Migrant Justice—an organization that represents many of the state's dairy farm workers—and many more food-chain workers in every sector of the industry from around the world. We sat on the dock overlooking Lake Champlain as a much stronger wind sent waves rolling in hard from the high peaks of the Adirondacks on the distant shore. It was hot and Kalpona wasn't feeling well. I told her she should come back to Vermont some summer soon, to get some quiet, some peace. To rest. She imagined bringing her mother with her and enjoying the green quiet.

Triangle, Tazreen, Rana Plaza haunt Kalpona Akter. Haunt me. Haunt so many. In 1985, I interviewed garment union organizer Pauline Newman, who had worked at Triangle as a five-year-old and a teen, who had jumped into barrels to hide from inspectors and read poetry aloud on the shop floor with her fellow workers.

"I lost friends there," she told me in the middle of our long talk. Triangle memories ambushed her seventy-plus years later. Her gravelly voice dropped to a cracked whisper. "I lost so many friends." Newman told me she was on the road, organizing for the ILGWU, when news of the fire reached her. She knew that continuing to organize women garment workers was her only way forward, but for months she felt crushed by grief. The only way to keep from sinking under the waves of

Figure 8.2. Annelise Orleck and Kalpona Akter.
Photo by Elizabeth M. Cooke; photo courtesy of Annelise Orleck.

that grief was to bring more and more workers into unions, to demand better from employers. To demand more for themselves.

Kalpona, too, tries not to let the grief paralyze her. Her eyes filled with tears as she told me a story in a hotel in Montreal during the summer of 2016. All around us, activists were gathering for the World Social Forum—its famous motto: A Better World Is Possible. She spoke in a hoarse whisper of holding a wailing mother in her arms after the 2012 Tazreen fire. She described the feeling of dust in her lungs, thick in the streets of worker neighborhoods after Rana Plaza. "It's hard to live with these memories sometimes," she said in that same cracked whisper I had heard from Pauline Newman decades earlier. I asked if she ever went to the beach to rest, to recover her strength, to breathe clean air, which she told me is in short supply in the center of Dhaka.

"There is too much to do." She smiled tiredly. "I never rest." Then the flash of personal vulnerability evaporated and the fiery activist reappeared. "We want the jobs," Kalpona said over and over. "We want the jobs"—jobs that employ more than four million, mostly women, in her country. "We just don't want to die for them." Surely my grandmother Lena, Pauline, and the hundreds of women who worked and gossiped and fought for better working conditions at Triangle felt the same.

The Global Uprisings Against Poverty Wages

It was not accidental that the 2019 Burlington gathering that Kalpona attended brought together retail workers, fast-food workers, farmworkers, garment workers, and hotel workers from across the United States and around the world. By that time, low-wage workers had been organizing globally for more than seven years—staging remarkable one-day flash strikes that drew low-wage workers out of their workplaces and into the streets in hundreds of cities in more than forty countries around the world. Forty years of falling real wages, the erosion of union membership, and the gutting of employment protections through the "gig" economy had left them little choice. I heard that again and again as I talked to workers around the world between 2011 and 2020 while working on my book *We Are All Fast Food Workers Now*. "I have no choice. I have nothing left to lose." And they sat down to block traffic in Atlanta and in Manila. They held hunger strikes on Manhattan's Park Avenue and in front of Los Angeles City Hall. An uprising against poverty wages circled the globe.

Bangladeshi garment workers began to fight in earnest in 2006, and within a few years they were joined by hundreds of thousands of Cambodian and Burmese garment workers, women in India and Ethiopia and Honduras. In the era of Triangle, of my grandmother's strikes, organizing was done primarily by word of mouth, by whispers in the shops, by knocking on neighborhood doors. By the 1930s, the telephone had become a powerful organizing tool—expanding the scale of strikes so that, in 1935, 1948, and 1951, Jewish and African American and Polish women waged national campaigns against the high cost of meat, bread, and milk. In the twenty-first century, smartphones have revolutionized the scope and modes of organizing again.

"My workers did not always have water," Kalpona told me. "But they had smartphones." She remembers seeing Dhaka garment workers on the factory floor watching on their phones the celebrations of Cambodian garment workers when they quadrupled the minimum wage for garment workers in that country in 2014. When thousands of low-wage workers flooded the streets of Manhattan on April 15, 2015,

I watched as marchers uploaded their own videos and downloaded videos of workers' marches in Kathmandu and Manila, Tegucigalpa and Abuja. I saw a middle-aged home-health-care worker download a photograph of a teenage garment worker in Bangladesh smiling shyly as she held up a sign with the words BANGLADESHI WORKERS SUPPORT THE $15 MINIMUM WAGE. Labor's rhetoric was international in my grandmother's day, but it had to be actualized via time-consuming and expensive modes of travel. As a result, only a select few could participate in face-to-face international gatherings. Today new technologies, especially smartphones, enable workers to connect electronically in all kinds of ways—in conversation, through watching videos of one another's protests and strikes, and by posting their own nonprofessional videos of speeches, protests, hunger strikes, and more.

The ghosts of Triangle were on picket lines in Kalamazoo in 1912, when Pauline Newman, still grieving for friends lost in the fire, went to organize workers there, who were on strike against sexual harassment in the shop. In 2018, young McDonald's workers displayed the same militance, the same anger at being grabbed and groped and insulted on the job. Triangle, Tazreen, Rana Plaza, the grills of thousands of McDonald's around the world are linked together as symbols in the twenty-first-century global uprising against poverty wages, against sexual violence, for a living wage, for decent labor conditions, for respect.

Lena and Kalpona are bookends bracketing the history of the global garment industry—mechanization and speedup after the invention of electric sewing machines in the early twentieth century, and in both eras, the subcontracting, the fight to unionize, the endless flights of capital in search of manufacturing sites without labor laws, unions, or environmental regulations.

The smoke. The death.

Lena and Kalpona, separated by a century, embody the heart, the brains, the militant spirit of the young women who have made and continue to make clothing. The ready-to-wear revolution was just beginning when Lena was young, when most people still wore homemade clothing. By 2011, when I first met Kalpona, the fast fashion revolution was well under way. It had lowered clothing prices, quadrupled the number of workers in the global trade (almost all of them women), and sparked an epidemic, an addiction in the affluent capitals of the world to cheap, colorful shirts and jeans and skirts. By the second decade of the twenty-first century, Americans were buying five times the number of items of clothing as they had bought in previous eras. The English and Europeans were not far behind. Lena and Kalpona were both products of seismic manufacturing shifts, of earthshaking zeitgeist shifts.

These garment workers, these girls, these women are militant symbols of their times. From Brighton Beach to Dhaka, spanning more than a century, Lena's and Kalpona's voices still carry the stories of the fight for justice.

PART THREE

TEACHERS

CHAPTER 9

Teaching the Triangle Fire to Middle School Students

▼

Kimberly Schiller

M y mother was a Long Island revolutionary. She taught me from an early age to be an activist. As an elementary school student in culottes and jumpers, I would tag along to the next rally, endorsement soiree, election-results party, and press conference. By the time I was eleven years old, I had attended many of my mother's political meetings. In 1993, when I was eleven, I helped her collect signatures outside our local King Kullen grocery store, urging people to sign a petition for Ben Zwirn, the Democratic candidate for Nassau County Executive. Some people shooed her away, while others took our clipboard and signed. I felt excited as I watched my mother, unafraid and relentless, walk right up to people and discuss the direction Nassau County was heading and how we needed a change from the same old politics.

I grew up in Levittown, a hamlet in Nassau County, Long Island, founded by William Levitt after World War II. Its purpose was to be a suburban haven where returning soldiers could put down roots, get married, and buy a house. Levittown is a middle-class community with both blue- and white-collar workers, union and management, living side by side. When I was growing up, politics on Long Island, particularly in our neighborhood, was for the most part red and conservative. Many held on to the "good ole days" of the 1950s. My mother has always been a proud New Yorker with a sharp tongue, wise words, and a staunch inclination toward activism. Her politics often differed from those of our neighbors and local politicians. When local politicians and our school board president and trustees saw my mother coming, they shuddered. They knew they were in for an earful.

In 1989, after years of rallies, town hall meetings, and three-minute commentaries at school board meetings, my mother got the attention of Governor Mario Cuomo. She wrote a letter to the editor of *Newsday*, a Long Island newspaper, calling for Governor Cuomo to have a conversation with her regarding the high property taxes on Long Island. Governor Cuomo responded with a promise to visit. When that day came, it was all hands on deck. News reporters lined our quiet, suburban, cookie-cutter street with giant antennae and other equipment that looked monstrous to me.

As a second grader, all I knew was that I could stay home from school because the governor was coming to visit. To stay home from school was unheard of in my house unless you were sick. But I was more excited about the delicious chocolate-covered strawberries that were teasing me from our dining room buffet than the hoopla about to happen. Yet when I looked out the window and saw hundreds of people with handmade signs in support of my mother, a few megaphones, families, and men in suits all around my house, I understood that my mother was the catalyst for all this excitement and felt proud.

My mother, with vibrant red hair, a crisp white shirt, and pleated black dress pants, stepped out of our house to shake the governor's hand, with my father, my kid brother, and me in tow. In Levittown, people are quiet, happy to gossip and complain about local issues. All talk, no action. My mother, on the other hand, was trying to make a difference, to keep Levittown affordable for middle- and working-class people, and to uphold the dream that her parents had when they moved east from Brooklyn thirty years earlier. Smiling, she shook the governor's hand, looking him straight in the eye.

My mother's strength and courage inspired me as a child of eight, just as Frances Perkins's determination would inspire me as an adult, though it would be a long time before I could truly find my own voice and confidence.

Figure 9.1. Governor Mario Cuomo's visit. From the left, Kimberly's mother, Carolyn Fevola; her father, Ronald Schiller; Governor Mario Cuomo; and Kimberly. The photo was taken in the family's dining room in Levittown, New York, May 1989. Photographer unknown; photo courtesy of Carolyn Fevola.

School was my favorite place because I was able to let my mind run free and learn about others outside of my small community. When I was nine years old, I decided that I wanted to be a teacher. I used to torture my kid brother with short stories and handmade dittos. In high school, I noticed how my tenth-grade English teacher, Ms. Evans, wove bigger ideas through the texts and vocabulary we studied. I saw myself in Scout, idolized Atticus, and empathized with Jay Gatsby. During my junior year of college, I registered for a women's history course. Professor Klee introduced me to Sarah and Angelina Grimke, Alice Paul, Ida B. Wells, Jane Addams, Victoria Woodhull, and Shirley Chisholm. The chapters in the textbook Professor Klee assigned moved along with just enough detail to arouse my curiosity, as the literature I had read in tenth- grade English had done. Later, while studying to become a teacher, I would turn to the lessons of Ms. Evans, Professor Klee, and my mother to shape my pedagogy.

Midway through the semester of my junior year, flipping through our women's history textbook, I came across a photo of the Asch

Building ablaze while water from fire hoses stretched to reach the top floors of the building but fell short. Two or three pages of text accompanied the photo, but there was not much explanation aside from basic facts: the date, the factory owners' names, and the number of victims. I do not remember what my professor said when I asked about the tragedy. I only remember feeling a deep connection to the victims and an urge to visit the site of the fire.

Earlier in the semester, after reading about Victoria Woodhull, I had created my own walking tour of the sites where she once lived, or was jailed, and had felt sad to see many traces of this history had been lost. On Great Jones Street, for example, I discovered an eyesore of a parking lot instead of the former residence of Ms. Woodhull. I hoped the Asch Building had not suffered a similar fate. I marked the date of the fire's anniversary in my calendar and vowed to visit the site then, if not sooner.

New York City has always been my refuge, so vibrant and full of opportunities, and a welcome change from Levittown. I was shocked to learn that the Triangle fire had occurred there, and so close to my beloved Washington Square Park. I had spent plenty of time in the park by myself, and with friends, chatting on benches, listening to indie music, reading books. How did I not know about the tragedy that had happened just one block away? On the days leading up to the ninety-first anniversary of the fire, and my first visit to the Triangle building, I often thought about the victims. What could I do for them? How would it feel to be there on the anniversary of the fire?

On the ninety-first anniversary, armed with a bouquet of multicolored carnations, I traveled into the city in the early morning. I sat next to other silent commuters on the Long Island Railroad. In Manhattan, I meandered through Washington Square Park on my way to the Asch Building, now renamed the Brown Building. I tried to imagine what it would have felt like walking to work, as so many of the workers had done that Saturday ninety-one years ago. It felt very different to be in Washington Square with this "new" information. I still admired the beautiful arch and the redbrick houses that line the park, but an uneasy feeling overtook me.

As I approached the building, I examined it from all angles. I counted the floors up to the ninth, shaded my eyes as I looked upward, and tried to imagine what it would have been like to be up there, and how it would have felt to watch from the ground. Both images were dizzying. I felt chilled, not because it was a blustery day, but because of the thoughts racing through my mind. I looked around. The Brown Building did not seem to strike anyone else. Passersby continued to walk, bothered by my "touristy" presence in the middle of their sidewalk. I felt isolated. It was as if I were a roadblock before their destination. I needed to do more than just pay my respects. But what could that be?

For the next several years, I returned to the Brown Building on the anniversary of the fire and left a bouquet of flowers. Once, I saw a wreath with a sash dedicated to the victims and realized that others also remembered. As I continued to visit, on the anniversary and other times during the year, I also realized the passersby weren't apathetic; they just didn't know. I decided that I would do whatever I could to teach others about the Triangle fire.

As I continued researching the history of the fire, I was moved by what Frances Perkins wrote. The tragedy was "seared on my mind as well as my heart—a never-to-be-forgotten reminder of why I had to spend my life fighting conditions that could permit such a tragedy." Perkins brought her words to life by putting all of her energy into improving working conditions in New York State and, later, the nation as our secretary of labor. I wasn't secretary of labor like Ms. Perkins, or a rabble-rouser like my mother, but I did have an audience in my students. I wanted to spark the same interest in important topics as my teachers had once done for me. They understood that their purpose in the classroom was not solely to check homework, correct grammar, and grade papers, but to develop a love of learning, and give us the tools to discover what impassioned us. They opened doors and hoped that we would walk through them. I remember when Ms. Evans had assigned *To Kill a Mockingbird*, and how passionately she had read Atticus' words: "You just hold your head high and keep those fists down. No matter what anybody says to you, don't you let 'em get your goat. Try fighting with your head for a change." I remembered the strength in Ms. Evans's voice. I realized that Professor Klee and Ms. Evans were activists as well as teachers.

I was in the midst of my first year teaching English to sixth graders at a school for gifted and talented children on the Lower East Side when I decided to teach the Triangle fire. My kids were spunky, immature (at times), and lovable. They were voracious readers, and a few of them persuaded me to begin a book club. We read novels like *The Giver*, *The Tale of Despereaux*, and *Eragon*—wonderful novels, but in the genres of fantasy and sci-fi. I was looking for something different to share with them. Then I read Mary Jane Auch's historical fiction, coming-of-age novel *Ashes of Roses* (2002).

Ashes of Roses is a compelling tale that follows Rose Nolan, a sixteen-year-old Irish immigrant, just a few years older than my students. The novel describes Rose's desire to assimilate—a tribulation familiar to my students then, but also now, almost two decades after I started teaching the Triangle fire. It is an emotional roller coaster that culminates with the protagonist and her friends struggling to escape the fire at the Triangle Waist Company. This book helped me bring Triangle history into my classroom. My club of sixth graders devoured the book. They were enthralled by the events and the protagonist. I was cultivating the empathy I had hoped for, but not at the level that I wanted, mainly because my students needed more time to mature. It wasn't until I began teaching eighth-grade English on Long Island, fifty miles from the Asch Building, that I was able to blend the lessons into a meaningful unit that affected my students deeply.

The population of students in my district is diverse. There are students who have never lived anywhere else, as well as students who come from thousands of miles away, like the characters in *Ashes of Roses*. Many of those who have come here from other places have faced treacherous conditions unimaginable to me and the native Long Island students. The different groups, however, play for the same sports teams, take the same classes, and move between social worlds seamlessly. The challenge of appealing to different kinds of readers leads a teacher to contemplate many factors when selecting a text. Is this a compelling protagonist? An intriguing story line? Is it relatable or dated? Is it readable? What prereading is needed? What support do I need to provide as we read? My commitment to including the Triangle fire adds another layer, but *Ashes of Roses* answers all my pedagogical questions. There are no magical flourishes, futuristic sci-fi qualities, or utopian/dystopian societies in *Ashes of Roses*, features that many popular YA books now include. Instead, the narrative is populated by authentic characters living in the moment with the hand they are dealt, coming to terms with real-life issues, and battling adversities.

We started with a prereading activity. I took down my usual proofreading and writing- process posters and replaced them with a large map of the world, then asked the students to list their nationalities anonymously on a small piece of paper; finally, I added a pin for every nationality. Our world map grew. It became a tactile exploratory terrain. Although our ancestors hailed from different regions and continents, we were all here now with the same intent: to learn and grow—just as Rose does in the novel. After our heritage map was established, I introduced accounts of immigrants who came through Ellis Island around the same time as Rose and were about the same age. I assigned a group of students to each account and they read it together, examining the hardships, why each immigrant sought refuge in the "land of the free," and what that person's experience was like after arriving in the United States. One group read about Theodore from Greece; another read about Helen from Syria; others had Molly from Germany, June from Palestine, Caren from Sweden, Paulina from Sicily, and Estelle from Austria. We added additional pins to represent these people. My intention was to cultivate a sense of community in our classroom and build on that feeling as we read *Ashes of Roses*. When we finally began reading, I watched as even my most reluctant students turned the pages eagerly. Together, we witnessed each of Rose's adversities. We felt her awe when she saw the Statue of Liberty for the first time. We read the words Rose repeated from "The New Colossus": "'Give me your tired, your poor, your huddled masses . . .' Well, we were poor, all right, and after two weeks crammed into the bottom of the boat . . . we certainly qualified as tired, huddled masses.'Here we are, America,' I whispered. 'We're just exactly what ye ordered.'" When Rose searched for a job to support her family, we empathized with the alienation and disillusion-ment she experienced as she was shunned for her brogue and for being a "greenie." We felt her elation when she found a job at the Triangle and felt like a "somebody," a real American working girl. At the end of the novel, we felt Rose's heartbreak and despair when she saw her hope for a new life in America shatter after the fire. But we also felt Rose's conviction when she pledged to make sure her friends and the fire would not be forgotten.

As we read the last pages of the book, my students' interest in Rose grew. It compelled them to want to learn more about the fire. They asked, "How could this happen?" "Why didn't anyone get in trouble?" "There were kids my age working there?" "Why couldn't they be saved?" "Can we see the building?" "What do you mean this is still happening in our world today?" I was still a student of the fire myself, and it was difficult to answer their questions, but I turned the conversation back to current issues. Even though my students' circumstances may not be as dire as those of the Triangle workers, some have faced many chal-lenges. Feeling alienated, as Rose does in the novel, is not an unusual feeling for my eighth graders. Some struggle daily to find hope and compassion, just like Rose.

When I realized that teaching the Triangle fire could go beyond reading a book, I knew I had to place emphasis on the victims and sur-vivors, and their stories. So, we read about garment workers Daisy Lo-pez Fitze; Catarina, Lucia, and Rosaria Maltese; Katie Weiner. We read about elevator operator Joseph Zito. We read about the Uprising of the 20,000 and Clara Lemlich's powerful words as she stormed the stage at Cooper Union. We built a memorial with illustrations of the Statue of Liberty and lines from Emma Lazarus's "The New Colossus." Our emo-tional connection with the material fueled class discussions about in-justice, assimilation, and integrity.

In 2011, on one of the coldest days of the year, I took a small group on the Long Island Railroad into Manhattan, a far-off place for some of them. We gathered in Union Square, bundled up tight in scarves, hats, mittens, and earmuffs. It struck me that my teenage students were braving the cold to honor people they had never met. They chanted,

Figure 9.2. Eighth-grade students from J. Taylor Finley Middle School, in Huntington, New York, at the Triangle fire commemoration in 2019. Photo by Kimberly Schiller; courtesy of the photographer.

sang, and danced with the eclectic group of musicians and activists who led the procession. Together, we marched with thousands from Union Square to Washington Place and Greene Street. It was a new experience for my students, who have possibly marched down our local Main Street with their cumbersome instruments during the Memorial Day parade, but never in this context, upholding the memory of the 146 victims of the Triangle fire. Without complaint, they solemnly held shirtwaists aloft on bamboo poles, each bearing the name and age of a person who had died in the fire, speaking to their peers about the shirtwaists they were carrying and the compelling symbolism of each.

My thirteen- and fourteen-year-old students listened attentively to the stories of survivors and victims of that distant day in 1911. I noticed them squinting up at the shirtwaists as they swayed in the crisp breeze. I smiled. It was so different from the solitude I had felt nine years earlier when others had indifferently strolled past me. There were scores of people, young and old, including elementary school children wearing cherry red firemen's hats, who looked at my eighth graders like they were the "big kids" with worldly wisdom.

On our way home, I asked my students to journal about the day. I did not require a specific type of writing, prose or poetry, or an illustration. Whatever they felt, I wanted them to express it honestly. Some sat pensively by themselves, scribbling away, while others spoke to their peers, building a plan for their journals. Back in class the next day, we shared our experiences. Some gave a heartfelt impromptu description of the day and others read from their journals aloud. Watching and listening as my students taught their peers, I smiled and wept.

On a typical day, my middle schoolers are usually searching for a pencil seconds before class begins, or racing to their desks to beat the bell, or concentrating on how they can get their nerve up to talk to their latest crush, or managing precarious stacks of binders and scattered papers as they carry them into their next class. These are the issues that concern them, not an event that happened one hundred years ago. But on the day of the commemoration, they become engrossed in the story of Triangle, mesmerized by the sight of the building. They try to imagine what it felt like to stand on the ledge of the ninth-floor windows and face the decision of jumping to their death or burning. Through empathy, they begin to understand their own place in history.

My students discuss what they have learned about the Triangle fire with family, friends, and, at the site, with curious strangers who approach them. They can explain the history behind the fire, what transpired that day, how lives were affected, and the safety laws that were established as a result. Some former students say to new students, "Oh, you have the Triangle teacher," giving a knowing nod. This is when I know that I am making good on a promise that I made to the workers at Triangle.

My work teaching the Triangle fire has shaped my own understanding of my place in history and expanded my commitment to labor activism. In 2012, I met Jane LaTour, a unionist, activist, labor historian, author, and an all-around amazing woman. With her encouragement, I began working with a cohort of the New York Labor History Association. With Jane as our guide, our cohort worked to get young people involved in labor history and events. We built on the New York Labor History Association's mission statement to be "a bridge between the past and the present" by showing labor documentaries like *Farewell to Factory Towns?* and cosponsoring an evening of short films at the Workers Unite Film Festival. In 2013, I was elected to the New York Labor History Association's board. I have also served on the board of the Frances Perkins Forum, and most recently, I was elected district vice president of my own union local, the Associated Teachers of Huntington. As district vice president, I have worked to overcome hurdles, such as mobilizing members within my local to vote against the New York State Constitutional Convention (Con-Con), which would have made labor laws, including those enacted after the Triangle fire, vulnerable to attacks by right-wing groups. In June 2018, we rallied together against the foreboding *Janus* case, which could cause more challenges for unions to organize and mobilize their members.

To help defeat the Con-Con, I assembled a PAC (political action committee) of colleagues across disciplines and grade levels. Together, we compiled informative flyers to distribute; devised a one-on-one plan to meet with many members prior to the vote in November; sent postcard reminders to vote no; and held a phone bank. After our victory against the Con-Con, we were faced with the *Janus v. AFSCME* case, which aimed to destroy public-sector unions by allowing members to opt out of paying dues while forcing the unions to continue representing those members. Even before the Supreme Court passed down its disheartening ruling, my local had already affirmed a recommitment from our members. In a post-*Janus* world, we continue to fight to keep what so many have won for us. Connecting the history of Triangle and other past struggles for justice to our current times, as I do in my teaching and my work with the New York Labor History Association, helps steel us for this fight.

As a teacher, and now as a mother, I have found the strength that I hoped I would find one day when, as an eight-year-old, I watched my mother shake hands with the governor. I am committed to inspiring future activists to speak in their voices. Realizing that my roles as a teacher and an activist are intertwined enables me to bridge more worlds with my middle schoolers. While I was serving on the New York Labor History Association board, Jane LaTour introduced me to Rachel Bernstein, cofounder and cohistorian of the LaborArts organization. Rachel invited me to bring my students to the Clara Lemlich Awards, an event held at the Museum of the City of New York that honors women over eighty years old who have been lifelong activists on behalf of the disenfranchised. My students were paired with these revolutionary women. They toured the Puffin Gallery for Social Activism with their activist mentors. They were able to ask their activist counterparts about their involvement in labor activism, what inspired them to become labor activists, and what motivates them to keep going. We all came away from the event with the knowledge that a person is never too old to fight for what is right—or never too young.

CHAPTER 10

Remembering the Triangle Fire in California

▼

Laura E. Ruberto

Why watch how other people live unless we see
something to apply to our own lives? Learn it. Live it.
—Dorothy Bryant, *Miss Giardino*

A few years ago, my daughter Alma came home from school with a worksheet about the Triangle Shirtwaist Factory fire. It was chock-full of details. It used simple language while also leading students to consider themes of immigration, women's lives, workers' safety, and public protest. The worksheet posed questions such as "Why were working women being treated so poorly?" and "Why were the doors locked?" It noted the specificity of place, New York City, multiple times and explained that many of the workers were poor young women and that most were Italian or Jewish immigrants. Alma seemed surprised when I told her that I knew about these women, their work, and the fire that had caused their deaths. I pulled down from a bookshelf an oversize coffee table book of reprints of *The New York Times* headlines and turned to March 26, 1911, the day the fire made it onto the front page. We looked at the ghastly photograph of the building aflame and read the article out loud together.

As pleased as I was that my daughter's public school was including this labor history lesson in the curriculum, I also wondered if it was the best way to introduce an eight-year-old California girl to the Triangle fire. What impact could the story have on my daughter, a Generation Z child born thousands of miles away from and a hundred years after the disaster? How should California children learn about the Triangle fire in the twenty-first century?

These questions stayed with me because they reflected so squarely my own professional and community work: scholarship on Italian and Italian American women and labor issues; teaching at Berkeley City College (an urban community college); pro-migrant/feminist activist work and other public service projects. Indeed, a great deal of my adult life has circled around issues central to the Triangle fire story: gender, migration, and labor. I have not incorporated these issues haphazardly in my life. Instead, I have done so with purpose and deliberation. While my interest in the Triangle fire as a scholar of Italian and Italian American culture is obvious, what is less apparent is how commemorating the lives lost in the fire has led me to bring to the surface other, less well known stories of migrant suffering and exploitation. Sharing the story of the fire with my daughter led me to reflect on history, location, memory, and my own relationship to the Triangle fire. What happens to the history of the fire when it is remembered far from where it happened? How can we make this story matter in other places and other time periods?

At its heart, the Triangle fire is a story of society's disregard for human life, a disregard that becomes starker when we consider it occurred in a city of great wealth. This dichotomy between exploitation and wealth exists historically, and now, in California. My deeper understanding of the fire's ongoing relevance has come from connecting it to similarly charged California-based events, in particular one that occurred three thousand miles from and thirty-seven years after the fire—the Los Gatos Canyon plane crash of 1948, which killed the twenty-eight Mexican citizens, all migrant workers, on board. Like the Triangle fire, this tragedy is marked by the loss of life of immigrant workers and a neglect of their histories. Like the fire, this story of the trials of immigrants and working-class people in the United States has inspired creative expressions and political work by individuals and communities. Through my involvement with centennial Triangle fire commemorations, I found I could bring the Triangle story to California. Also, by connecting the fire to the Los Gatos plane crash, I could reinforce the importance of both tragedies—and, hopefully, encourage greater dialogue, activism, and change.

In 2010, I joined the San Francisco LaborFest Northern California Triangle Fire Coalition, which was organizing events for the upcoming centennial of the fire. I led the organizing efforts for what became the Berkeley-centered events: LEARN—SHARE—SEW: Berkeley City College Remembers the Triangle Shirtwaist Fire and Immigrant Women Workers. The events had two broad participants/audiences in mind: the Berkeley City College (BCC) community and the non-college community within the city of Berkeley and its environs. The fact that over 50 percent of BCC students are the first in their families to attend college and that many come from immigrant families sharpened the significance of bringing the story of the fire to campus, as did tapping into Berkeley's vibrant liberal culture. Set in the heart of downtown Berkeley, BCC's campus—little more than one large five-story building—is overshadowed by the University of California at Berkeley, whose main campus begins 1.5 blocks away. BCC often goes unnoticed even by those who walk by daily. With its visibility on the streets of Berkeley, the Learn—Share—Sew project helped create a public presence across the geography of the city.

The Learn theme became embedded in the BCC curriculum. Professors Shawn Doubiago and Elizabeth Wing incorporated the Triangle fire in their Women's Studies and Humanities courses, respectively, and involved students in the public programs. The Learn theme ensured that our community within and beyond campus knew the basic history of Triangle (many people did not know about the fire or the protests and changes in labor laws that ensued). A series of faculty talks and documentary film screenings offered historical contexts for the greater Berkeley community to discuss the fire and its memorialization as well the meaning of the fire in contemporary times.

In an effort to extend beyond the local—and connect with initiatives in New York City—faculty, staff, students, and community members chalked the names and ages of the 146 Triangle victims on the sidewalks around a one-square block of downtown Berkeley, giving the entire project greater visibility within Berkeley's cityscape.

Figure 10.1. Laura E. Ruberto chalking outside Berkeley City College.
Photo by Shanna Hullaby; courtesy of the photographer.

Groups of twos and threes took to the streets, fat chalk and lists of names in hand, stopping to explain when passersby asked what cause they were supporting or in what performance-art pieces they were taking part. The colorful scroll of victims' names boldly written out passed by the main entrances to Berkeley City College and Berkeley's City Hall, connecting the two main supporting institutions. This urban action gave the entire series more visibility and led other local folk to become involved. Poet and political activist Arnold Passman joined later planned events by reading from Julia Stein's poetry anthology, *Walking Through a River of Fire: One Hundred Years of Triangle Factory Fire Poems.* Another Berkeley resident, Evelyn Velson, happened upon the chalking event and contacted me, curious to learn more about the commemoration, because, as she modestly mentioned, she was the daughter-in-law of Clara Lemlich Shavelson, the same Lemlich who

Figure 10.2. Artist Melanie Shapiro shows author Michael Parenti how to sew a memorial ribbon. Photo by Laura E. Ruberto; courtesy of the photographer.

was, Velson wrote in an email, "the sparkplug that started the uprising of the 20,000 workers and the real start of the ILGWU." Velson could not attend the commemorative events, but she sent other community members our way.

The third component of the program, Sew, focused on the labor of the Triangle workers. Given how important sewing was to the victims' livelihood, I wanted the commemoration to include the act itself, to evoke the materiality of the work. So I invited Oakland-based artist Melanie Shapiro to develop a project that would showcase the act of sewing and tie it back to the fire and the workers. She created a sewing corner and set up a table where participants could sew their own personalized memorial ribbon. Laid out on the table were vintage fabric swatches and colorful ribbons, as well as pins, needles, and thread. For those who did not know how to sew, she demonstrated how to thread a needle and piece together fabric through simple stiches. The image of Shapiro with needle and thread in hand, talking others through sewing, reminds me of Joanna Clapps Herman's description of sewing as an act that requires intimacy with the tools of the trade as well as dexterity, skill, and accuracy: "The needle is held precisely between thumb and forefinger," she writes in her essay in *Embroidered Stories*, "the thread is licked between the lips and tongue, the end of the thread is bitten sharply off with the front teeth so that the tip is clean and wet and will slip easily through the tiny eye of the needle."

I was happy to capture in a snapshot a particularly meaningful encounter of Shapiro and Michael Parenti sewing together. Parenti, a political scientist, author, and activist spoke about how his own Italian immigrant family's working-class background had shaped his understanding of labor and class politics. Shapiro, a Jewish American woman born and raised in California, had learned about the fire from her family and had been touched by how young most of the victims were. She prepared memorial pins, each with the name and age of a person killed by the fire, creating a simple visual reminder of the victims' individuality.

After the event, Shapiro sent a similar set of pins to performance artist Annie Lanzillotto, who wore them later in the New York City centennial commemoration (the Berkeley events took place in the weeks leading up to the actual anniversary in order not to conflict with the events occurring across the bay in San Francisco). The cultural alliance created between artists and activists spanned geography in a material way.

During one of the Learn events, I gave a public lecture that connected the fire with the Los Gatos Canyon plane crash. My lecture was shaped by contemporary and local concerns related to these historical events—from the continued exploitation of immigrant labor and prejudicial immigration reform in the United States to the challenges against ethnic studies programs and the educational disenfranchisement of minority students in our public schools. I hoped that discussing these tragedies together would encourage a dialogue on the need for social justice and progress in the contemporary moment.

On January 28, 1948, a small, chartered plane carrying thirty-two people left Oakland, California, for the El Centro Deportation Center near the Mexico border. The plane crashed near Coalinga, in Fresno County. The Mexican men and one woman had come to California mainly through the Bracero program, the temporary migrant visa program that brought tens of thousands of Mexican workers to the United States. They earned paltry wages and worked in abject conditions.

The accident was brutal: Dismembered bodies flew out of the falling plane and scattered in a valley where the plane, itself a burning mass of metal, plastic, and fabric, had crashed. Firefighters, police, and civilians rushed to the scene, but there were no survivors. In the days and weeks following the disaster, only the bodies of the U.S.-born crew (the pilot, copilot, flight attendant, and a guard) were identified. The other twenty-eight people—commonly referred to as "deportees," although their legal status was more complicated than that term suggests—were never officially identified. Parts of their bodies were never recovered. Three days after the crash, they were buried in an unmarked mass grave at the Holy Cross Cemetery in Fresno; some of the twenty-eight caskets were interred empty because the complicated work of recuperating and connecting body parts was never completed. No effort was made to contact the family members of the deceased Mexican citizens. Nevertheless, news spread across the Central Valley, first by word of mouth throughout the migrant worker community, and later through newspaper and radio stories, and several hundred Latino farmworkers and their families attended the funeral. (Tim Z. Hernandez has documented this story with much more detail than I do here.) The mass grave was left unmarked until some years later, when someone anonymously placed a simple bronze headstone on the grave with the following inscription: 28 MEXICAN CITIZENS WHO DIED IN AN AIRPLANE ACCIDENT NEAR COALINGA CALIFORNIA ON JAN. 28 1948. R.I.P.

An official list of the dead was never released. Newspaper coverage from the era is sparse and the English-language media was often full of misinformation; only the Spanish-language press noted the Mexican victims' full names, as Hernandez's careful research shows. *The New York Times* described the victims as follows: "The group included

Mexican nationals who entered the United States illegally, and others who stayed beyond duration of work contracts in California. . . . All were agricultural workers." The names of the dead, when noted at all, were often written inconsistently, with typographical errors—Ramon Paredes became Ramon Perez; Apolonio Placencia became Apolonio Placenti—making the work of identification undertaken years later nearly impossible. In the immediate aftermath and for decades to come, no one except the victims' families seemed concerned with such details. Only in the last dozen years or so have there been public reflections on the events and the lives lost. In 2008, one local resident of Coalinga recounted to a journalist the scene of the accident:

> I was born and raised in Coalinga and can remember going to the crash site the day after the incident. My father, older sister, and I viewed the crash and even though I was about six years old at the time, I can remember it as if it happened yesterday. It was a cold and damp day and even though the reports were that the site had been cleaned up, this was not the case. The sadness of seeing the meager possessions of the passengers and the total lack of respect by those who had the task of removing the bodies will be something I will never forget or forgive.

I read these lines out loud in Berkeley as I laid out the bare details of the crash.

Like others, I first learned about the crash through the song written by Woody Guthrie, "Plane Wreck at Los Gatos," sometimes called simply "Deportee." Guthrie wrote the song as a poem. Martin Hoffman later added a melody. It seems that Guthrie never recorded it. Most accounts say it was not sung publicly until the late 1950s. We know nothing about Guthrie's relationship to the crash itself. We only know that he was living in New York City at the time. That he made note of it suggests more about Guthrie's political commitment than it does about the public conversation around the tragedy. Guthrie's song, and the life of the song itself, has done more to transmit the memory of the events than anything else. Many notables in the American folk and country music world—Joan Baez, Johnny Cash, Bob Dylan, Arlo Guthrie, Dolly

Parton, Pete Seeger, Bruce Springsteen, and Lucinda Williams—have made this song part of their repertoire. With each rendition comes another example of how creativity and storytelling can shape and historicize experiences and connect those who combat social injustice.

In each version, the lyrics name the victims—albeit with generic Spanish-language names—recognizing the humanity that public discourse had disallowed them:

> Goodbye to my Juan, goodbye, Rosalita,
> Adios mis amigos, Jesus y Maria;
> You won't have your names when you ride the big airplane,
> All they will call you will be "deportees."

The use of personal pronouns— "Some of us are illegal, and some are not wanted"—makes the victims' plight everyone's story and reminds listeners of the cost of progress and the need for basic human rights for immigrants and workers in the United States:

> Is this the best way we can grow our big orchards?
> Is this the best way we can grow our good fruit?
> To fall like dry leaves to rot on my topsoil
> And be called by no name except "deportees"?

The song remains mostly a critique of the greed of U.S. capitalism and the need for sympathy and respect for the underprivileged.

In 2011, Hernandez, a writer and educator, uncovered the identities of the victims as well as other details about the crash. He traveled around the United States and to Mexico to locate, meet, and record oral stories of a few victims' family members. He spearheaded fund-raising to have a new headstone placed at the grave in Fresno in 2013. All the victims were finally named. His book, *All They Will Call You,* whose title comes from the refrain of Guthrie's song, details many of these oral histories and recounts details about the crash that had never been told before. He also worked with musician Lance Canales to produce an extended version of Guthrie's song, which includes the real names of the victims. His work of historical recovery in the memory of migrant lives and their labor parallels the memory work around the Triangle fire, both fundamental processes for shaping collective memory and histories. While I did not have Hernandez's work to inform my presentation on the Los Gatos Canyon plane crash (I did not learn about his work until the publication of his book in 2017), I had used the lost lives and stories of the working migrants of that plane crash as the core narrative to bring the history of the fire to California—and, in turn, connect California's stories to the legacy of the fire.

Again and again, the history of the Triangle fire takes me back to other stories about exploited and forgotten immigrant workers. My knowledge of the fire has long led me to other voices, other injustices, and other teaching moments, academic research, and creative work. I can't, though, yet say what effect that Triangle fire elementary school worksheet might have on my daughter. I wonder what stories her memories might hold on to and how they might direct her as she grows up. But my own experience with the Triangle fire continues to be further shored up from such exchanges. These are the exchanges, the teaching moments outside a classroom, on which I act and imagine a different world.

I have consistently been absorbed by the role memory serves in the construction and reconstruction of history and the narrativizing of real lived experiences. The memory work inspired by disastrous events such as the Triangle fire and the Los Gatos Canyon plane crash are hopeful signs for me of the ways we can educate and activate change. The full significance of the Los Gatos Canyon plane crash and the Triangle fire have yet to be fully understood, but I remain optimistic that continuing to remember them will lead to a bolder, more generous future.

CHAPTER 11

Teaching the Girls
The Triangle Fire as Affective History

▼

Jacqueline Ellis

The image that startles my students most is of an empty space: a hole next to a shop window ledge; a burned wooden plank leaning against a stone wall, pieces of mangled metal receding into a dust-covered background. What was a sidewalk skylight has been shattered by the force of a girl's body hurtling through it. Before viewing this image, my students have contemplated photographs of the burned factory, of the fire hoses unable to reach the ninth floor, of the girls' bodies lined up on the sidewalk and arranged in open coffins. They are shocked by those images, but their reactions to this photograph are visceral. The students sense the girl's desperation as she steps from the window, and the sound of her body as it crashes through the glass and lands on the ground. The scene around the hole has been cleared, but the space that is the shape of the girl's body is empty. The image evokes mourning, shock, anger. It is an image of the aftermath of the Triangle fire and of the expendability of the girls who died in it. It is also a concrete representation of Rose Schneiderman's speech after the fire: "This is not the first time girls have been burned alive in this city. . . . There are so many of us for one job it matters little if 146 of us are burned to death."

When I teach the Triangle fire, my students analyze survivors' narratives, obituaries, poetry, and family pictures as a way of reconstructing the lives of the dead girls represented by the empty space in the photograph. We also consider these sources to understand the contemporary experiences of girls working and dying in factories. I show them *Made in Thailand*, a documentary about a fire at the Kader Toy Factory in 1993. Like the Triangle, the Kader Factory's workforce is made up of primarily young women and girls who assemble commodities in dangerous conditions for low pay. Like the Triangle, the absence of safety regulations leads to a fire. Like the Triangle, doors are locked, and fire escapes are inaccessible, so girls are trapped. Like the Triangle, girls must decide whether to jump from the window or die in the flames. One girl describes her experience of the Kader fire: "Everyone was clawing and fighting at the door. We couldn't breathe. I ran to the window.... I ran to the window again. I couldn't see the ground. I called for my parents. I jumped and landed on [the] bodies of my friends below. I didn't know if they were dead. Someone dragged me away." As she tells her story, the young woman sits at a work desk strewn with the components of a Lion King toy waiting to be stuffed. Throughout the documentary we see images of the commodities manufactured at the factory: pieces of material sewn together, then pushed onto a metal pipe that inflates them with the white fiber that ignited the Kader fire. The girls and young women who made the toys at the Kader factory recognize the disparity between how little they are paid and what price the toys will fetch. They understand the cheapness of the materials, the disposability of the product. This knowledge mirrors their employers' view of them as easily exploitable workers.

I began my scholarly career by analyzing literature by and about working-class women and the politics of representation in response to images of working-class women and girls. I have situated women and girls working in assembly plants as theorists of globalization, where feelings are central to workers' understanding of the economic and political systems that shape their lives. I have also written about affect—specifically anger—as a mode of self-identification and resistance, interwoven with my emotional life as the white mother of a Black girl. These elements are integral to my teaching the Triangle fire. Yet when my daughter lines up her soft toys on her bed—the worn-out Piglet we bought her as a baby, the bear dressed in a taekwondo suit—I don't often think about the girls and young women who made them. I don't usually consider their back pain, their aching tendons, their exhaustion, how little they are paid or how dangerous their jobs are. My mind is on my daughter and how much she cares for these toys.

In my essay "Working-Class Women Theorize Globalization," I wrote about Elena, a maquiladora worker in Mexico who uses affect to critique consumer capitalism. Describing her job assembling Miss Piggy dolls, Elena says, "Nothing in the world would make me buy one of the dolls for myself or my daughter. I hate them." My students consider Elena's feelings as a worker and as a consumer when they reflect on the geographic and economic spaces between the things they buy and the young women and girls who make those things. They look at the labels on their clothing so that we can note down the countries where their T-shirts or hoodies were manufactured. They use the list to contemplate the relationship between their own bodies and those of the young women and girls who manufactured their clothes. I play "Are My Hands Clean?" by Sweet Honey in the Rock. The lyrics help my students to map the locations of the raw materials and to visualize the steps in the manufacturing processes of a garment they might buy at a store in the United States. With an embodied sense of their position in the global manufacturing process, the students reflect on their emotional responses to the question raised in the song's title: shame, empathy, pity, apathy.

Most of my students are the first generation to attend college, come from immigrant families, or are themselves immigrants. They balance college with work and family responsibilities and they do not want to feel guilty about buying two-for-ten-dollar T-shirts at the Children's Place or a Disney-themed toy from Target. Their social locations bring up other feelings. After our class on the Kader Toy factory fire, one student, with tears in her eyes, tells me about relatives who work in garment factories who "look like the girls" we saw in the documentary. Another student nervously tells the class about her mother, an undocumented immigrant who supports her family by selling homemade desserts. Another speaks with pride about an aunt—also an immigrant—who runs a sweatshop. She describes the aunt as having achieved economic stability for her family: the American Dream. The students' feelings reveal the affective processes that delineate their immigrant experiences: sadness about family members left behind, fear about being undocumented, and a sense of belonging that comes with becoming assimilated to American capitalist ideology.

For my students, discourses about globalization, consumerism, international labor laws, and trade agreements that circulate in academic spaces are abstractions. But their emotional relationships to the texts we study are concrete. As pedagogy, affect provides a context for my students to explore the experiences of girls who are workers and of girls who are activists. We consider how girls' emotions have been and continue to be used as a way of diminishing girls' experiences and voices. We recognize how girls deployed affect for protesting and organizing before and in the aftermath of the Triangle fire and in the wake of more recent horrors. We can think about how girls' experiences relate to our own and to those of our families and communities. Affect can integrate the legacy of the Triangle girls into the work of contemporary girl activists—it is a means of "talking to the girls."

Clara

I was fifteen during the miners' strike that shut down the coal industry in the United Kingdom from 1984 to 1985. My father worked as a millwright in a brick factory and was the shop steward of his union. My family talked about politics, socialism, and strikes in the car rides back from my grandparents and in front of the television during the news. I learned that unions and labor politics were masculine and that strikers were always men: miners, shipbuilders, steelworkers. There were no unions at my mother's clerical jobs, none for the shop assistants or the lunch ladies, or for the other jobs my friends' mothers had. Britain had its first woman prime minister, but we didn't talk about feminism except as something for women who had enough time to think about such things.

The working-class identity that was a defining part of my household was at odds with the culture of the city where I grew up. Most adults in Peterborough worked in factories or assembly plants but voted for the Conservative Party and in support of Margaret Thatcher's government. There was no tradition of organizing and striking like there was in Yorkshire mining towns or cities like London or Manchester. There was also no aspiration or upward mobility—education beyond the age of sixteen was ridiculed: "I would never go out with a boy who stayed on at school instead of getting a job," one girl said to me. Taking extra exams and thinking about university were not for the likes of us. But my mother insisted that my brother and I go to college and have experiences that had been denied her as a girl. So at eighteen, I left Peterborough and went to university in East Yorkshire. Later, I went to graduate school in Massachusetts and eventually moved permanently to the United States.

In college, studying 1930s proletarian literature was a way of asserting my working-class identity in spaces that were overwhelmingly middle-class. Focusing on American women authors, I explored a new feminist identity. I researched the history of working-class women in the United States and, later, went to a conference at the Center for Working-Class Studies in Youngstown, Ohio. Tillie Olsen autographed my dog-eared copy of *Tell Me a Riddle*. I learned about the Uprising of 1909, the Triangle fire, and Clara Lemlich. I made intellectual connections, but, as an immigrant, I still didn't feel at home. At a closing event in Youngstown, I stood uncomfortably in a circle, holding hands with academics and activists who were singing "Solidarity Forever." Most were my parents' age, had been part of the social movements of the 1960s, or had participated in demonstrations and strikes at steel plants or car manufacturers. They were immersed in research about working-class communities, literature, or folk music. My hand felt warm and clammy against somebody else's fingers. I had no sense of what political solidarity felt like. I avoided making eye contact and didn't sing along, even though I knew most of the words.

As I continued to research working-class women's lives in the United States, I identified with girls like Clara Lemlich, a union organizer like

Figure 11.1. Portrait of Clara Lemlich, 1909. Photographer unknown; photo courtesy of the Kheel Center for Labor-Management Documentation & Archives at Cornell University.

my father and a working-class girl like me. She was defiant and unapologetic about being a girl. Years later, when I ask my students to analyze reports of Lemlich's speech at Cooper Union, I emphasize Samuel Gompers's description of her as a "frail little girl with flashing black eyes" and a "tremulous" voice. We discuss the incongruity of those details in relation to Lemlich's speech. They think about their girlhoods—or those of girls and women they know—in comparison with Clara's. They talk about girls being expected to clean and cook and about having less freedom to stay out with friends compared to their brothers—stories that are alternately propelled by resentment, resignation, defiance, or acceptance. We laugh about the girlhood pleasures of buying new clothes or getting a manicure. The emotional contours that frame our discussions of girlhood—in early-twentieth- century garment factories and in our own lives—help my students to understand the activist legacy of the Uprising and the day-to-day lives of the girls killed in the Triangle fire.

We consider the activist identity Lemlich performed in opposition to socially constructed views of girls as passive, frivolous, innocent, and apolitical. In one photograph, taken in 1909, she wears a white shirt with a high collar that almost meets her jawline and a thin dark-colored tie knotted at the neck. Her hair is curly and parted to the side. Her eyebrows are arched. She doesn't smile. Her eyes are heavy-lidded, looking downward toward the viewer. Through her clothes, hair, pose, and expression, Lemlich adopts a masculine identity that reflects her desire to be taken seriously as an activist. Students notice her purposeful integration of opposing identities. The shirt and the tie are part of her girlhood, like the strikes and the books and the sewing and the bruises. She embodies wisdom that comes directly from her girlhood experiences—from working, from studying, from organizing, from violence.

Samuel Gompers described Clara as someone "who feels and suffers from the things pictured." To him, her emotions were emblematic of feminine weakness embodied by a girl who needed to be saved from exploitation. Nevertheless, girls' emotions were intrinsic to the Uprising. A *McClure's Magazine* article described one garment worker, Natalya Urosova, whose "lips trembled" as she recalled the moments before the girls in her shop walked out of their jobs: "Oh it excites me so . . . yet, I can hardly talk about it." At Cooper Union, Clara recognized the girls' listlessness, their frustration, their boredom at having to listen to more than two hours of speeches. Lemlich knew her fellow girl workers felt "discontent and hatred of their bondage," that they were "anxious for . . . change." Later, Clara described the centrality of affect to her organizing work: "I had a fire in my mouth. . . . Audacity—that was all I had—audacity!"

The emotional dynamics that precipitated Clara Lemlich's activism—anger, sadness, love—also animate Bangladeshi organizer Kalpona Akter's work to improve the lives of girls working in the global garment industry. In 2013, after the Savar garment factory building in Rana Plaza, Dhaka, collapsed and killed 1,134 workers, most of whom were young women and girls, Akter visited the site. She wanted to help the victims and their families. But she also wanted to collect evidence for which brands were sourced at the factory to frustrate the cover-up of responsibility she knew would follow. She stuck her hands into the rubble and found a package of labels that read "made with love." The irony stung and angered her. More so when she realized the labels she found were for clothes that were to be sold by the Children's Place. She told a reporter, "American companies know this is happening. We've told them, 'Remember these human faces. You killed these girls.'" When Akter reaches into the physical space where girls' bodies have fallen, what she feels connects Rana Plaza to Clara Lemlich to the Triangle fire to girls who are workers and to girls who are consumers. Placing girls at the emotional center of this trajectory also allows immigrant girls, activist girls, working-class girls, girls of color—girls like many of my students and, in some ways, like me—to recognize themselves in these histories and to consider their place within them.

Emma

Using affect as an analytical tool, my students also study the girls who are at the forefront of March for Our Lives—the movement for gun control that formed in the aftermath of the mass shooting in 2018 at Marjory Stoneman Douglas High School in Parkland, Florida. I show them Emma González's Twitter profile picture and ask them to describe what they see. They notice González's pose, cradling her hands on either side of her face; they notice her smile, the dimple in her right cheek, her red lipstick, the way she has pulled the sleeves of her black shirt over her hands. They describe her as sweet, relatable, girlie. Some students notice that Emma's hair is short; others think that it looks pulled back into a ponytail. The profile picture is a counterpoint to the portrait of Clara Lemlich they have looked at earlier, where femininity is purposefully decentered in favor of an image that allows Clara to shape her girlhood identity to fit what union activists were "supposed" to look like. In contrast, Emma's profile picture defies media images that mark her as masculine—her shaved head, her military-inspired clothes, and her unsmiling expression (often read as anger). Significantly, for Twitter—one of the sites from which she conducts her activism—Emma has chosen an identity that conforms to more traditional signifiers of girlhood.

Similarly, in profiles and interviews, Emma roots her identity in girlcentric tropes. She describes herself as a "typical" teenage girl: "I am so indecisive that I can't pick a favorite color, and I'm allergic to 12 things," she writes. "I draw, paint, crochet, sew, embroider—anything productive I can do with my hands while watching Netflix." Emma's emphasis on girl culture—reminiscent of Clara's love of hats and of my students' classroom discussions of manicures and pop music—contrasts girlhood pleasures with the violence of events like a school shooting, police beating union activists, or girls dying at Rana Plaza or at the Kader Toy Factory or in the Triangle fire. This juxtaposition is echoed in Emma's description of her friend Carmen Schentrup, who was killed in the Parkland shooting. Emma details how their everyday girlhood activities contrast with the horrific circumstances of Carmen's death: "We had science together. I got my period one day and didn't have a pad, and Carmen gave me one—what a queen." She remembers eating pizza, watching movies with her friend who is now dead: "I still have one of her party invitations taped up on my mirror."

Like Clara, Emma has a strategic relationship to girlhood. And, like Clara, Emma uses emotions to mobilize her audience. In her speech at an antigun rally in Fort Lauderdale, Emma relied on anger, shock, and incredulity interspersed with descriptions of everyday high school experiences—tests, papers, classroom debates. When I play the video of her speech, my students are impressed that Emma had done her homework: She presented data, histories, expert opinion. They also notice her raw emotions and her refusal to keep them in check, despite the risk of being dismissed as hysterical. She was angry when she described "the students who are now suffering from PTSD, the students who had panic attacks during the vigil." She wiped away furious tears as she yelled back to television pundits who blamed the shooting on the assailant being ostracized at school: "You didn't know this kid!" she cried. "He wouldn't have harmed that many students with a knife." She was angry at the shooter's parents and neighbors, who gave him access to guns despite his expressed "homicidal tendencies." Sometimes, Emma's anger was sarcastic—her tone was derisive as she noted President Trump's connections to the NRA. It turned to fury as she screamed the dollar amount Trump's presidential campaign received from pro-gun lobbyists. She yelled so loudly into the microphone that the speaker crackled.

Like Rose Schneiderman's speech at the Triangle fire memorial, Emma's speech at the March for Our Lives rally was about the mobilization of grief. When she stepped onto the stage, Emma was more composed, more confident than she had been in Fort Lauderdale. Her voice was steadier, lower-toned. She smiled before speaking. Her speech had the rhythm of a spoken word poem as she named the students who were killed and described teenage activities that each child "would never" do again. She ended the speech with six minutes of silence, which made the crowd at the rally uncomfortable. Some people chanted, "Never again." Others called out Emma's name. Sometimes the only sound was Emma's breathing. Listening to the tape of her speech in class, students shift in their seats, shuffle papers, fidget with the lids of Dunkin' Donuts cups. The silence was a space as evocative as the holes in the concrete left by the body of a falling girl at the Triangle or of the space in the rubble at Rana Plaza that Kalpona Akter reached into to pull out labels that read "made with love" from children's clothes. Emma held the space with her emotions—her trauma, her grief; with the tears that rolled down her cheeks as she stared straight ahead.

González's critics have directed their personal attacks against her self-representation as a girl activist. One Republican candidate for the Maine House of Representatives called her a "skinhead lesbian" with "nothing to say unless you're [a] frothing at the mouth moonbat." Emma describes becoming a "skinhead" as a practical choice connected to girlhood experiences: "I looked terrible in a ponytail!" She also characterizes cutting her hair as an act of self-care: "[I]t sounds stupid, but it [long hair] made me insecure; I was always worried that it looked frizzy or tangled. What's the best thing to do with insecurity? Get rid of it."

Emma's appearance is also self-consciously queer. Reflecting her Latinx identity, her queer activism was inspired by Sylvia Rivera's speech at the Stonewall uprising. The shooting at the Pulse Nightclub—where 90 percent of the victims were Hispanic—led Emma to recognize how her identity related to the systemic homophobia and racism that precipitate hate crimes and gun violence. Her profile picture, her hairstyle, her clothing, her friendships, her rhetorical approach, her gender expression, her sexuality, and her ethnicity combine with her reliance on emotions. The feelings associated with being a queer Latinx girl are key to Emma's activism.

"I . . . cry a lot," she says. "But crying is healthy and it feels good . . . Crying is a kind of communication, and communication is awesome."

My students and I manage our tears as we learn about the girls who died or who were traumatized at the Triangle fire, at the Kader Toy Factory, and at Rana Plaza; and as we watch and listen to the girl activists at the March for Our Lives rally. When eighteen-year-old Edna Chavez, a member of the Community Coalition organization in South Central Los Angeles, described having learned to "duck from bullets before [she] learned how to read" and watching her brother die after being shot, she held back her tears. We do the same. We smile, relieved, when we see nine-year-old Yolanda Renee King, Martin Luther King, Jr.'s granddaughter, walk on the stage, hand in hand with Marjory Stoneman Douglas activist Jaclyn Corin. We laugh when we see Renee wave and urge the crowd to join her in a call-and-response chant: "We. Are going to be. A great generation!" King's palpable joy at speaking at the rally brings us respite from the grief, the anger, the fear, the anxiety, and the outrage that are integral to the calls to action from Edna Chavez and Emma González, but we still feel the weight of the experiences they described and the political urgency their emotions embody. Some students look down at their desks; others look up from their phones, eyes narrowed, mouths tense. I sit next to the lectern, looking down. I think about my daughter, who looks like Renee. I recognize the same righteousness, the same nervousness, the same self-conscious smile. I think about her goofing around at her elementary school, cracking jokes as the teacher closes the classroom door and ushers the fourth-grade students into the corner of the classroom, trying to get them to be still and quiet and small so that a shooter outside might pass by to the next classroom or to another school or to a different neighborhood or town or state to kill children who are not these children, who are not my daughter.

Naomi

"She's a little Black girl fan-girling on George Clooney!" a student exclaims in response to a clip of eleven-year-old Naomi Wadler—another March for Our Lives activist—appearing on *The Ellen DeGeneres Show*. Wadler described a phone call from Clooney, who invited her to speak at the rally in Washington, D.C. She smiled and expressed admiration for the actor's celebrity status. She recounted how nervous she was to speak to him. The student's comment highlights the perceived incongruity of Naomi's crushing on an actor whose fan base is more likely to be middle-aged white women. The student's observation about Naomi's feelings toward Clooney led to a wider class discussion of her self-representation in relation to socially constructed ideas about girlhood. Her awkward walk onto the stage, the little wave to the audience, her broad smile and bouncing curly hair, her cropped pants, and ballet flats all presented a girlhood identity in line with social conventions. Naomi was confident as she talked to Ellen. She looked the host directly in the eye and was engaging as she described what it was like to speak at the rally. Through her affect, she performed girlhood as she recalled overcoming her nervousness before she began speaking ("When I went on, the first thing I said was 'Hi'... and then everybody was, like, heeeyyy") and in her description of how "I [fell] off my chair" after speaking with Clooney.

Naomi emphasized typical girlhood tropes throughout the conversation with Ellen. She mentioned hanging out at a friend's house when her mom's phone "blows up with text messages." She talked about math tests and about her mentions on Twitter and Instagram. Then Naomi described how the death of her mother's friend in the Parkland shooting inspired her to organize a walkout of sixty students at her school. It wasn't until the last few seconds of the six-and-a-half-minute interview that Naomi mentioned race, specifically Black girls: "We added an extra minute to honor Courtlin Arrington, a Black sixteen-year-old in Alabama who was shot. And we decided to do that because I feel way too often Black women are shot and their names aren't remembered. And they're not valued as much."

A photograph of Courtlin Arrington appeared in the background for a few seconds as the audience applauded. The camera returned to Ellen and she told Naomi she was proud of her. Unlike George Clooney, Courtlin Arrington was not discussed. The audience did not learn that Courtlin was planning on attending nursing school after graduation. Nor did they know that she was shot at school by a classmate on March 7, 2018, ten days before the planned school walkouts on March 17, after the Parkland shooting.

Before Naomi walked onto Ellen's stage, an excerpt from her speech at the rally was played for the audience. In the clip, Naomi explicitly emphasized race: "I am here today to acknowledge and represent the African American girls whose stories don't make the front page of every national newspaper. . . . I represent the African American women who are victims of gun violence, who are simply statistics instead of vibrant, beautiful girls full of potential . . . I'm here to say never again for those girls, too." Despite the foregrounding of Naomi's girlhood identity, the elision of her activism made visible the marginalization of race from representations of girlhood. Hence, my student's comment that highlighted the default emphasis on whiteness in relation to girlhood and their insistence on emphasizing Naomi's identity as a Black girl.

In class, we consistently return to the question of how race, ethnicity, social class, or immigrant status determines who gets to be a girl in what context: in media representations, at school, in the household, in public spaces. In early-twentieth-century garment factories, girlhood was synonymous with exploitability, but being Jewish or Italian or immigrant or poor meant that girls were seen by employers as workers, not children. Unless accompanied by a respectable upper-class member of the Women's Trade Union League (WTUL), working-class girls who protested on public streets were viewed by police and magistrates as prostitutes, not innocent girls. After the Triangle fire, activists emphasized the victims' girlhood as an organizing strategy to elicit sympathy that would lead to mobilization and protest. In class, we talk about why the deaths of girls of color are viewed as less important than the deaths of white girls. I introduce images, from 2015, of Dajerria Becton, a fifteen-year-old Black girl who was pinned to the ground by a white police officer at a Texas pool party. She is wearing a bikini. The officer jams his knee into her back. In the video, we hear Dajerria scream for her mother as the white officer presses down on her almost naked body. Her emotions—fear, humiliation, anger—energize our discussion. My students recall their own encounters with police and describe the ways in which girls of color are often treated as adults. One student talks about regularly making dinner for her family from the age of ten. Others describe being responsible for their younger siblings, taking care of grandparents, or translating for their mothers at the doctor's office. Girls of color talk about hypersexualization and nod in recognition when a classmate describes being sent home from school for wearing a tank top and an above-the-knee skirt while white girls wearing the same clothes went unnoticed by school officials. I recount how my daughter's fourth-grade teacher told me that a white girl could not be a bully because she was so cute and adorable and because my daughter did not cry when she reported that the white girl had threatened to have her brother kill her. We read *Girlhood Interrupted,* which foregrounds the significance of affect to social perceptions of Black girls. The data supports our experiences. In comparison with white girls, Black girls are perceived as knowing more about adult topics and more about sex; Black girls are viewed as more independent and, crucially, in relation to our classroom discussions of girls' emotions in both historical and contemporary contexts, less in need of comfort, support, protection, and nurturing.

Black women and girls were excluded from the shirtwaist unions of the Triangle era, and most white employers and workers opposed their being hired at all. The WTUL made efforts to reach out to the Black community through churches and local women's clubs, but only to urge them not to cross picket lines. Black girlhood is absent from representations of garment workers as passive employees, feeble victims, or ardent activists. Girls' race—their connection to whiteness and their differentiation from blackness—was not addressed. Similarly, gender, working-class, and ethnic identities have been integral to the fire's recognition as a vital event in U.S. history, but race is often marginalized from these narratives. Focusing on affect is a way of addressing these silences. Thinking about the 1909 Uprising or about the Triangle fire as part of an affective history of girlhood identities and activism gives students an opportunity to explore these events from more inclusive, intersectional perspectives.

We compare Clara Lemlich's and Emma González's affective organizing strategies to Ida B. Wells's use of emotion as a young woman activist. When, in 1884, a conductor demanded that Wells move from the ladies' car of a train to the smoker, she refused. When he tried to physically remove her from the car, she bit his hand. She described this event later: "[T]he moment he caught hold of my arm I fastened my teeth in the back of his hand. I had braced my feet against the seat in front and was holding to the back, and as he had already been badly bitten he didn't try it again by himself." Students gasp and laugh when they hear Toni Morrison read Wells's description of this incident in the documentary *A Passion for Justice*, but they also notice her feelings, particularly in relation to the white passengers, who "seemed to sympathize with the conductor" and cheered when Wells was dragged out of the train. Emotion also motivated Wells's decision to sue the railroad company after this event. Her righteous rage was balanced by relief when she initially won her case. When that decision was reversed on appeal, however, Wells described her reaction as bookended by optimism and disappointment: "I have firmly believed all along that the law was on our side and would . . . give us justice. I feel shorn of that belief and utterly discouraged . . ."

Wells's feelings that the legal system would never provide justice for Black people has clear ramifications for contemporary Black girls like Dajerria Becton and Courtlin Arrington, whose experiences are sidelined when girls' histories are written and girls' stories are told. Black girls appear only briefly in these narratives: in a viral video clip, as a quick background image, or as a couple of paragraphs in the histories of early-twentieth-century girlhood activism. Teaching the Triangle fire has made it possible for me to create pedagogical opportunities for constructing more inclusive narratives. The deadly working conditions experienced by the girls at the Triangle Factory are replicated for girls of color working in the contemporary global economy. The girl-centered activism that precipitated the Uprising of 1909 is reimagined in the activism of contemporary girls of color like Emma González and Naomi Wadler. The discourses that delineate girlhood and shape the lives of real girls are redeployed in new contexts: White girlhood and the emotions of white girls are privileged, while girls of color navigate racist systems and perceptions that negate their feelings and minimize their pain. The complexities of girls' emotions provide a means for my students to recognize themselves and to look for the places where marginalized girls' voices might be heard. Exploring these narratives helps my students understand the ways that social, political, economic, and cultural systems intersect with girls' lives, including their own and those of girls they know. We learn that studying the Triangle fire means telling stories, not just of the girls who died but also of girls whose stories have yet to be heard.

Postscript: After the completion of this essay, as of May 2021, Emma González's pronouns are they/them. They no longer identify as a girl and prefer to be known as "X González."

PART FOUR

MOVEMENTS

CHAPTER 12

Solidarity Forever!

▼

May Y. Chen

The Chinese sewing workers told me the biting wind came from 146 ghosts. On a cold, windy day in late March 1985, I stood with a crowd of union leaders, workers, and retirees on Washington Place, near Washington Square Park, in Greenwich Village. New York University students rushed by and looked at us, wondering what was happening.

The fire truck raised its ladder up, up, up, but it could not reach the floors where the people once worked. Bagpipes played "Amazing Grace." The Fire Department officer rang the bell as each victim's name was called. I felt so moved, so sad, so cold, and so committed to making people care about the lives of young immigrant women workers.

Again, in the 1990s, on a blustery day in late March, I stood on Canal Street in New York's Chinatown, where a huge crowd had gathered around a fire truck for another commemoration of the Triangle Shirtwaist Factory fire. At the time, I worked for the Education Department of Local 23-25 of the International Ladies' Garment Workers' Union (ILGWU), and we were conducting workplace fire drills. There were hundreds of factories around Canal Street, in dozens of old five- to ten-story brick buildings. This year, a brave colleague stood at the window on an upper floor and waved her hands, yelling "Help! Help!" The big fire truck raised its ladder. It slowly extended up, up, up to the window.

A fireman climbed up the ladder, hoisted her over his shoulder, and carried her down safely to the street. Cameras flashed. Everyone cheered.

My life experiences and the women in the union have taught me the importance of collective efforts, teamwork, and mutual support that I did not learn in school. Collectivity was not part of our curriculum. When I was a kid, I often thought that being a girl was a big disadvantage. Being Chinese and from an immigrant family made it even harder. Within the family, adults (especially fathers and grandfathers) placed the highest value on boys "to carry on the family name." Outside, in school and the neighborhood in suburban Massachusetts, I was sometimes taunted as a "Chink," an enemy from "behind the bamboo curtain." Even though I was born in the United States, people treated me as a foreigner. It's no surprise that I grew up rooting for the underdogs.

I was a quiet and studious girl. But I wasn't a "girlie girl." I liked to run around, climb fences and trees, and wrestle with other kids. I hated frilly, uncomfortable clothes and shoes, but school dress codes required girls to wear dresses and skirts. As I grew up, I appreciated how women played a strong role in my family, and how things were changing from generation to generation. My grandmother lived in Hong Kong and grew up at a time when they still bound and crippled the feet of young girls. Her feet were unbound midway through the process, but she still needed special shoes. My mother would order shoes for her in Boston and ship them to Hong Kong.

My mother and all the aunties were capable, outspoken, and opinionated women who encouraged their daughters to get a good education and jobs, and to contribute to the family and community. Dozens of cousins stayed with us during college vacations. They encouraged my dream of attending Harvard-Radcliffe, and I was accepted into the class of 1970. The gender ratio was out of balance—one female for every five male students. Women lived in the Radcliffe dorms, some distance from where the classes were held, and were not allowed to use the undergraduate library in Harvard Yard. There were only a dozen or so Asian women students, including international students.

In a period of tremendous political and social movements, I became an activist. I fought for the civil rights of women and minorities. I protested the Vietnam War. It was during college that I also started reading and learning about unsung heroes and heroines in American history. When I participated in antiwar teach-ins and campus-wide student strikes, I was about the same age as Clara Lemlich, the young Ukrainian immigrant worker who led the 1909 garment workers' strike. There were huge meetings in the Harvard football stadium. I admired the student leaders who rallied the crowd with their passionate speeches, just as Lemlich had done when she had called for the Uprising of the 20,000. I discovered that May Day and International Women's Day were inspired by American labor struggles, but Americans celebrated Labor Day and Mother's Day instead of these historic events. Together with many college friends, I fought for the rights of the poorest and most exploited so that we could all rise together.

As college graduation approached, I started looking for a job. It was shocking to discover that many job recruiters interviewed only men and that jobs for women were fewer in number and mostly clerical. I read many of the early feminist books that discussed the earnings gap and other workplace and social gender inequities: *The Feminine Mystique* (1963); *Sisterhood is Powerful* (1970); *Our Bodies, Ourselves* (1971, written by the Boston Women's Health Book Collective, which included college classmates). As an Asian woman, I suffered humiliating sexism and racism; men sometimes approached me as if I were one of the stereotypical prostitutes they saw in movies and on the Vietnam War news.

One incident stands out. It was the first time I went to a bar, right in Harvard Square. In those days, there were not many Asians in the college, so I went to the bar with several white friends. We studied the menu and ordered drinks. It was fun hanging out with friends in the dark, cozy space, feeling "grown-up," until three or four loud guys came over to taunt and harass me, the only Asian woman in the place.

"Hey baby, sexy girl, Suzie Wong . . ." they said. They were white, maybe returning Vietnam Vets, probably drunk.

I told them I was a local college student. My friends intervened: "Leave her alone. She's with us. She's our classmate at Harvard."

The bullies pushed back: "What? You don't want to share the gook girl with us?"

The bar manager came over and asked us to leave. My harassers got to stay. Why was I, the victim, getting the boot, along with my friends? Our education and upbringing made no difference.

Discovering Asian American Activism

After college, I moved to California, where I began to learn about organizing and teaching. Asian Americans of various nationalities (Japanese, Chinese, Filipino, Native Hawaiian, and others) had fought for and won an Asian American Studies Center at UCLA, where I worked as a research assistant. Not only had Asian ethnic nationalities worked together but they also supported Black, Latinx, and Native American students, fighting for programs for each group. The Third World Solidarity movement helped everyone. We read and learned about the histories of diverse groups and found ways to work together for common causes. Founded in 1969, the UCLA Asian American Studies Center initiated many community and campus-wide projects. Many advocates and activists shaped and supported this important new institution. Faculty and graduate students taught classes and published journals and books, including the radical newspaper *Gidra*, which reflected the history, feelings, and experiences of Asian Americans. As part of my work with the Center, I taught a class about Asian women and participated in programs to celebrate International Women's Day.

After graduating from UCLA, I worked in jobs related to community organizing, education, and services in Los Angeles's Chinatown. As a community organizer, I brought my passion for women's rights to some memorable programs. One was a basketball league for girls at the local recreation center in Chinatown, which previously had leagues only for boys. We college and postcollege women volunteers formed a team called "Sisters," and played every week against energetic,

Figure 12.1. Asian American activists Yvonne Wong Nishio and May Ying Chen protesting the displacement of Little Tokyo residents, Los Angeles, ca. 1978. Photo by Alan Ohashi; courtesy of Visual Communications Media Archive.

Figure 12.2. Little Friends Community Playgroup rally at Los Angeles City Hall (May holding her baby), Los Angeles, 1977. Photo by Eddie Wong; courtesy of Visual Communications Media Archive.

fast-moving high school girls' teams. Another program was the Little Friends Community Playgroup in Chinatown, which evolved into a full-time day-care center after some years of community mobilizing.

At the end of 1979, I moved to New York City. By that time, I was married and had two small children. I was working part-time and volunteering in the community, teaching English to immigrants and supporting tenant and labor organizing. Among the Chinatowns across the United States, the one in New York was the largest and most complex, with dozens of organizations, including progressive groups and leaders. There were large community rallies and demonstrations about U.S.-China relations, housing, and job opportunities. Some of the community-service activities that started as volunteer efforts led to new organizations, which remain solid, effective institutions today, such as the Chinatown Health Clinic (now the Charles B. Wang Community Health Center), the Chinese American Planning Council (CPC), and the Chinatown History Project (now the Museum of Chinese in America, MOCA).

As I met and worked with people in Manhattan's Chinatown, I heard about the International Ladies' Garment Workers' Union (ILGWU) and the sewing factories in the neighborhood. The garment workers, mostly women, were lively and sharp. There were hundreds of factories in Chinatown, and workers would exchange stories about which ones were better or worse. They also exchanged useful information about schools, community services, and other resources. As a newcomer and working mother, I got valuable tips from them. I also learned about the classes and outings sponsored by Local 23-25 of the ILGWU. And I realized that Local 25 was the historic shirtwaist makers' union of Clara Lemlich and other "rebel girls." It was the union of the Triangle Shirtwaist Factory workers.

One large building full of garment factories stood right across the street from the Chinese Progressive Association's community storefront, where I taught a weekend English class. One day, I heard loud noises and commotion coming from the building. It sounded like people were locked inside. They yelled and pounded on the doors. The police or firemen finally came to break open the doors. Thankfully, there was no fire or major emergency, but I heard the echoes of history, of women workers sewing and suffering through the ages, locked into a factory on the weekend, as they pushed to finish the bundles of pretty clothes to be shipped out.

In the summer of 1982, I witnessed a new iteration of the Uprising of the 20,000 as Local 23-25 workers in Chinatown rallied and went on strike to defend their union contract. A group of Chinese employers thought they could play on the Chinese workers' ethnic sympathies to get rid of the union. Chinatown bosses said, "We're all Chinese, so you can trust us to take care of you." The Chinese workers knew they would lose benefits and rights if the union contract was not renewed. They wanted equal treatment and the same rights and benefits as other garment workers in the industry. I was in a large crowd of striking union workers, where I ran into many of my English students. Some women were pushing strollers with their toddlers. Everyone was excited to be part of something so huge. Most of the women were young wives and mothers who rarely got to speak up in their family or community. Chinese tradition had them quietly following their fathers, husbands, and, even in old age, their sons.

One of the most moving accounts of the 1982 strike appeared in a memoir, "Memories of the 1982 ILGWU Strike in New York Chinatown," by union factory worker and leader Katie Quan. She describes the rally in Columbus Park on June 24, 1982:

> There were nearly 20,000 Chinatown garment workers crammed into the park, all wearing union caps and carrying picket signs and banners. From the stage, union steward Mrs. Shui Mak Ka told the crowd that the contractors are "mistaking a fisheye for a pearl," and retirees club president Mr. Kai Bong Wong shook his finger in rage as he rallied the crowd to fight. A minister prayed for our success, and [Local 23-25 manager] Jay Mazur declared that "We Are One!" After the rally the whole crowd marched through the streets of Chinatown. It was an exhilarating moment. Thousands upon thousands of Chinese immigrant women garment workers had come together to stand

Figure 12.3. 2011 Triangle Fire Centennial: Union Solidarity—Bangladeshi labor leaders Kalpona Akter and Babul Akhter with Local 23-25 members Sing Kong Wong, Lana Cheung, and May Chen. Photo by Rocky Chin; courtesy of the photographer.

up for themselves. This was a day I had dreamed for, and this rally proved that it could be done.

Quan cites a Chinese proverb that resonated with me: "When fire singes the hairs on the skin of the women workers, they will rise up like tigers." I began to see more and more examples of peace-loving, law-abiding, hardworking Chinese women who fought back when provoked. They only needed good leaders, a support group, and a just cause.

The 1982 strike was a turning point in Chinatown for the status and power of workingwomen. We found respect in the union—and self-respect. The patriarchal Chinatown power structures began to change. These changes endure today. Thirty-six years later, in 2018, I marched with the union in New York's annual Labor Day Parade. I walked up Fifth Avenue with an elderly Chinese woman, a veteran of the 1982 strike, who chanted with her daughter and taught her grandchildren, "We Are One! We Are One!"

A Whole New World

After the 1982 strike, I landed a job with Local 23-25 and enjoyed a long career in the union (1983–2009). In 1984, I was hired to work full-time for the union's groundbreaking Immigration Project. We helped thousands of union members and their families become American citizens, sponsor relatives, and defend themselves during factory raids by government immigration officers. Next, I moved to the Local 23-25 Education Department, later becoming a union officer and, eventually, manager of Local 23-25. I made lifelong friends among my colleagues and workers. Colleagues and friends said that we put Chinese immigrant workers into the pages of American labor history with the strike. The union made us strong.

For me, working inside the union wove the history, stories, and traditions of the ILGWU with the issues and concerns of current-day immigrant garment workers. I already had over a decade of experience working in Chinese immigrant communities and studying the history and issues of Asian Americans. I used to insist that the Asian American and Chinese American experiences were unique—and that we needed to assert ourselves, especially since we were, and still are, so invisible in American history and media. I joined the union to explain, integrate, and represent the Chinese community.

The union was a new experience for me, with its long history of so many diverse ethnic groups, cultures, languages, and traditions. Working in the union opened my eyes to the broad similarities of immigrant workers' experiences, workplace problems, and the hopeful aspirations of immigrant families. I discovered that the stories of Chinese union members were unique and yet similar to those of current union members from Central and South America, the Dominican Republic, Haiti, Italy, Mexico, Africa. And these current union members had much in common with garment workers from one hundred years earlier, in the period of the Triangle Shirtwaist Factory, even as the languages and cultures were different. The workers, especially the women, enjoyed freedom and friendships with their coworkers. They earned, saved, and spent their own money, and they banded together for decent pay and working conditions. They got married and had children, and dreamed of a better, happier life for their families, including good schools and more opportunities for the next generation. They loved all the foods and the plentiful markets and stores in New York. Many of them continued to celebrate and adapt their traditional customs in America.

In 1985, when I attended the first of many annual commemorations of the Triangle Factory fire, we mobilized union members and retirees to participate in the ceremony. The union staff went to every factory to pull out the workers during their lunch hour. There were hundreds of factories in Manhattan, from Midtown to Chinatown. Every workplace knew and heard about the annual commemoration. Hundreds of sewing workers would attend, especially from Chinatown, which was so close to the site. Planning meetings were held at the union office to discuss the mobilization efforts and the program. The program aimed at making the historic tragedy relevant to current issues of workers' safety and workers' organizing. The union had a strong Health and Safety Department to train workers about fire safety, how to use the fire extinguisher, and how to avoid fire hazards. There was also training on "ergonomics" and how to create a safe work environment and prevent injuries. We encouraged workplace fire drills, such as the dramatic one on Chinatown's Canal Street with a fire truck and ladder. Speakers at the Triangle Fire Commemoration included young people from Students Against Sweatshops, international garment workers and their advocates, and workers struggling to organize unions in their workplaces. I remember workers from chicken-processing plants in the South talk about serious injuries suffered on the job, and workers who spoke about the horror of witnessing coworkers die in industrial laundries, some caught in the huge machines or collapsing from heat exhaustion.

I retired from the union in 2009 but continue to participate in the annual Triangle Fire Commemoration. It is always moving to watch the fire ladder extend yet fail to reach the floor where the fire flared, and listen to the reading of the 146 victims' names. There are so many friends and supporters at the event: retired and current union members and staff, family members of the Triangle workers, artists, activists, scholars, teachers, and students. This is one annual event that brings people together.

The union and its memory of the Triangle Factory fire have taught me about solidarity. Triangle links past and present in solidarity. It links people of different backgrounds and places in solidarity. It links workers with different jobs fighting for safe workplaces in solidarity. Triangle links the experiences, struggles, and hopes of women workers and immigrant workers in solidarity. Every year, the ceremony renews my belief in the power and importance of coming together, of solidarity.

Worker Solidarity Across the Decades

Sometime in the 1990s, while I was moving or cleaning up my union office, I came upon old cassette tapes of Leon Stein's interviews with Triangle fire survivors. I listened to Stein talk to family members of the survivors, who were surprised to discover that the factory fire as remembered and described by their mothers or grandmothers was a significant historic event, not just a crazy story told by an old lady. I felt guilty about having closed my ears too many times to the rambling stories of my family elders who had lived through historic times.

As I listened and reflected on the Triangle survivor interviews, and later researched and read more of them, I was struck by the connections with the lives of garment workers I knew. They also worked in factories where workers were paid for each section or operation based on the number of pieces of garments that they completed. Some workers put in zippers, sleeves, or waistbands. Each piece had a price. Others operated special machines to make buttonholes or overlock seams. Workers often moved around from shop to shop, following the work with better prices. I could hear workers conversing about common themes and experiences across the decades, and across the globe.

I recently joined efforts to write down the stories of Local 23-25 Chinatown garment workers through a project called We Built New York, led by writer-artist-teacher-activist Esther Cohen. Many of these stories were posted online in 2018 by PBS in honor of Asian Pacific

American Heritage Month. This project gave me the opportunity to sit down, listen, and write down the experiences of many longtime friends: Alice Ip, Connie Ling, Agnes Wong, Duan Yee Lam, Biyao Chen, sisters Bonny and Cindy Leung, Hung Mau Chang, Betty Fung, Lana Cheung, and others. They talked about the tough decisions and adjustments they had made in coming to New York, and how they got jobs and learned to sew in the factories. Their coworkers and the union welcomed them and taught them what to do. We shared our complaints about the unequal treatment of girls in the traditional Chinese family. We also talked about all the things we had learned from being in the union. The union had been a school for so many of us. Almost all these workers took English and civics classes with the union, and many celebrated with coworkers in the factories when they became U.S. citizens. Finally, we shared stories about happy and sad times at work, as well as in our families and communities.

These Chinese workers' stories evoked the stories of Triangle workers. There was Mary Domsky Abrams, who talked about her committee for settling piece rates and also described how the factory girls happily celebrated the engagement of a young coworker. Celia Walker Friedman told the story of coming to America when she was only five years old, learning to speak English without an accent, and being called a "Yankee" by her coworkers. Rose Hauer talked about singing and doing her "little act" in the dressing room at the end of a long workday, much as modern-day Chinese songbird Bik Ngan Sek talked about singing all day in the factory to entertain her coworkers. The factories were a highly social and sociable environment, a big family, a community.

Schooled by the Union

The union's organizing history at the Triangle Waist Company was one major reason why the fire has been remembered for more than a century. The workers and organizers had taken part in the 1909 Uprising of the 20,000 and pushed for two years to get the Triangle employers to accept the union, to no avail. On the day of the fire and every day, the factory doors were locked to keep union organizers out, as much as to keep workers inside. The Triangle Waist Company was never a union shop, even though many of the workers were active union supporters.

Reading about this history and other difficult labor campaigns, I appreciated the tenacity of the Triangle workers and the union before and especially after the fire. I learned that unions cannot win every battle in the labor movement, but that pushing back, speaking up, and bringing workers together can build collective support and solidarity for future victories.

As the "union of immigrants," the ILGWU supported and embraced the complexities and diversity of the workers' cultural backgrounds. Different languages and idioms were part of the colorful conversations we heard in the factories and union offices. Many workers and union staffers told me how they were "brought up by the union" and received all their education in the union—schooling that their family and poor circumstances could not provide in their younger days. The union was an amazing and inclusive environment. My job involved teaching English, civics, and workers' rights, but I learned so much more than I taught the workers.

I was fortunate and grateful to come from a family that valued education for girls as well as boys. I received a strong American education in free public schools, as well as the family's financial support to attend college and graduate school. But it was working in the union that gave me the most invaluable education about leadership and solidarity. Meeting and working with people from so many different countries and backgrounds, I came to love and understand the power of the union to bring diverse people together and give us all a voice and respect. Many of the disadvantages we faced, I learned, could be overcome through our collective efforts. Even if we did not win every fight, even if things did not turn out perfectly, we put in our best effort. I was no longer the shy and voiceless little girl of my childhood and youth.

Chalk

In late March 2019, I decided to take my older grandchildren, ages nine and six, to learn about the Triangle fire. We read a few children's books: *Fire at the Triangle Factory*, by Holly Littlefield, and *The Triangle Shirtwaist Factory Fire*, by Jessica Gunderson, and a book about Clara Lemlich, *Brave Girl: Clara and the Shirtwaist Makers' Strike of 1909*, by Michelle Markel. The annual ceremony was scheduled for the fire's anniversary, March 25, which fell on a Monday, a school day, but we headed out the day before, on Sunday, to visit the building, now a college classroom building. We read the plaque on the building and walked across the street to look at the upper floors. I told them about the big factory, and how the ladders of the fire trucks were not long enough to reach and save the workers. We looked at the roof and thought about the workers who were able to escape by going up. And we thought about the sad story of workers who jumped to their death.

Next, we went to the sidewalk in front of an apartment building on Thompson Street where Rosie Grasso had lived. She was sixteen when she died in the Triangle fire. We posted and handed out flyers about the fire, and some passersby stopped to watch as we chalked Rosie's name. Some asked us, "What's going on?" Some said, "Thanks for keeping this history alive."

The kids chalked "Rosie Grasso, Age 16, Lived at 174 Thompson Street, Died March 25, 1911, Triangle Factory Fire" on the sidewalk in front of the building with colorful words and images. My granddaughter said, "We did this chalk project to tell people that Rosie Grasso lived in this building. It was weird, because normally we chalk and draw in the playground, park, or garden." My grandson said, "I drew lots of triangles and flames for the Triangle fire."

The next day, after the annual commemoration ceremony, I walked by the apartment building with a couple of union friends. I was so disappointed to see that the kids' chalk work had been completely erased. The building's super was there with her young son and said that the landlord had told her to wash it away.

"Why are you messing up my sidewalk?" she asked.

"Rosie Grasso lived in this building with her parents." we said, "more than one hundred years ago and died in the tragic fire just a few blocks away. Rosie was an immigrant from Italy and one of the younger workers in the factory. We remember her and the other workers by chalking their names on the anniversary of the fire."

The building super's inquisitive young son was interested.

My friends and I bent over the sidewalk with our chalk and wrote once again "Rosie Grasso, Age 16, Lived at 174 Thompson Street, Died March 25, 1911, Triangle Factory Fire." Other chalkers walked by and told us about fancy Greenwich Village buildings where the cleaners waited to erase the chalk as soon as the chalkers were done. At least this super respectfully waited for us to leave before taking out her bucket and hose. Down on the Lower East Side, near Chinatown, where I live, many of the chalk drawings remained in place for days or weeks, until footprints and rain erased them.

It's cold and blustery—the breath and spirits of 146 young ghosts joined by generations of social justice supporters, heroes and heroines. I look at our work on Thompson Street and walk around the neighborhood to check out numerous other chalk drawings. Many of them are beautiful works of art. The chalk may be washed away by water hoses or rain, but the memory and collective experiences live on. The union and the community have created actions and traditions across time and ethnic lines. They have built the solidarity that binds us together. I feel so cold, so emotional, and so confident in the power of solidarity.

CHAPTER 13

Remembering Family

Labor Activism and the Triangle Fire

▼

Michele Fazio

W hen I teach the Triangle fire poetry, I place public memory and lived experience at the center of discussion. I want my students to reflect on the impact of class inequity on our lives—socially, culturally, and politically. Often, students react viscerally to poems by Paola Corso, Chris Llewellyn, Mary Fell, Safiya Henderson-Holmes, and Carol Tarlen. "The poems are written in a way that the reader can feel the pain," one student noted, "as if they were the victims of the fire." "These works inflict sadness," another student wrote, "as they place you on the sidewalk watching the flames or on the window ledge preparing to jump." Students feel the power of this poetry to document social struggle and promote action. As one student put it, "This [history] SHOULD make people angry." Repeatedly, student responses advocate for worker justice: "The Triangle fire poems represent how cries for justice were merely silenced by [privileging] products over people." Some students reflect on contemporary immigrant and migrant labor: "This history of harsh labor conditions has been repeating itself over and over again and does not seem to stop." Comments such as these close the temporal, geographical, and cultural gaps that would otherwise keep the memory of these tragedies buried in the past. They illustrate how teaching working-class literature awakens students' class consciousness and awareness of the psychological and cultural violence of erasure. I teach in the rural South, a region with its own history of industrial manufacturing. My students draw connections between the Triangle fire and local disasters, such as the 1991 fire at the Imperial Foods processing plant in Hamlet, North Carolina, which killed twenty-five workers trapped behind locked doors. A few of my students admitted to knowing family members and neighbors who had died or were injured in the Hamlet fire.

Teaching the fire is personal for me. I tell my students that I am drawn to its legacy because of my grandmother, Angelina (Scelfo) Fazio, who worked as a dressmaker in union shops in New York City from 1903 until she retired in the late 1950s. I know very little about the early years of her life as a young girl who arrived from Sicily in 1900, except for the few fragments of stories that she told at holiday meals. I feel as if I know more about her wardrobe than I do about her. As the youngest member of the third generation of a large Italian American family, I knew Nana only as a venerable, beloved matriarch. She was petite, soft-spoken, and reserved. She often lapsed into Italian when she wanted to keep the conversation private, though she spoke little. She preferred to nod and smile at her children and grandchildren gathered around the dining table. An accomplished seamstress, she dressed herself in clothes impeccably designed and sewed by her own hands. She was proud of the hemlines she stitched, edgings that were barely discernible to the eye. Her creations—an impressive collection of smartly tailored skirt suits for herself and stylish cocktail dresses for her daughters—appear in family photo albums, each marking the passing decades of her life.

Some memories lay trapped, suspended in time, forgotten until something triggers their telling. One such memory from my childhood stands out. Long after the platters of antipasti, breaded cutlets, and macaroni had been consumed, my parents, aunts, cousins, several siblings, and I sipped from demitasse cups of espresso laced with anisette as my then ninety-one-year-old grandmother began to tell stories of participating in trade union strikes and protests for a living wage. She had started working at the age of nine. She described long, tedious days in the garment industry, where, at age sixteen, she cut, measured, and

Figure 13.1. Angelina (Scelfo) Fazio, sixteen years old,
1911, New York City. Photographer unknown;
photo courtesy of Michele Fazio.

Figure 13.2. Angelina (Scelfo) Fazio, pictured in the dark dress on the
left, with her children at a May Day celebration, 1920, New York.
Photo by unknown family member; courtesy of Michele Fazio.

sewed. Nana also recounted stories of marching in May Day parades and singing songs of resistance, which is how she met the man who became her husband, Vincenzo Fazio, a member of the First Executive Board of Local 89 of the ILGWU.

I was surprised to learn that she and my grandfather had fought side by side to promote workers' rights. Because he had died in 1945, when my father was a teenager, my grandfather was a stranger to us all. I could not imagine how this stoic, elderly woman—my grandmother, whom I had only seen cooking in the kitchen—in her youth had fought against industrial capitalism and sometimes won. Although I did not understand fully the significance of her participation in the early-twentieth-century labor movement, I wanted to hear more stories and urged her to continue talking. I see now that the act of eating and storytelling in the privacy of our home was an integral part of my immigrant grandmother's expression of her Italianness to her American-born grandchildren, as Simone Cinotto explains in his discussion of the historical and cultural relationship that Italian Americans have with food. Home and the passage of time created a safe space for her to speak aloud the names of long-dead radical activists of the Italian American Left, such as Carlo Tresca, Nicola Sacco, and Bartolomeo Vanzetti. The pressure to act "American," socially and politically, surely weighed upon her, a woman who lived as a widow for over forty years.

"The fire was bad, very bad," she said as her voice stilled. The room, too, fell silent as the clatter of silverware scraping dessert plates stopped, allowing the weight of her words to settle in. I sat quietly by her side, transfixed by the world she described. As she relived the trauma of that fateful day, she became quiet. Her eyes lost focus and her lips pressed together in a thin line. Nana, at least in my memory, had always maintained a pleasant demeanor. She smiled proudly at her family as she observed her English-speaking grandchildren, a boisterous bunch always on the go. This time was different. She was someone else, somewhere else. She was recalling the horror of watching women leap from the windows. No one moved at the table. We imagined what witnessing this event must have been like for her and how close she had been to death. She worked just a few steps from the Asch Building. At last, Nana's hands moved across the tablecloth. She smoothed out its creases, a decisive act that signaled she had reached the end of her story. *Finito*. I never experienced a moment like that with her again. I have never forgotten it.

I had never heard of the Triangle fire before that day. Nearly a decade after hearing my grandmother's story, in June 1997, I attended the third Biennial Conference of the Center for Working-Class Studies at Youngstown State University. There, Janet Zandy presented a paper on the Triangle Shirtwaist Factory fire. I was moved by her discussion of contemporary poets writing about the fire—the same ones I now teach—and realized, quite profoundly, that *this* was the fire in my grandmother's story. Zandy's words about the violence of this "collective tragedy" against workers prompted me to dig deeper into my family history.

Excavating the past, I have learned, is an emotionally painful process. Some memories are not treasured family heirlooms. They are repressed for good reason. During 1997 and 1998, I interviewed family members. Often, they were reluctant to talk about the past. I also collected stories from my father and older siblings, who were more willing storytellers. Nonetheless, many gaps remain. Historical records in archival repositories document a chronological time line that corroborates the stories of how my relatives survived two Red Scares, assassination attempts, FBI raids, and the destruction of printing presses. What had begun as a single story about my grandmother's work history soon turned into the discovery of multiple threads of my family's involvement in the Italian American labor movement, revealing a tapestry of radical resistance that had been obscured for almost eighty years.

As New York became an epicenter for union activism, my grandfather Vincenzo and his brother Raimondo, who had immigrated to the United States from Sicily in 1903, joined the front line of the garment workers' labor struggles. Within two years of their arrival, they became members of the fledgling Industrial Workers of the World (IWW) and were soon immersed in the wave of labor strikes during the early twentieth century. Both brothers advocated for workers' rights through the tenets of syndicalism, a socialist ideology, Marcella Bencivenni writes, that espoused direct action in the workplace through strikes and other forms of resistance. Vincenzo and Raimondo were hard-line labor radicals who fought for good wages and safe working conditions before and after the Triangle fire.

Raimondo wrote extensively. In 1911, he published a booklet, *Socialism and Syndicalism*, that advocated for the union's power to uphold worker solidarity. He also served as the editor of several Italian radical newspapers, including *Il Proletario* (*The Worker*), the official newspaper of the Federazione Socialista Italiana (FSI), and, later, the antifascist *Il Nuovo Mondo* (*The New World*). His activities as an organizer were documented in numerous news publications, such as *Cronaca Sovversiva*, an anarchist newspaper published in Barre, Vermont, that featured announcements of Raimondo's scheduled talks in New York City, in which he defined socialism and its goals. On December 13, he gave a speech during the Uprising of 1909; it was reported in the *New-York Daily Tribune* under the headline GIRL STRIKERS FIRM: WAISTMAKERS UNDAUNTED BY FAILURE OF ARBITRATION. Outlining the strike committee's demands for recognition of the union, Raimondo, along with labor activists Hugo Lupi, Publio Mazzella, Antonio Cravello, and Alessandro Giusti, spoke for the Italian strikers, expressing their ongoing commitment to the strike.

On March 2, 1912, the children of striking workers in Lawrence, Massachusetts, were sent to New York to secure their safety as violent exchanges between workers and police escalated. Raimondo, then secretary of the FSI, and nurse activist Margaret Sanger met them at Grand Central Station. As *The Sun* reported, "The children were marched to a restaurant, followed by a rapidly increasing crowd. They appeared to be highly delighted over the attention they drew." Raimondo actively supported the strikers, serving, according to Michael Miller Topp, as part of the delegation that traveled to Washington for the "congressional investigation into police violence." He also wrote, as Rudolph Vecoli has stated, in defense of IWW organizers Arturo Giovannitti, Joseph Ettor, and Joseph Caruso, who had been accused of the murder of striker Anna LoPizzo.

My grandfather remained active during those years. He traveled more extensively than his brother to participate in rallies and protests across the Northeast. He distributed pamphlets during strikes that

Figure 13.3. Vincenzo Fazio (middle) with union friends, 1911.
Photographer unknown; photo courtesy of Michele Fazio.

involved Italian immigrant women in New York (Uprising of 1909), Massachusetts (Lawrence Textile Strike of 1912), and New Jersey (Paterson Silk Strike of 1913). This time line mirrored that of my grandmother's work in the garment industry. I imagine their paths crossed at a protest or organizational meeting. Perhaps my grandfather handed out flyers outside her workplace or she attended an event where he or Raimondo was speaking. Nana told me they fell in love instantly—he was a "handsome man," she said. She gave no other details except that they married in 1914, joined the ILGWU, and raised five children on factory wages, often working side by side assembling ladies' garments.

In 1935, as unions gained more power, my grandfather formed an insurrectional movement on behalf of the Italian Dressmakers' Union, "Le Garibaldine," named after the Italians who had fought with Giuseppe Garibaldi. He placed a two-page advertisement in two Italian newspapers, *Il Progresso Italo-Americano* and *Corriere d'America*, listing his demands for a self-governing union and increased financial transparency for a movement of "PURE UNIONISM." Serving as chairman of this faction, he accused ILGWU officials of spending the hard-earned union dues of the working poor on what he called "Pleasure Trips." He was later charged by Luigi Antonini, ILGWU's general secretary, and other members of the executive board with betrayal. They said he was a Communist who incited others to "overthrow the organization" and expelled him from the very union he had helped to create. Fellow worker Rose Ceraolo, Le Garibaldine's secretary, was also removed from any association with Local 89. My discovery of his case in the ILGWU papers at the Kheel Center for Labor-Management Documentation & Archives at Cornell University in 2016 provided political context for a story my grandmother proudly repeated on many occasions. My grandfather had been "blacklisted" and banned from working at union-run factories, which forced him to do piecework at home to make a living. My grandmother, though, only told that she had been the sole wage earner of the family for several years and kept the family afloat during the Great Depression.

While my grandmother's name may not appear in labor archives or books on Italian immigrant women's participation in the labor movement, she stood in solidarity with others in the name of worker justice. Her signature appears on Rose Ceraolo's appeal in the ILGWU papers, in which Ceraolo petitioned to be allowed to return to work. Most likely, my grandmother used her birth name to avoid any association with her husband's activity. Nana also told the story of serving dinner to Tresca on several occasions. I have no doubt that she not only knew what the men were discussing but also fully supported their political views. And, knowing her, she must have taken a seat at the table. Wives and daughters, as Jennifer Guglielmo argues, were involved in supporting labor activism at work, in the community, and at home.

Nana's devotion to her husband was inextricably linked to labor activism. This I learned when, after her death, in 1989, I found a political speech written on two fragile, yellowing pieces of paper, which she had kept in her nightstand for over forty years. I read with trepidation my

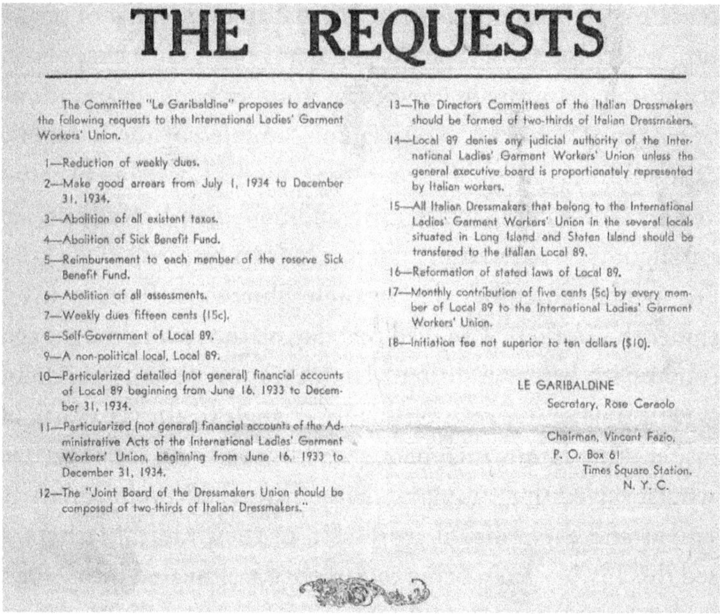

THE REQUESTS

The Committee "Le Garibaldine" proposes to advance the following requests to the International Ladies' Garment Workers' Union.

1—Reduction of weekly dues.

2—Make good arrears from July 1, 1934 to December 31, 1934.

3—Abolition of all existent taxes.

4—Abolition of Sick Benefit Fund.

5—Reimbursement to each member of the reserve Sick Benefit Fund.

6—Abolition of all assessments.

7—Weekly dues fifteen cents (15c).

8—Self-Government of Local 89.

9—A non-political local, Local 89.

10—Particularized detailed (not general) financial accounts of Local 89 beginning from June 16, 1933 to December 31, 1934.

11—Particularized (not general) financial accounts of the Administrative Acts of the International Ladies' Garment Workers' Union, beginning from June 16, 1933 to December 31, 1934.

12—The "Joint Board of the Dressmakers Union should be composed of two-thirds of Italian Dressmakers."

13—The Directors Committees of the Italian Dressmakers should be formed of two-thirds of Italian Dressmakers.

14—Local 89 denies any judicial authority of the International Ladies' Garment Workers' Union unless the general executive board is proportionately represented by Italian workers.

15—All Italian Dressmakers that belong to the International Ladies' Garment Workers' Union in the several locals situated in Long Island and Staten Island should be transferred to the Italian Local 89.

16—Reformation of stated laws of Local 89.

17—Monthly contribution of five cents (5c) by every member of Local 89 to the International Ladies' Garment Workers' Union.

18—Initiation fee not superior to ten dollars ($10).

LE GARIBALDINE
Secretary, Rose Caraolo

Chairman, Vincent Fazio,
P. O. Box 61
Times Square Station,
N. Y. C.

Figure 13.4. "Le Garibaldine." Reform advertisement placed by Vincenzo Fazio. ILGWU. Local 89. Luigi Antonini correspondence. 5780/023. Courtesy of Kheel Center for Labor-Management Documentation & Archives, Martin P. Catherwood Library, Cornell University.

grandfather's handwriting, difficult to understand in places. "A Lumi Spenti" ("Lights Extinguished"), written in Italian and dated 1945, reads like a manifesto that reflects on and questions the future of the American Labor Party. This communication was to be my grandfather's final act of defiance. He died of a cerebral hemorrhage shortly after writing this speech. My grandmother held on to those two pages, as opposed to a lock of his hair or some other memento. She also kept a collection of old, overlooked books in the family's bookcase. One of them, *Gli italiani di New York*, published by the Labor Press in 1939, contains the program for the twentieth anniversary of the Italian Dressmakers' Union, ILGWU Local 89. The program included a radio adaptation of Giacomo Puccini's *Madame Butterfly* and speeches by Fiorello La Guardia, New York City mayor; Arturo Giovannitti; and Luigi Antonini. It also included an address by Eleanor Roosevelt. The rest of the book is a survey of cultural achievements prepared by the Workers of the Federal

Writers' Project. Raimondo's name is listed alongside that of poet Giovannitti, writer Pietro di Donato, and many others in a chapter on the history of Italian culture in New York. Another book my grandmother kept, *Dynamic Democracy*, by Antonini, compiled by the Italian Labor Education Bureau and published in 1944, marks Local 89's twenty-fifth anniversary. These items, which my grandmother so carefully preserved, bring to light vital parts of my family's hidden history.

For me, to remember the Triangle Shirtwaist Factory fire is to remember the workers who died that day, all those who fought against class oppression before and after March 25, 1911, *and* my grandmother. Recovering my family's relationship to Triangle history is a form of activism. Yet other family members, second-generation sons and daughters who survived the trauma of living through a revolutionary labor movement and the political repression of their radical fathers, suppressed this history from being told as they assimilated into American society. I write this story to reconstruct the history of the working class as a legacy to uphold, not disavow.

Teaching the Triangle fire through the lens of working-class studies has led me on a journey to explore the relationship between archival research and family history, and their dual objectives to document collective memory. This approach informs my research on the legacy of working-class ethnic communities and how they are memorialized today. I do not know whether my grandmother would welcome my efforts to speak about the family in such a public manner. I only know her story stays with me. Year after year, it reminds me of what we stand to lose by forgetting the past.

The wool, silk, and lace my grandmother once held in her hands is now stored in old trunks, tucked away in the back of closets. These remnants of her needlework evoke her skillful touch and furrowed brow. I imagine her bending over the cloth, needle in hand, completing one stitch at a time. Each thread binds my life to hers—as do her stories.

CHAPTER 14

They Were Not There

A Rumination on the Meaning of the
Triangle Shirtwaist Fire to Black Garment Workers
in Early-Twentieth-Century New York City

▼

Janette Gayle

I t's a sweltering hot summer day in New York City in 2018. An immigrant of West Indian origin and a historian by vocation, I'm on yet another research trip for a book I am writing on Black women who worked in the New York garment industry in the early twentieth century. After spending hours in an un-air-conditioned room at the New York Municipal Archives, poring through the business records of garment shops that might have employed Black women, I finally give up and leave with precious little more than I started with. Once again, I am reminded that trying to find Black garment workers in the historical records before World War I is not unlike looking for needles in haystacks. Disappointed and frustrated, I head back to East Williamsburg, where I am staying with my son, who lives in one of those trendy loft apartments that once housed a garment factory.

As it did in its previous life, the loft houses a bank of floor-to-ceiling windows that stretch across the width of the apartment. The windows let in a copious amount of light, but they barely open. The poor design of the windows, coupled with air-conditioning that doesn't work, makes me feel hot and closed in. Adding to this rising sense of claustrophobia is the realization that there is only one door to get in and out of the loft. I also know that there is only one flight of stairs that would allow me to exit the building, having had to climb them once due to a malfunctioning elevator. So much for safe, modern urban living. A momentary flash of fear grips me as I wonder what would happen if a fire broke out in the building under these conditions. This momentary flash makes me think of the panic and terror that must have engulfed the garment workers who lost their lives in the Triangle Shirtwaist Factory fire on March 25, 1911.

A monumental event in the history of the garment industry and the labor movement, the Triangle Shirtwaist Factory fire revealed to the general public the intolerable conditions that garment workers labored under to produce affordable ready-made clothing and fueled efforts to enact protective labor legislation. A highly visible tragedy, the fire gripped the attention of New Yorkers and paused the pace of this perpetually moving city as the white press exposed the horrors of the conditions that had led to the fire and its grim result. Despite all of this, to my surprise and frustration, I discovered that there was not one report of the fire in the city's Black press. Why this glaring omission?

One hundred and forty-six young women perished in that fire.
There was not one Black woman among them.
They were not there.

For a long time, I wanted to write an essay about Black garment workers and their connection to the Triangle fire. But I couldn't, because as I went about my research, I came to the realization that they simply were not there. I came to see that rather than the story's being a history of invisibility, it was a history of exclusion. As it turned out, my struggle revolved around the reality that Black women were not in the building at the time of the fire. In fact, in 1910, one year before the fire, a mere 188 Black women worked in the industry. Statistically insignificant, they composed barely .003 percent of the female garment industry workforce. Moreover, unlike the Jewish and Italian garment workers who toiled in buildings like the one that housed the Triangle Waist Company, the Black women who worked in the industry were employed in the various small garment shops that dotted the outskirts of the Garment District. Although they were isolated from women who worked in factories, I wondered how the Black women who worked in the industry felt about the lack of attention the Black press paid to the tragic event. Were they outraged or saddened? Did they protest? Or did they feel powerless to do anything about galvanizing Black public attention to the fire and the conditions that caused it? We may never know the answers to these questions—the historical record is silent on the matter. Why were so few Black women employed in the garment industry? At this time, employers did not hire Black workers in most industries, including the garment industry. In addition, Jewish and Italian immigrants, with a sprinkling of native-born whites, composed the bulk of the labor force that made the garments. Despite the limitations on the number of immigrants from most of Asia, the pre–World War I period was a time of open migration to the United States. Reflecting the pro-immigrant sentiment expressed in Emma Lazarus's poem "The New Colossus"—"Give me your tired, your poor, / Your huddled masses yearning to breathe free"—millions of immigrants from Eastern and Southern Europe streamed into New York, providing more than enough labor to supply the garment industry's needs. There was simply no need to look outside the Jewish and Italian communities for workers.

The composition of the garment industry workforce was part of my awakening to how race worked in the Americas. In the British West Indies, where I came from, Jews and Italians were not part of the working class. Classified as white in the racial landscape of Britain's island colonies, both Jews and Italians were the owners and managers of businesses, not factory workers. How strange it was to my West Indian conception of race that in the United States they were not considered white, or at least not fully white, and that they earned their living by the sweat of their brow.

The second reason for the paltry number of Black garment workers is slavery's terrible legacy of racism, an indelible stain left on American society. From as early as the mid-1600s, legislators in colonial America enacted a series of laws to distinguish between Black and white women based on race. The statutes reflected white colonists' ideas about the place that Black women would occupy and the role they would play in colonial society. For example, the labor of Black women was taxed (a tax levied on their owners), while the labor of white women was not. The prevailing logic categorized Black women as agricultural workers—producers—and therefore taxable. White women, on the other hand, were categorized as dependents, even though their labor was critical to the household economy. Furthermore, enslaved Black women were assigned the additional role of being the reproducers of the slave workforce. The children of enslaved Black women legally inherited their mothers' status, even if their fathers were free. And just in case it wasn't clear before, in 1705 the Virginia Assembly enacted a law that made it clear that the distinguishing factor between servants and slaves was race: Servants were white; slaves were Black. In the eyes of white America, blackness became indelibly associated with slavery and racial inferiority, a poisonous belief that has survived largely intact into the present. The legacy of this badge of inferiority and degradation had the effect of locking nearly all Black women and men out of the burgeoning industrial economy of the early twentieth century. As was true in other industries, in the rapidly growing New York garment industry native-born white workers flatly refused to work alongside Black women. Jewish and Italian immigrants may or may not have arrived in America with preconceived notions of Black inferiority, but in America, where race was closely associated with social mobility, many came to take on the attitude of their native white American colleagues.

The Triangle Shirtwaist Factory fire spurred the formation of influential groups that lobbied the New York legislature in Albany to enact labor legislation that mandated better building access and egress, fireproofing requirements, the installation of alarm and sprinkler systems, better eating and toilet facilities for workers, and a limit on the number of hours that women could work to fifty-four hours per week. On paper, these laws made New York State the leader in labor reform in the nation. In reality, the environment in which workers toiled in the garment industry continued to be grim. Unsafe working conditions, low wages, long hours, and little or no protection against firings and layoffs remained the order of the day. Despite this, Black women still desired jobs in the industry. Why?

Perhaps, like me prior to starting my research, Black women were not aware of the suboptimal conditions that existed in the city's garment shops and factories. After all, there were few Black garment workers to tell the tale. With little or no exposure to the physical conditions in the industry or the rigors of garment factory work, did they understand that the only thing that mattered to employers was that their employees perform with speed and accuracy? Did they understand that task repetition—sewing seams, hemming garments, putting in sleeves, trimming garments—was all that workers did from the moment they went to work until the moment they left at the end of the day? Did they know that all this would be performed under the watchful eye of a supervisor who could be kind but also cruel? Very likely not. However, if they did know, they still pursued jobs in the industry. Why? Because given the limited range of occupational opportunities available to Black women in New York City, a job in the garment industry was one of the few options, apart from domestic service. While entry-level jobs in the industry did not necessarily pay better than domestic work, there was the potential for advancement for those with talent and an eye for detail. Moreover, in the hierarchy of work in early-twentieth-century New York, a garment factory job trumped domestic service because of the deeply embedded notions of servility associated with that occupation. For Black women, a job making beautiful or even plain dresses and shirtwaists was better than scrubbing floors, cooking meals they were not allowed to eat, looking after children who were not theirs, having to address their charges as "Miss" or "Master" while being addressed by their first names, wearing uniforms that marked them as servants, and being constantly vulnerable to verbal and sexual abuse by employers, conditions with which Black women were only too well acquainted.

Wanting better out of life, young Black women, often with the encouragement of their parents, prepared themselves for jobs in the industry by attending the Manhattan Trade School for Girls. Founded in 1902 by a group of progressive-minded philanthropists, the school offered a rigorous one-year dressmaking program designed to equip young women with professional sewing skills. While most of the students were first- and second-generation Eastern and Southern European immigrants, a few Black women were enrolled. Their stories, recorded on the school's report cards, give us some insight into who they were, their path to the industry, and their experiences in the garment shops.

Take Helen Page, for instance. After successfully completing the tenth grade at Flushing High School in New York, Helen enrolled at the Manhattan Trade School for Girls in 1913. Helen and her parents were part of the early-twentieth-century migratory diaspora that brought thousands of Blacks from the American South and the British West Indies to New York City. Her father, John, worked as a messenger and her mother, Geneva, was a homemaker. This family arrangement placed Helen somewhere between the upper rungs of the working class and the lower rungs of the middle class in Harlem's Black community. There would be no working as a domestic servant for their daughter if they could help it. It is not hard to imagine that with ten years of schooling under her belt, Helen had no desire to become a domestic servant. Upon graduating from the Manhattan Trade School for Girls in 1914, she found work in a dress shop doing hand sewing. Helen worked in the industry for several years, although she never advanced beyond the entry-level position of finisher.

Other Black graduates of this school did not fare as well as Helen did on the job market when she graduated in 1914. Violet Baker is a case in point. The child of West Indian immigrants, Violet was described by one of her instructors at the school as a "good girl" whose work "is so good [that] I am promoting her on fine garments." Armed with her dressmaking certificate and recommendations, Violet sought a job as a finisher at a dress shop. She never had a chance to show her skills. The manager took one look at Violet and dismissed her. A note from the shop's manager was placed in Violet's file at The Manhattan Trade School for Girls: "I did not know you were sending me a colored girl. Cannot use her." We do not know how many Black women like Violet sought jobs in the industry but were turned down. There is no way to tell, but given the widespread anti-Black sentiments of the day, it is highly unlikely that she was the only one.

I did not know you were sending me a colored girl. Cannot use her.

It has been at least ten years since I first saw those fateful fourteen words. Yet they never fail to shock, sadden, and anger me each time I read them. For far too many Black people, the sentiment expressed in those words is still a stark reality. I came face-to-face with the reality for the first time in my life as a migrant in America. Let me be clear, anti-Black prejudice exists in the West Indies. However, its experience is complicated and mitigated by the way in which factors such as color and class are expressed in West Indian society. A milk chocolate–complected woman from the upper echelons of the Jamaican middle class, in Jamaica I was not in any way hindered by the color of my skin. More important, from a societal standpoint, I was not considered Black. It was only upon my arrival in America that I learned that I was in fact "Black." This seeming transformation could only be accomplished in a society in which the complexity of color was reduced to the binarism of "Black" or "white." To my dismay, I was now what W. E. B. Du Bois referred to as "a problem."

What, exactly, did that mean? It meant that I was first seen by others and defined by them through my race. In other words, I was no longer just "Janette Gayle," but "Black woman Janette Gayle," or "Janette Gayle, the Black woman." On the one hand, this brought me a degree of inclusion into the Black American community, although this inclusion was always incomplete because I was marked as a foreigner. On the other hand, in the eyes of white people, the mark of "blackness" placed me outside the scope of full citizenship. In 1903, Du Bois proffered the concept of double consciousness to explain the psychological impact that the burden of race placed on African Americans. According to him, double consciousness produced a "sense of always looking at one's self through the eyes of others, of measuring one's soul by the tape of a world that looks on in amused contempt and pity." While, as a Black woman in America, I felt the power of this concept, as an immigrant Black woman, I experienced another layer of the alienation described by Du Bois. Seen as Black by white Americans and foreign by African

Americans, one might say that I experienced a triple consciousness. This triple consciousness became an important motivating factor. It became one of the more important reasons for my decision to pursue a degree in African American history. Understanding this history and living with it as a force in my life has made me keenly aware of the obstacles that Black people in America have faced and continue to face in overcoming structural racism and anti-Black prejudice of the kind that Violet encountered.

How utterly frustrating the experience of being denied a job in a garment shop because she was "colored" must have been for Violet. To have left their homeland in search of a better life for themselves and their children and to come face-to-face with this rejection must have angered Violet's parents. To have invested time and energy into preparing herself to make the most of the opportunities that America purportedly offered must have been at least frustrating for Violet. But it might also have made her determined to fight back—to demand a place for herself in the garment industry.

As a Black immigrant myself, I understand the motivations of these women who were determined to take advantage of the opportunities they believed New York City held open to them. But, like them, I also ran afoul of ideas that sought to circumscribe what others thought was my place in American society. Like many of the women I write about, when I came to the United States in the mid-1990s, I first worked as a domestic servant. While the conditions in which I labored were much improved from what they had been in the past, the work remained low status and low paying. For me, my job as a domestic servant was a stop-gap on the way to fulfilling other ambitions; it was part of my path to making the most of being in America. My employers thought otherwise. When I expressed my desire to earn a college degree, they questioned why I would want to do that, since I was "so good at what I was doing" for them. In their imagination, my *proper* place as a Black immigrant woman in American society was in service to them. My way of escaping this fixity of place was through a university education.

Earning a college degree opened up a whole new world for me. Although I had always believed in the necessity of fighting injustice, I entered university politically naïve and largely ignorant about workers' struggles. In fact, if I were to be totally honest, coming from a middle-class background in my West Indian homeland, I was not terribly sympathetic toward unions. What an eye-opener it was for me to begin to study the history of worker exploitation in industrial capitalism, the divisive role that race and gender played in the American working class, and the terrible conditions under which workers toiled and continue to toil in the "First World"—all of which opened the door to calamities such as the Triangle fire and many other injustices. Seeking to understand this history and tantalized by fleeting references to Black garment workers in a few historical studies, I set off to learn who these women were and what motivated their determination to make a place for themselves in the New York garment industry. I soon realized that just as academia was my escape from my employers' fixed idea of my place in American society, so was the early-twentieth-century New York garment industry for Black women. Understood as "domestics" by white Americans, these women tried to escape the fixity of place through the garment industry. It was this desire to transcend their prescribed place that drove their determination to push their way into the garment shops and factories from which they had for so long been excluded.

World War I opened up opportunities for Black women to be hired as garment workers. The exigencies of war meant that the industry's traditional labor supply from Eastern and Southern Europe was disrupted as transatlantic passenger shipping was displaced by the transportation of wartime goods, such as uniforms and blankets. The decline in the number of "white" immigrant workers and the need to fill orders for the government created the conditions necessary for Black women to get jobs in the industry. And get jobs they did.

By 1920, the number of Black garment workers increased to 2,450. The influx was so great that it led Benjamin Schlesinger, the president of the ILGWU, to announce to the assembled delegates at their annual convention that "colored women workers are invading the ladies' garment trades." I think, somewhat cynically, to myself that first they excluded Black women; then, when they needed them, they let them in but called them invaders.

Who were these colored invaders? Most were southern African American migrants, the majority hailing from Virginia, Maryland, and the Carolinas, followed by British West Indian immigrants, from all the islands, but mainly from Barbados and Jamaica. The smallest number of these workers were native-born Black New Yorkers. Mirroring the composition of the Black population in New York City, the newest entrants into the garment industry were 60 percent African American and 40 percent West Indian. Many were married, but most were single. They ranged in age from fifteen to fifty-nine, but most were in their twenties and thirties. Before they were hired in the industry, the majority had worked as domestics, while others had been housewives. A few had earned their living as self-employed dressmakers, and some—like Helen Page, Violet Baker, Beatrice Carter, Bessie Smith Coles, Elsie Gross, Vivian Farley, Cecelia Jones, Helen Seeley, and Floria Pinkney—entered the industry as trained garment workers.

As the names of these women and snippets of their history became visible to me, I wondered what, if anything, they knew of the Triangle fire. Did they know that the lives lost in the fire not only galvanized the push for protective labor legislation but also energized the push to organize female garment workers? Did they know about the bravery and determination of young Jewish women such as Clara Lemlich, Fannia Cohn, and Pauline Newman, who were at the forefront of that struggle? Whether Black garment workers knew it or not, they were heirs to the legacy of that momentous struggle. However, as the ILGWU was soon to discover, organizing Black garment workers was neither simple nor easy.

On the face of it, organizing Black garment workers should not have been a difficult task. Though numerically sufficient enough to be a cause for concern to the union if they were not organized, Black garment workers were a tiny percentage (barely .04 percent) of the female garment industry workforce. Moreover, they were almost entirely concentrated in the ladies' wear segment of the industry, making it easier for the union to access them. Finally, Black women were among the most exploited workers in the industry. The overwhelming majority of Black women labored at low-wage, labor-intensive, entry-level positions with little to no job security. Given their position, the union rightly believed that they would be receptive to the union's message. And yet, the ILGWU found that the path to winning the allegiance of Black garment workers was fraught with challenges. Memories of old histories lingered long in the minds of African Americans, memories of when the white working class wanted nothing to do with Black workers and adamantly excluded them from membership in their unions. West Indians were not so burdened with these memories, but they were nevertheless cautious of joining with white workers.

Influential voices in the Black community inveighed strongly against Black women joining the ILGWU. Marcus Garvey, Kelly Miller, and W. E. B. Du Bois were the most vocal. Garvey, head of the multi-thousand-strong Universal Negro Improvement Association (UNIA), warned his followers that if Black workers unionized and succeeded in securing wages equal to those of their white counterparts, employers would no longer hire them and would replace them with white workers. In an article entitled "The Negro as a Workingman," Howard University professor Kelly Miller sounded a similar refrain. He reminded Blacks of the violence perpetrated by the white working class against Black workers and warned them that to join forces with "the restless ranks [of white workers] which threaten industrial ruin would be fatuous suicide." Du Bois, founding member of the National Association for the Advancement of Colored People (NAACP) and editor of the Black magazine *The Crisis*, was also skeptical of interracial labor organizing. Weighing in on the issue in an editorial, Du Bois opined that although Blacks were "theoretically part of the world proletariat, practically they were not part of the white proletariat." Instead, Black workers "were the victims of white workers 'physical oppression, social ostracism, economic exclusion, and personal hatred.'"

While voices warning Blacks against joining forces with white workers held sway in editorials and UNIA meeting halls, a small cadre of voices advocating interracial labor solidarity was emerging on street-corner podiums, in the Black press, and in homes, and was gaining some momentum in the Black community. Chief among these voices was community activist and labor leader A. Philip Randolph. A Socialist,

Randolph was convinced that labor organizing was essential for Blacks to improve their economic status. He urged Black garment workers to join forces with white garment workers in the ILGWU. Not to take this action, he believed, effectively undermined the strength of the labor movement. Whom to believe was the quandary that Black garment workers faced.

Who would I have believed? Garvey, who reinforced a sense of Black pride and dignity and preached a gospel of Black economic self-reliance; or Miller and Du Bois, who told Blacks that trusting white workers to look out for their interests was folly; or Randolph, whose message encouraged interracial labor solidarity? This was a difficult choice. I believe that I would have decided that if the union wanted me to join, it would have to court me. That is exactly what the union had to do.

Enlisting the aid of Randolph and the handful of other pro-union advocates in Black New York City, ILGWU leaders worked hard to woo Black garment workers into the union. Demonstrating the seriousness of their intention, the union held several meetings in Harlem. Anxious to reassure Black garment workers that they would be treated fairly, speakers at the meetings addressed issues pertaining to relations between union members as well as the attitude of union leaders toward the members. Speakers also focused on the material advantages of joining the union, such as the forty-hour workweek and wage increases that the union had recently won. The response to the organizing drive was promising, with as many as one hundred Black garment workers attending some of the meetings. But while the union piqued the interest of some Black garment workers, relatively few became members. It was going to take more than meetings and speakers to persuade Black women to join the union. The reasons were complex. First, Garvey's influence was deep and hard to dislodge. Moreover, the bitter conflict between Communist and Socialist factions that consumed the union for several years in the 1920s made it an unattractive organization for workers, Black or white, to join. Thus, by the end of the decade, the union had very little to show for its efforts to woo Black women into the fold.

This state of affairs might have remained the same had it not been for the Great Depression. Descending upon the nation in late October 1929, the plunge in the economy created conditions that began to shift Black garment workers' response to the union. Initially, the change was gradual. However, as unemployment in Black New York City soared and as household income plummeted, Black women's wages—always important to the survival of their households—became even more vital. The constraints in the labor market caused by the depression initially caused Black garment workers to resist anything that would put their jobs at risk. As a result, the majority remained unorganized.

While the status quo seemed fixed in place, events in the garment industry outside of New York that were about to unfold would soon change that. In May 1933, a strike by five thousand garment workers in the Philadelphia dress industry reenergized organizing efforts in New York City. While these changes were implemented in the union at the local level, events were unfolding at the federal level that further invigorated organizing activity. Pressured by union leaders and pro-labor lobbyists, on June 13, the U.S. Congress passed the National Industrial Recovery Act (NIRA). A foundational part of President Roosevelt's economic recovery plan, the law gave workers the right to join trade unions of their own choosing, free from the interference, restraint, or coercion of their employers. Though conceptually groundbreaking, the law was weak, given that no enforcement mechanism accompanied it. Moreover, the structure allowed management the opportunity to create codes that established uniform wages and hours. The law gave many small garment manufacturers the ability to set the prevailing rates and conditions in the industry. On its face, this seemed to give employers undue advantage vis-à-vis workers. Convinced that the legislation imperiled workers, union leader Charles Zimmerman argued that it was imperative for garment workers to organize in order to staunch the power of employers to control the labor market.

Far from the panacea the government had hoped it would be, the law further galvanized the union into action. In early July, union leaders met and voted to hold a strike in August. Notices were sent out to garment workers warning them "not [to] wait for the Recovery Act to hand [them] down anything from heaven," but to organize and "help swell the ranks of [unionized] dressmakers in their militant struggle ... for higher wages and better conditions." With funds in the union's treasury dwindling, pamphlets and posters advertising the strike in the Black community were minimal. While this might have been an impediment to the organizing effort, it was countered by person-to-person communication. We can imagine that as converts to the union cause, Black union members such as Lillian Gaskin, Violet Williams, Edith Ransom, Eldica Riley, Ethel Atwell, Maida Springer, and Winifred Gittens spent time and energy convincing their sister Black garment workers to join the strike.

Their efforts paid off. On the morning of August 16, when the call to strike went out, Black garment workers did the very thing they had previously refused to do since the union had begun courting them in 1920. Acting decisively and in solidarity with their fellow workers, they laid down their tools, walked off the job, and enrolled in the union. Remembered in union lore as the Uprising of the 60,000, the Dressmakers' Strike of 1933 marked a critical turning point for the ILGWU. Reversing over ten years of decline, membership swelled to above its peak in 1920, before the internecine fight between Communists and Socialists that had nearly destroyed the union. The strike marked a milestone in the history of the relationship between the union and Black garment workers, as thousands signed up to become members. Almost overnight, the number of unionized Black garment workers rose from a few hundred to well over four thousand. The tide had turned. In the following months, Black garment workers continued to join the union in record numbers, setting a trend that spanned the next three decades.

Welcomed into the membership, Black garment workers enthusiastically engaged in the life of the union as they worked to take their place in the ranks of the organization. They participated in elections, served on committees, worked as shop delegates, represented the union at conventions, played on sports teams, held dances, and attended classes. Taught by veteran union organizers, these new members learned how

Figure 14.1. Black ILGWU members. Many, if not all, of these Black garment workers joined the ILGWU in the months following the 1933 Dressmakers' Strike. Photographer unknown; photo courtesy of the Kheel Center for Labor-Management Documentation & Archives, Cornell University.

the union operated, what their rights as workers were, and how to organize. They were also taught the history of the union. It was not until then, some twenty years after the Triangle fire, that Black garment workers learned about this tragic event that was instrumental in generating the protective labor legislation to which they were heirs.

Did Black garment workers wonder why they had not heard about the Triangle fire before, especially when it had happened in the city where they lived? What did the deaths of the 146 Triangle workers mean to once excluded, now included Black women in the garment industry labor force? Were they sorrowful and angered and pained? In the deep recesses of their hearts, did they also feel that the fire was a rare instance when their race had saved them? There is no definitive answer to these questions. Answers probably incorporate all, or some, or, perhaps, none of these. My best hope is that the knowledge of the tragedy of hopeful young immigrant women at the Triangle Waist

Company and the protective labor legislation that their deaths brought about somehow helped to build bonds of interracial labor solidarity in the New York garment industry.

Bonds of solidarity between Black and white garment workers were demonstrated on May 13, 1937, when delegate Gittens addressed the General Executive Board and other delegates at the ILGWU's twenty-third convention. Speaking on behalf of her fellow Black union members, Gittens expressed her "appreciation for the opportunity given to us to find our place in the ranks of our class and to share in the benefits, duties, and responsibilities of trade union life in America." There is every reason to believe that the appreciation voiced by Gittens in her speech was genuine. After all, well before most other white-run unions had either refused to include Black workers or even organize them in separate chapters, the ILGWU had included them directly in its membership. However, I believe that there was more underlying what Gittens said. For while it is true that the union gave Black garment workers the opportunity to *find* themselves in the ranks of their class, it is equally true that by forcing themselves into the garment industry workforce and actively engaging in the life of the union, Black garment workers *made* a place for themselves in the American industrial working class, a class from which, for much of American history, they had been consciously and systematically excluded on account of their race and their gender.

The Triangle Shirtwaist Factory fire was a seminal moment in the history of the New York garment industry. The deaths of young women in the fire are rightly remembered and commemorated as a terrible and unknowingly made sacrifice that led to improved conditions in the garment industry. Heirs to this legacy, Gittens and the workers for whom she spoke are almost invisible in the history of the garment industry and the labor struggles that it engendered. As I look back, I realize that my determination to make these women visible was an animating concern driving my research and scholarship. I knew that understanding their successes and struggles was key to understanding the shape of the early-twentieth-century labor and civil rights movement, and I feared that the dearth of research on these pioneering women reflected an attitude that their contributions were not important. Indeed, when I first started down this research path, some around me questioned the efficacy of my work. After all, there were only a few thousand Black garment workers. Why bother? While I was discouraged by this argument, I was also emboldened to continue my work. Not to do so would give credence to the belief that numerical preponderance determines historical significance. Throughout my research, nagging voices of uncertainty about the value of my work dogged me, but my drive to uncover heretofore hidden histories won out. As it turned out, not only were Gittens and her fellow Black garment workers part of the first cadre of female Black workers to be organized; they were also at the forefront of the struggle for civil rights in New York. If I had given up, this important history might never have been brought to light.

PART FIVE

MEMORIALS

CHAPTER 15

Chalk and Smoke, Fabric and Thread

Reflections on Feminist Commemoration and the Triangle Fire

Ellen Wiley Todd

I stand at the south entrance to Union Square Park. It's March 25, 2011. I'm in my last decade of university teaching and research as a feminist art historian of U.S. art. Sunshine and a brilliant sky illuminate the manicured park and the neighborhood. The park bustles with hundreds of eager, warmly dressed parade participants, many of them students. Some chat in groups. Others distribute banners, large placards, and high-necked blouses embellished with name-bearing sashes and floating on tall poles. I enter the park to request the privilege of carrying one of these blouses and join the procession to commemorate the one hundredth anniversary of the Triangle Shirtwaist Factory fire.

Beginnings

In 1993, I published *The New Woman Revised: Painting and Gender Politics on Fourteenth Street,* a book that features paintings by four urban realists I had written about in my dissertation. During the Depression, from their studios these artists had observed and depicted women in their neighborhood: women striding past bargain emporia or posed to view a store window in their own latest fashions; teenage office clerks from insurance companies or banks sharing a lunchtime ice-cream cone with friends; weary millinery workers leaving their shops at the end of the day. Many of the women who inspired this art would have been first- or second-generation immigrants, perhaps daughters of Triangle workers. In my book, I considered the works of these four artists (Kenneth Hayes Miller, Reginald Marsh, Raphael Soyer, Isabel Bishop) in relationship to women's work and consumerism in this lower-middle-class (and sometimes politically radical) neighborhood. While mainstream art schools, commercial galleries, and museums still preferred art without politics, my project used social and feminist art history to reveal the gendered and class content of these paintings.

I had always thought that my second book would apply feminist approaches to identity politics to interpret the work of one of these artists. But by the time my sabbatical started, in 1995, art history had shifted from single-artist studies to social histories and widened its scope to include visual culture studies. This enabled the study of multiple images around a single subject—including images that were not considered "high art." I had been gripped by political cartooning from alternate publications in the Depression, often made by painters who moved beyond their art school education and the slim economic possibilities it provided. And then there was photography, with a full spectrum of producers, from untrained amateurs to photojournalists to fine artists. I wanted a project that worked the boundaries between different kinds of images, practices, and institutions of art.

As a feminist art historian, I wanted to keep thinking about women as historical actors and about women and work. And I wanted to stay in New York City. Ultimately, I decided that a single event or movement might provide an ideal focus. Thanks to the feminist and labor historians whose work had introduced me to the Triangle fire in graduate school, I found my subject just eight blocks below the Union Square of my four dissertation artists. I began using art historical methods to compare news photos and editorial cartoons in New York's newspapers across the political spectrum. Sandwiched between the demands of life and workplace, my Triangle project encountered twists and turns as I struggled through the competing challenges of its multiple disciplines: art history, visual culture studies, women's and labor history.

Then the study of a 1930s mural, discovered at the High School of Fashion Industries, expanded the chronological scope of the project and included painting.

The visual object is my point of departure to understand the Triangle fire. I write as a historian of images, not events. My investigation revolves around detailed observation and description of objects. Visual forms reflect and enact history, whether through reportorial representation or documentation, or through more symbolic systems. The Triangle fire challenged my aesthetic boundaries as it brought me to images of a working-class, immigrant disaster, marked by horror rather than beauty. The Triangle community enabled my participation in the history and legacy of Triangle itself through a remarkable set of encounters with new friends in annual commemorations.

A central premise of my thoughts on Triangle's visual production is that newer forms of commemoration recall older types. In particular, three twenty-first-century commemorative works embody both Triangle's early commemorative history and early-twenty-first-century commemorative concerns. The first, a 2010 piece titled *Drawn in Smoke*, by feminist artist Harriet Bart, takes us to an uptown Manhattan gallery space. Its main work is an exhibit of 160 small drawings made with smoke, each bearing the name of a victim penned in the delicate script of the era. The drawings are assembled into a monumental wall-size grid of remembrance. The second tribute is the annual *Chalk*, the brainchild of artist/filmmaker Ruth Sergel. The third project, the *Shirtwaist Kites*, created by musician and cultural worker Annie Lanzillotto, was organized with playwright and performance artist LuLu LoLo and many others. As designed for the Triangle centennial, this performative work featured 146 individualized, handmade shirtwaist blouses, one for each victim. Festooned with sashes bearing victims' names on the front, their ages on the back, the shirtwaists were carried on tall poles in the "Procession of Shirtwaists" from Union Square to the site of the fire on the day of the centennial. The three commemorations range from the solitary recognized artist making "high art" for the uptown gallery audience to groups of multiethnic communities staging creative performances in public urban spaces for politically activist purposes. All three projects juxtapose individual units (paper, chalk, or cloth tributes) with monumentally communal ones (grids, neighborhoods, masses of shirtwaist kites). All three name the victims; all three use fragile or ephemeral materials to signal the lost traces of lived embodiment—the working, wearing, and suffering of Triangle workers who died in the fire.

These three contemporary memorials relate visually and conceptually to earlier ones. Together, they extend a dual typology of commemoration that originated at the time of the fire: participatory works that are fluid, public, and performative; single works of art made by individual artists that fall within some form of mainstream art production in their own historical moment. The interfaith funeral procession on April 5, 1911, on New York City streets after the fire exemplifies the participatory tradition. Approximately 400,000 mourners, including garment union representatives, families, and city dwellers converged on Washington Square from Madison Square and the Lower East Side of Manhattan. At its symbolic heart was a white horse-drawn hearse draped in black netting, typical of Italian funeral processions. It carried a simple coffin that evoked Jewish funeral traditions. The coffin was unmarked, standing for the seven then unidentified victims of the fire. This participatory and highly symbolic demonstration was staged in response to the city's refusal to release the unidentified bodies for the funeral procession, caused by the fear of unruly demonstrations from the immigrant population of New York's "foreign" districts. The parade, striking for its silence, followed mourners through rain-drenched streets.

Triangle marchers were not welcome at the simultaneous funeral performance staged at the edge of the Evergreens Cemetery in Brooklyn, where the city owned a plot. There, the city officials who had denied the release of the seven unidentified victims quietly transported their separate coffins for a formal interment. These administrators commissioned an "official" work of sculpture to mark the shared grave site, and thereby initiated the second commemorative tradition: the single work of art by an established artist, working within official institutions of art. Funding for the memorial design came from Progressive Era elites who administered the Red Cross Relief Committee for the Charity

Figure 15.1. Evelyn Beatrice Longman, *The Triangle Fire Memorial to the Unknowns*, 1912. Marble, nine feet, ten inches high, including pedestal. The Evergreens Cemetery, Brooklyn, New York. Photo by Ellen Wiley Todd; courtesy of the photographer.

Organization Society of the City of New York. Until I discovered her identity in the Red Cross archives, no one remembered the memorial had been designed by sculptor Evelyn Beatrice Longman. In 1909, she became one of the first female sculptors awarded associate membership in the National Academy of Design. As a young worker from a poor background, she was an appropriate choice to plan the memorial for the workingwomen of Triangle.

Longman produced a monument for the graves of the then unidentified victims of the fire buried in the Evergreens Cemetery. The sculptural relief features a partially draped female mourning figure, carved in the classical style of Longman's traditional training. The figure's crouched pose, bowed head, and clasped hands encircling the neck of a Greek-style krater provide the allegorical model for anguished yet dignified mourning—a tradition well known and acceptable to social elites wishing to acknowledge the tragedy and let it be forgotten. But to my contemporary eye, the bent figure also argues for an oblique reference to Triangle women's suffering. The powerful figure is compressed into her niche—a visual analogy to Triangle workers bent over their machines and constrained by the conditions of regimented factory work.

Another early single-artist example for Triangle imagery appeared in 1938 on the auditorium walls of the Central High School of Needle Trades (today New York's High School of Fashion Industries). There, the educational board of the ILGWU commissioned the experienced federal government muralist Ernest Fiene to paint *History of the Needlecraft Industries*. Two monumental murals include allegories along with portraits of industry notables and anonymous workers. The culminating scene of the first mural, which portrays the early history of the garment industry from immigration to sweatshops, features a depiction of the Triangle fire.

Here, the demands of art and history collide, revealing a tension between the mural as a record of garment history and as a work of art with powerfully signifying art historical references. Fiene staged the scene as a combined Renaissance Pietà and Lamentation. The fallen Triangle fire worker, a Christ-like male martyr, slumps in the lap of the Madonna surrogate surrounded by female mourners. True to 1930s labor iconography, the Jesus figure wears the sleeveless laborer's undershirt, while the women appear in the plain long dresses of early-twentieth-century workingwomen. The 1930s choice of Christian iconography might have addressed the substantial audience of witnesses, survivors, and young garment trainees of Italian heritage, but it ignored important historical facts. Female immigrants in their teens and twenties dominated the roster of victims over workingmen. While a Pietà provided a deeply understood and profoundly religious shorthand for suffering, it left the patriarchal notion of the Christian male worker in place. Moreover, the Christian Pietà left out the young Jewish women who constituted a large part of the workforce in the garment industry.

Figure 15.2. Ernest Fiene, the Triangle fire, detail from *Victory of Light Over Darkness,* from *History of the Needlecraft Industries,* 1938–1940. The High School of Fashion Industries, New York. Photo by Ellen Wiley Todd; courtesy of the photographer.

This mural illuminates the contradictions between how history deploys factual reportage and how images either distort that knowledge or probe established accounts to reveal additional layers of understanding. Fiene was trained in Renaissance mural techniques and New Deal pictorial rhetoric. He paired those conventions with the male union leaders' demands for a monumental "work of art" that would favor stories of men's labor struggles and achievements. His mural is filled with revelatory contradictions between art historical precedents and the facts on the ground. As single-artist works, Longman's sculpture and Fiene's mural provide precedents for Harriet Bart's contemporary memorial.

To the Uptown Gallery for Contemporary Art

Two days before the Triangle centennial, I visited the Driscoll Bab-cock Galleries to view feminist artist Harriet Bart's monumental 2010 *Drawn in Smoke*, a grid of 160 smoky shapes and names commemo-rating the Triangle fire.

Bart's work was placed along a lengthy wall in five rows of notebook-size drawings. Each one contained an individualized abstract pattern made with candle smoke manipulated by the artist's hand. Each paper bore a victim's name in scratchy nineteenth-century script. On the wall opposite *Drawn in Smoke* hung an earlier garment-themed work by the artist, *Garment Registry* (1999). This work mirrored the grid form with rows of ironed and folded women's housedresses, inserted into envelopes of translucent paper and mounted on clipboards. Between the two wall grids of packaged dresses and smoke drawings, a simple wooden table under a bare lightbulb contained Bart's 2001 artist book *Garment Register*. It incorporated pages listing women's names and their union dues, accompanied by photos and pieces of vintage fabric.

As an art historian, I initially understood this three-component room as installation art (big spaces filled with large assemblages of material), minimalist structure (grids, rectangular components), and feminist art production (new manipulations of unusual materials that evoked women's lives and labor). But as a participant in the Triangle commemoration, I experienced the visual emphasis of the artist on the working, living, and suffering of Triangle's victims. In my mind, each of the three works—*Drawn in Smoke*, *Garment Registry*, and *Garment Register*—contributed to an ensemble that explored the conditions of garment labor in the context of the Triangle fire. Placed together in the gallery, they gave tangible form to the women's working lives, to the products of their labor, and to their deaths. With its roster of names and dues in a book, *Garment Register* lent historical identity and agency to anonymous workers. In *Garment Registry*, the rows of packaged housedresses were both labor's products and stand-ins for the clothed and living garment workers. Their "bodies" were held on clipboards signifying the Progressive Era factory foreman in charge of a

Figure 15.3. Harriet Bart, *Drawn in Smoke* (detail), 2010. Installation view at Weisman Art Museum, Minneapolis, 2020. Soot and ink on paper, each drawing 11 7/8 by 8 inches. Photo by Rik Sferra; courtesy of the photographer.

bureaucratic process for managing rows of workers bent over machines. This ominous industrial rationalization and the tragic results of its dehumanizing processes became clear as these "workers/dresses" faced the smoky forms of Triangle's lost victims on the opposite wall. There, Bart's *Drawn in Smoke* read as a palpable trace of the fire itself, and of the corporeal residue of burned bodies.

Bart's gridlike structure with names invoked Triangle participants' long-standing quest to chronicle the identity of all the victims. The historical *inaccuracy* of her list of names resulted from her use of an early roster of 160–162 names compiled before 1999 at Cornell University's Kheel Center. At no time between the fire and its one hundredth anniversary, when the revised roster appeared, did anyone possess an authoritative list of all 146 victims. Rather than faulting its inaccuracy, I prefer to understand her piece in both historical and feminist terms. The earlier set of names represents the multiple decades during which these women were marginalized or forgotten.

Bart's work offers a legitimate political critique of labor's conditions and its consequences. But the viewing of this horrific beauty occurred in an exclusive commercial gallery, historically a space of class and social exclusion. Moreover, individual victim sheets were for sale as reproduced prints, allowing viewers to symbolically "own" a victim. I wonder if this paradox between the aesthetic and commercial/political can be mediated. Perhaps their purchase and relocation in private domestic spaces participates in a commercial system that was part of their exploitation. But we may also honor them with beautiful traces that offer a meditative reprieve from sorrow and suffering. Perhaps the contemplative gallery space muted the work's political voice. My hope is that conversation, education, and the work of historical remembering and critique can offset some of the uncomfortable paradoxes of this component of participation.

A Return to the Streets

Public and performative modes have dominated contemporary memorial practices. They have strong ties to a broader mode of activism for social justice. They also speak about the breakdown of boundaries in the post-1970s art world to include performance and the incorporation of any imaginable material. The *Chalk* and *Shirtwaist Kites* projects belong to the typology of public memorializing that began at the time of the fire with the two dramatic funeral processions.

Once I learned about Ruth Sergel's *Chalk*, I knew I wanted to participate. In 2009, I introduced myself to Ruth, via email, as an art historian who worked on the fire, and as someone who might find the bending and chalking a bit awkward, owing to arthritis. Crucially, I *really* wanted to chalk with others rather than alone. Ruth's generous welcome led me to some wonderful chalkers. I joined the Remember the Triangle Fire Coalition and participated in the first committee to establish a permanent memorial. These activities culminated in the week of events at the one hundredth anniversary of the fire: speaking engagements, attending lectures and performances, visiting exhibits, and, best of all, walking with everyone in the frigid cold of the anniversary procession. I was accustomed to isolated scholarly work. Now, involved in participatory, experiential scholarship, I began to reflect on the dual modes of commemorative Triangle fire art.

In March 2010, after the Triangle fire commemoration, I met up with Lisa Merrill, Mary Anne Trasciatti, her daughter Bridget Caslowitz, and others, and we set off to chalk. Ruth had given us several names. After watching an experienced chalker, I was ready to try my hand at remembering Lizzie Adler in blue chalk. A Romanian-born worker, in this country for just three and a half months, she was twenty-four when she died. I took a deep breath and began. I pictured her as my long-lost companion, whom I now wanted to honor. The physical labor was stalled by the effort to make color appear on the pebbly pavement. In the end, my result failed to meet my aesthetic aspirations (bold, colorful, and thick letters, perhaps a flourish of period ornament). But I wrote Lizzie's name in big capital letters, then filled the slab to give her the entire pavement in front of her home. Even if thin and quavering, my penmanship evoked Lizzie's presence. As I sat for a photo next to Lizzie's sidewalk panel, I imagined her perched on her stoop, visiting with family or new friends after her recent arrival in America.

My suburban childhood sidewalks were far removed from the tough pavements of Manhattan's Lower East Side. Chalk, a tool and symbol for education, gave me a privileged access to knowledge acquisition and dissemination, a schooling denied to many immigrant women, or cut short by labor demands invading their lives. These young immigrant garment workers found pleasure and agency on urban streets, whether socializing, going to movies or dance halls, or purchasing small ornaments and trimmings to fashion their own homemade waists. Whenever I chalk, I remember the totality of their tragic *and* pleasurable lives. Chalking outdoors feels like gratifying subversion, defacing a sidewalk, taking a small risk in service of the larger good.

Although *Chalk*, which Ruth has described as "active collective memory," is ephemeral work that vanishes within days, sometimes hours from when it has been completed, I see a connection between the

Figure 15.4. Ellen Wiley Todd chalks Lizzie Adler. Triangle Fire commemoration, New York, NY, 2010. Photo by Mary Anne Trasciatti; courtesy of the photographer.

memory work that it enacts and a longtime women's studies clothesline project staged on many U.S. college and university campuses, including George Mason, where I used to teach. To protest acts of sexual abuse, affected students painted T-shirts naming their experiences, to remember the acts perpetuated on themselves or friends. The individual works are suspended on clotheslines in groves of trees around campus. Over time, they have multiplied as contemporary students leave them in the historical archive and new ones are made. As their numbers grow, they become more forceful in their collective statement, empowering others to speak out, and inspiring more progressive action against sexual abuse.

On the cold, bright one hundredth anniversary of the fire, the shirtwaist kites continued the work of remembering and witnessing. They animated the procession from Union Square to the site of the fire. Positioned on poles of differing heights, they could be seen from everywhere. They floated, as one participant suggested, like angels above the crowd, guarding us and recalling for us the lives and tragic deaths of the workers—or danced in the streets, amid other banners from fellow unions. The brightly colored waists, adorned with lace, buttons, and fancy trim, grew increasingly more vibrant as the day progressed. My own chalking ghost, Lizzie Adler, received a bright pink waist, trimmed in black lace. It raised her up from where I had chalked her name to a march on the streets.

Shirtwaist kites fluttered above the crowd of marchers. I asked to carry one of the few that had not been distributed. Thus, Jennie Stellino accompanied me on my centennial journey. Jennie, who came from Italy, had lived in the United States for four years. As one of the youngest employees of Triangle, she undoubtedly snipped threads, tied knots, and sewed buttons—and for her efforts, died at only sixteen. By the end of the commemoration, Jennie's kite merged with those of fellow participants. The shirtwaist kites felt celebratory yet mournful, fragile yet powerful, joyous yet twisting with the anger of a century's injustices, replete with historical memory and contemporary practices and meaning. The crowd that surrounded the kites on the chilly March day recalled another day, one hundred years earlier, when New Yorkers marched

Figure 15.5. Shirtwaist kites at the end of the 2011 Triangle Fire Centennial Commemoration. Photo by Ellen Wiley Todd; courtesy of the photographer.

in solidarity with and in memory of the dead workers. The image of the kites placed together respectfully on the street opposite the fire's site at the end of the ceremonies engendered a wrenchingly poignant recollection of the bodies lying in the street or at the makeshift morgue.

Like Lizzie Adler, her onetime coworker and my chalking muse, Jennie brought back memories of my teenage self and the fabric and thread of shirtwaists. When I was ten, my mother taught me to embroider. Patient by temperament, I delighted in the deliberate repetitive work of cross-stitches and daisy chains. In eighth grade, my sewing teacher despaired at the machine edging on my required gingham apron, plucked it out with her long nails, and sent me home to repair it. My distraught mother, who had recently completed a fine-tailoring course, took me in hand. While my teenage girlfriends boasted about finishing a skirt in two hours, my own carefully crafted wardrobe took long weekend and summer hours. Skirts were fully lined, zippers hand-sewn, seams turned over and finished with topstitching, and professionally pressed over a tailor's ham. I made blouses, tennis dresses, summer shifts, and wool jumpers. In addition to exacting quality control, my mother helped me choose appropriate patterns, fit them, and promised good-quality fabrics if I would make, rather than purchase, much of my wardrobe. In 1962, after weeks of careful work, I completed a beautiful shirtwaist dress. Made of silky French cotton foulard in forest green with a repeated cherry red figure, it reminded me of patterns in my deceased father's ties. With a shoulder yoke, set-in sleeves, a Peter Pan collar, buttonholes down the entire front, and a full gathered skirt, it was my most complicated and beautiful garment. I wore it all through high school.

I made few garments after high school, turning my attention increasingly to schoolwork. But sewing gave me a deep appreciation for fashion's craft, for all other aesthetic processes, and especially for fashion history. With no knowledge of Triangle, I discovered turn-of-the-century shirtwaists early on and looked for their contemporary imitations. Especially pleasing to my young eye were the so-called fancy waists with elegant adornment on the front. My formal photographic portrait at college graduation shows me in a fine cotton waist with horizontal tucks and a tiny embroidered blue-and-green ribbon. This preference survives in the turtlenecks or moderately embellished dress-up tunics of my mature life. Undoubtedly, this teenage training contributed to the visual and tactile sensibilities of my eventual profession.

But only Triangle and its histories finally afforded me the wider picture, the far more urgent and darker side of production and consumerist visual pleasures. Triangle taught me the histories of labor and garment making, work processes, and their economic and human costs. Triangle showed me the workplaces, their health hazards, their faulty construction, their prisonlike constraints. Triangle brought me to a far greater sense of community endeavor. Finally, Triangle helped me understand how new visual possibilities enable our political endeavors. *Chalk* and *Shirtwaist Kites* work together, complementary memory projects, each renewable. On the ground, we press chalk, recall the names, and bring them home. In the air, we hold the kites aloft, letting them float in a moment of freedom to imagine our own tentative hope and renewal.

CHAPTER 16

And They Returned Home
Italy Remembers the Triangle Fire Women

▼

Ester Rizzo Licata
Translated by Edvige Giunta

I wanted to bring them back home. They were there, on a long list: 146 names, the names of the victims of the Triangle Shirtwaist Factory fire. I recognized Italian last names, especially Sicilian. When a group of us, all women, read that long list on the stage of a theater in my hometown of Licata, Sicily, on March 8, 2012, a respectful silence enveloped the audience. It was then that I felt a deep desire to learn about and understand the lives of these fellow Italian women before they went to America, to give them the dignity of being remembered in the places where they were born and where they lived a chapter of their lives.

Before March 8, 2012, I had never heard the name Clotilde Terranova. Then some women with whom I shared an interest in the Triangle fire told me about her and that she had been born in our town. I felt the urge to learn more about this fellow Licatese. And so I began my research. With Cettina Callea, then president of the local chapter of FIDAPA (International Federation of Women in the Arts, Professions, and Business), I went to the Office of Vital Records. There, day after day, we looked through faded records corroded by time. There we found Clotilde's birth certificate. We patiently reconstructed her family tree and even identified her grandparents. In Licata, we looked for other traces of her life but found none. To anchor Clotilde more firmly to the history of our town, we decided, through FIDAPA, to place a commemorative plaque on the facade of the library: "To Clotilde Terranova, fellow citizen who died in 1911 at age 23 in the fire of the Triangle Shirtwaist Factory in New York. In memory of a life that was cut short, historic memory of a heroine who crossed the ocean in search of a better life; to pass on to the next generation the memory of a tragedy that gave rise to women's labor unions."

It was March 25, 2013. As I looked at Clotilde's name up there and read the words that would become so familiar to me, I could have felt satisfied. My work was completed. But something gnawed at me. The same force that had pushed me to look for traces of Clotilde, to work to get her remembered through that plaque, now drove me to continue my search. There were other Triangle women.

My interest in women's history, especially the stories of women that have been erased from official narratives, began in 1982, when I studied at the Istituto Superiore di Giornalismo (Journalism Institute) in Palermo. Not yet twenty years old, I researched women's history. I knew then that this research would become my life's work. After I completed my studies, for almost three decades I worked as a financial consultant, though I still dedicated my free time to researching women. I felt compelled to remedy the injustice and discrimination suffered by women whose historic contributions had gone unacknowledged. I wrote newspaper and encyclopedia articles. In 2013, I started to teach a course on women's literature at CUSCA (Centro Universitario Socio Culturale Adulti) in Licata, where I still teach today.

My research on Triangle history, which started with Clotilde Terranova, extended to the other Italian victims. At first, I had no plans of writing a book. But, in September 2012, when I met with the publisher Ottavio Navarra to discuss a different project, I mentioned my research. He suggested I write a book. Thus, *Camicette Bianche* was born.

For two years, I cross-referenced thousands of dates from the disembarkation lists at Ellis Island with birth records from dozens of towns in Sicily, Puglia, and Basilicata (Lucania). Many people became my collaborators. We were thrilled whenever we found the birth date and established the birthplace of a Triangle woman. During these two years, I traveled thousands of miles to Sicilian towns near the sea and in the mountains. I had the feeling of being accompanied, encouraged, sustained. By now, the women of Triangle were sisters. I felt deep affection and tenderness for each of them. I shared a piece of my life with them.

Once, I woke up in the middle of the night thinking about the name of Gaetana Midolo. I had searched for her in vain on the disembarkation lists at Ellis Island. Might her name have been erroneously recorded as a man's name? I got up and reviewed all my research. Finally, I found her: recorded as Gaetaneo Midolo from Noto. I waited for dawn with trepidation. I had the names of her parents from her American death certificate but needed to contact the town of Noto to confirm that she was born there. When the response came, it confirmed that Gaetana Midolo was indeed born in Noto. I could go and verify this—and finally hold her birth certificate in my hands.

In Sperlinga, after finding the birth record of Giuseppina Buscemi Carlisi, I asked to consult the records to search for Grazia Maria Gullo Floresta. I suspected she, too, was born in Sperlinga. Indeed, she was. She had lived on the same street where Giuseppina was born. There were many similarly inspired moments during my journey. These moments defied logic and rationality. I was guided by intuition. In the end, I was able to identify the birthplace of thirty-two of the thirty-eight Italian women who worked at Triangle.

Camicette Bianche was published in 2014. That same year, my publisher and the organization Toponomastica Femminile circulated a nationwide petition to name streets, gardens, and squares after Triangle fire victims in their birthplaces:

> The fire burned even the memory of their invisible lives. Their lives and their tragic deaths recall social injustices that exist even today. To record their names and their stories, told for the first time in Italy by Ester Rizzo in her book *Camicette Bianche*, has been first of all an act of gratitude and justice. In fact, it is thanks to their sacrifice that workers' rights and workplace safety regulations have been achieved. Thus, we appeal to the town halls so that they do not forget the story of these women. We do so to restore not simply a vague and generic memory,

but a tangible memory that is personal as well as symbolic, through the naming of a square, a street, a garden, or another public space that may give back to these women the place they deserve in the history of our country.

Our call was received with enthusiasm by local governments, schools, and community organizations. Today, the names of the thirty-two Triangle workers for whom I found a birthplace are mapped onto the landscape of Sicily and the other regions where they were born. In Marineo, following the ceremony that named a street in memory of Vincenza Benanti, a television reporter concluded the coverage of the event with the words "Welcome home, Vincenzina." There was something profoundly moving about the tender diminutive used by the reporter to mark this bittersweet homecoming. This posthumous recognition stands as symbolic compensation from the stingy land that once had forced these girls and women to emigrate, a land shining with sunlight but also marred by poverty and struggle.

And so they returned home: twenty-four Sicilians (Rosa Bona Bassino, Vincenza Bellotto, Vincenza Benanti, Giuseppina Cammarata, Giuseppina Buscemi Carlisi, Rosina Cirrito, Maria Anna Colletti, Giuseppa Del Castillo, Grazia Maria Gullo Floresta, Caterina Bona Giannattasio, Rosa Grasso, Elisabetta Maiale, Francesca Maiale, Caterina Canino Maltese, Rosaria Maltese, Lucia Maltese, Gaetana Midolo, Michela Nicolosi, Provvidenza Bucalo Panno, Vincenza Pinello, Concetta Prestifilippo, Maria Santa Salemi, Clotilde Terranova, Caterina Uzzo); five Pugliese (Anna Vita Pasqualicchio Ardito, Marianna Santa L'Abbate, Antonia Pasqualicchio, Maria Serafina Saracino, Teresa Saracino), two sisters from Basilicata (Maria Giuseppa Tortorelli Lauletti and Isabella Tortorelli); and a woman from Campania (Maria Michela Marciano Cordiano). These are the Triangle workers for whom I have established a birthplace with certainty. For the others—Laura Brunetti, Francesca Caputo, Albina Caruso, Anna Balsano Ciminello, Maria Francesca Massaro Miraglia, Jennie Stellino—my research has not been fruitful yet.

Figure 16.1. Ester Rizzo with the mayor and vice mayor of Potenza, Basilicata, in front of the house of the Tortorelli sisters, Armento, Italy, 2019. Photo by Giovanni Salvio; courtesy of the photographer.

I wanted my contribution to the history of the Triangle workers from Italy to serve as a bridge between their Italian life stories and their American life stories. Local community organizations have contributed to building this bridge. Many of the people who have helped me in this work live across the ocean. In 2015, a year after *Camicette Bianche* was published, Edvige Giunta and Mary Anne Trasciatti invited me to talk about my book in New York at the Italian Cultural Institute and the John D. Calandra Italian American Institute. During the trip, I met many people who have devoted their energy to the legacy of the Triangle fire, like LuLu LoLo, whose beautiful performance, *Soliloquy for a Seamstress*, moved me deeply. Mary Anne Trasciatti also invited me to sit onstage as a guest at the 104th official commemoration of the fire on March 25, 2015. As I stood there, in front of the Brown Building, I felt overcome by joy and sorrow.

I believed I had concluded my physical and emotional pilgrimage to places and official commemorations in New York City. I had one day left before my departure. That last evening, I had dinner with friends of my interpreter, Silvana Daventeri. There was a church in front of the restaurant. I read its name: Our Lady of Pompeii. I felt a shiver down my spine: This was the church where the funerals of several Italian Triangle workers had been held, the church where during those awful days the families in mourning had gone to receive comfort from their community. Although it was late—about 9:00 P.M.—I approached the large wooden door, pushed it open, and went inside. I was struck by the light of hundreds of votive candles. There was no one there. I stood still, silent. I looked at the central nave, where the bodies had been laid out over a century earlier. Suddenly, I understood that my journey had come to its end. From the cradle to the coffin, as I had written a year earlier in my book. I had come full circle.

Over the years, I have crossed paths with people who have traveled from New York to Italy, like writer Annie Rachele Lanzillotto, who witnessed by my side the dedication of the plaque to the twenty-four Sicilian Triangle workers in Avola. Annie and I traveled through Sicily to other towns, to other commemorative spaces. Together, we stood in front of the plaque for Clotilde Terranova in Licata and the one in Villafranca Sicula for Gaspare Mortillaro, the elevator operator who, with Giuseppe Zito, saved lives. I crossed paths with scholars, such as Andi Sosin and Joel Sosinsky, and descendants of Triangle workers, such as the late Anna Marie Landolfo, with whom I attended the dedication of a plaque to Maria Grasso and Concetta Prestifillipo in Cerani. These encounters served as a conduit for messages from descendants of Triangle workers. When she learned of the dedication of a plaque to her great-aunt in Palermo, the great-niece of Catarina Uzzo wrote me a letter: "My name is Linda Terrasi Falabella. . . . I think it's wonderful that you have not forgotten the women who lost their lives in the Triangle fire. . . . I'm truly honored that you want to remember my great-aunt. . . . God bless you." This letter is yet another thread that connects all of us across time and space.

The history and the names of the Triangle fire women have returned to Sicily, Puglia, Campania, and Basilicata, the regions where they were born and where there are now commemorative sites. And they have traveled throughout Italy. After I presented *Camicette Bianche* at the University of Rome Tor Vergata, the university devoted a day to the Triangle fire, as did the Department of Sociology of Roma Tre University. Similar commemorative events have taken place at the Ca' Foscari University of Venice. I have visited elementary, middle, and high schools all over Italy and recounted the Triangle story. The national union UILTEC (Italian Union of Textile, Energy, and Chemical Workers) chose March 5, 2016, as a day of national commemoration; other unions, CISL (Italian Confederation of Workers' Trade Unions), UIL (Italian Labor Union), and CGIL (Italian General Confederation of Labor) of Modena, together with UDI (Italian Women's Union), organized a large demonstration to remember the Triangle fire. Even the national press and television have paid attention. *Shirtwaists*, a musical directed by Marco Savatteri and performed on Italian stages, and the song "No Name," composed and sung by Francesca Incudine, illustrate how the story is inspiring Italian artists. The Triangle story has crossed the American and Italian borders and has touched the European cultural sensibility in places like the Italian Cultural Institute of Strasbourg and Saarland University, in Saarbrücken, Germany, where I spoke on behalf of the Italian women of Triangle.

On March 8, 2018, Toponomastica Femminile requested and obtained the dedication of a path in the public garden in Licata to Clotilde Terranova. The commemorative plaque has been placed on the path surrounded by trees, right near viale 8 Marzo. When I pass by, I feel a clear sense of having participated in and witnessed an act of posthumous justice.

The work continues.

CHAPTER 17

The Fabric of Memory

▼

Richard Joon Yoo

The Fashion Institute of Technology, New York City, March 16, 2019. Nests of needles and swarms of thread are strewn across four long rows of tables crammed with hands sewing. Fabric scraps are cut, then trimmed and fitted. The room fills and rustles with energy—the energy of people who have come to sew a three-hundred-foot-long ribbon. They sew in pieces of fabric from their lives or from scraps we give them if they show up empty-handed. Some come alone to sew a single fragment of fabric into the ribbon, then leave. Others stay to help others sew. People trim pieces of fabric to fit the spot they have chosen on the ribbon and take them to another table. There, each piece of fabric is photographed and written stories are archived. A rhythm of this work settles as the day progresses. I barely know how to use a needle and thread.

The tables, each sixty-six feet long, recede into what eerily resembles the horizon of a sweatshop floor. Along its length, the Collective Ribbon thickens with fragments of cloth and artifacts that people have treasured for years or made anew and that will now have a life in the fabric of memory of the Triangle Fire Memorial. I pace the long corridors between the rows of tables, slowly dodging the traffic of chairs as participants push needles and thread, in and out, through the thick fabric of the ribbon. Several volunteers find another patch that needs to be sewn into the fabric. Others stand or walk slowly, like I do, among the crowd. Perhaps they, too, are reflecting on how this work, having begun with the girls of the Triangle Factory, after over a hundred years of grieving and consequences from their deaths, will become a memorial for those very girls.

Here and there, I touch the fragments that people have sewn into the ribbon—worn cuffs from jean jackets and entire shirtwaists sewn as if billowing in the wind. The ribbon stretches along the length of each table as it takes on embroidered cloth faded and folded through decades in drawers: union patches, nearly blank squares of fabric—perhaps cut from a larger story—scraps from children's clothes, blue tablecloths from a grandparent's table in Italy, scarves, mundane prints from precious cloths, pieces embroidered with names, and pieces boldly embroidered with "146." The Collective Ribbon created from this patchwork will be etched into metal. It will become the texture on the stainless-steel panels of the Triangle Fire Memorial.

Almost six years earlier, in 2013, about a month before my first son, Lev, was born, Uri Wegman and I spent long evenings and weekends in my home working on a design competition hosted by the Remember the Triangle Fire Coalition. It was a design to build the permanent memorial for the Triangle fire. Uri and I both lived in Sunnyside, a short hop on the number 7 train from the site of the fire. Both of us had studied and worked and taught in New York City for years. It had deepened our knowledge of the city's history and architecture. We were well practiced at collaboration from years of working on art and architecture together. It was Uri who brought me into the studio of Sarah Oppenheimer; together, we had helped her design and build elaborate and complex aluminum, steel, and glass installations. An effortless natural dialogue and flow had grown between us as we went back and forth on design schemes for the memorial with joy and rigor. In cafés, we filled napkins with drawings and diagrams. We sketched, we spoke, we crossed out. We were guided by a desire to maximize the emotional experience of remembering the fire by utilizing a minimum of material. We refined what we wanted the memorial to do and tested multiple design itera-tions in search of the most direct and compelling realization.

It was spring. The plum tree outside the studio window had blos-somed with thick bunches of pink flowers: It was our backdrop when we submitted entry 30613D—our only marker on the anonymous in-ternational design competition. There were almost two hundred inter-national entries. What were the chances that two boys from Queens would win the competition?

My six-month-old, Lev, was finally asleep that December night when I received a brief email that read "We have announced a winner." I called Uri. We were overjoyed. We had no idea what the journey toward building the Triangle Fire Memorial would entail.

There would be countless community meetings, presentations to the Landmarks Preservation Commission, neighborhood board meet-ings, meetings with institutions and government agencies—New York University, the Landmarks Preservation Commission, the Department of Transportation, the Department of Buildings, the Public Design Commission. Over time, the design became more precise when some-thing pushed against it, as did the will and determination of the Re-member the Triangle Fire Coalition. Those who lived across from where the fire occurred thought the memorial would light up like a disco ball. They had misread an image, but we took their concern seriously and found we could reduce the sun glare by using Stoneglass, a stunning material that, appropriately, comes from Italy. The basic scheme that had won the design competition evolved into a feasible, immensely nu-anced, and more powerful design that would survive the intense forces at play in New York City. The challenges inherent in the process did not surprise us. Such challenges often occur in the realization of me-morials. We were astonished, however, to realize the extent to which the long, deep, worn, and tattered threads of the Triangle fire's history were intertwined in the thick fabric of New York City and its people.

Through this work, we met many people devoted to the memo-rialization of the Triangle fire—historians, activists, artists, writers, labor union members, and descendants of victims and survivors. We heard stories that had been passed down for generations. We talked to descendants who carried with them this distant and still heavy history. These encounters, these stories helped us understand that the memorial should be born from those whom it serves, that it should be a memorial *for* the public *from* the public. What could we do to endow the material with meaning that would reverberate from the past through the present moment? How could we engage the public? During the years it took for the memorial to get traction in the muck of bureaucracy, Uri and I went back and forth discussing these questions. We became increasingly more committed to engaging the public in the building of the Triangle Fire Memorial. Our gathering at FIT on March 16, 2019, to create a Collective Ribbon was born from this commitment. The Remember the Triangle Fire Coalition invited people to become, through their contribution and work, part of the Triangle Fire Memorial. For two days, people gathered at FIT to create a huge ribbon by sewing together smaller individual pieces of fabric donated by participants. The ribbon would be used to cast the main component of the memorial, which would then be mounted on the facade of the Brown Building, where the fire occurred in 1911.

Looking across the Great Hall at FIT on March 16 and 17, 2019, I realized that laying out hundreds of feet of canvas on these tables in four long rows was the very first step in the *fabrication* of the Triangle Fire Memorial. We were breaking ground for the memorial in that very instant when needle and thread penetrated memory and purpose. It was an unusual, though perfectly fitting, ground breaking: rows and rows of hands and thread and fabric and the projection of personal memory on this now very public document—the Collective Ribbon—and soon the Triangle Fire Memorial itself. Chairs pinned bodies to table edges. Elbows and forearms held the fabric in place. Needles made fingertips burn. The sound was different from the factory bustle in 1911. The purpose of our communal work was one the 146 victims could not have imagined. It was a tribute not just to their work in life but also to the activism and change their deaths inspired over one hundred years ago—and continued to inspire, at that very moment, at those tables.

Triangle Fire Memorial as a Catalyst

At the corner of Greene Street and Washington Place, a block east of Washington Square Park, you stand innocent. You take a step toward the darkened reflective panel that, at waist level, wraps along the facade on both sides of the Brown Building. At first, it reflects the building itself, but the reflection heightens as you approach. Circular glass orbs slide off the panel, revealing the beige facade that extends toward the sky, all falling into your field of vision as you look down into the dark mirror. Closer, names reveal themselves, written with bright blue sky, surrounded by the shadow of textured metal. Closer still, your own reflection appears. It is jarring to see yourself there. You are suspended in a pool of black light.

Floating between your reflection and the names is the etching of a text engraved in the black glass, a ghosted text. There, you encounter testimonies from witnesses and survivors. One reads: "... could not hear the cries ..." A few feet farther down the length of the memorial, as you walk the sidewalk from Washington Square Park, you read "... bent down and looked downstairs and I could see the fire come up. In the shop the girls were running around with their hair ..." Still a few steps further: "... the elevator did stop and the door opened at last, my dress was catching fire"; "... they would come down with arms entwined—three and even four together." And then Frances Perkins's words: "The window was too crowded and they would jump and they hit the sidewalk. Every one of them was killed, everybody who jumped was killed."

You stop. You stand on that sidewalk, still. You look into that black mirror, and see yourself, unblinking. Between the story and the names, there is your reflection. You are caught mid-sentence with the names and the changing city sky as backdrop. You blink in the black mirror. You proceed down the sidewalk. The moment expands as you traverse the length of the panel of the memorial. Your grasp of the fire thickens as 146 names pass by overhead. Between the reflective panel and the ribbon with the names, you enter a liminal space. Your reflection is suspended between the story of the fire and the names of those lost

Figure 17.1. The Collective Ribbon as a reflection of the shirtwaist factory.
Top photo by Richard Joon Yoo, March 2019; courtesy of the photographer.
Bottom photo, ca. 1910, photographer unknown; courtesy of the Kheel Center
for Labor-Management Documentation & Archives, Cornell University.

overhead. It places you—in relationship to the fire, its victims, and its consequences—as an intrinsic actor in the memorialization of the Triangle fire.

Turning the corner of the black mirror, and the building itself, you see in the reflection the metal cut with the names gently bending toward the sky. It rushes toward the one-hundred-foot height of the memorial, and back. You look down into the reflection, and realize it now shows the fall of the girls from the factory to your feet. You step back from the building and arch your neck uncomfortably toward that sky. Looking down again into that reflection, you are overcome by vertigo.

You see this ribbon of metal rising to the ninth floor, where most of the 146 worked. It seems as if it's pointing. Viscerally, you feel the distance, the depth to which those remembered had plummeted. In the act of looking downward into the reflection and the story, then upward, toward the trajectory of the ribbon, you retrace the witnessing of the fire—looking up . . . looking down.

This metal, cascading down from the ninth floor, is cast with the relief of a thousand fragments of fabric sewn together by those who gathered to remember and reflect on the fire by making a Collective Ribbon. In the metal, you see etched:

Long embroidered strands. ("This piece of fabric is from a tablecloth and napkin set my mom hand-embroidered for me.")

Names crocheted in circles. ("This fabric was chosen because it is symbolic of the wedding dress she would have worn the week she died.")

A crosshatch patterned print. ("I chose this fabric because of the grid pattern to represent NYC streets, to hold ourselves accountable.")

A scarf with paint. ("This fabric is a hand painted scarf with velvet on one side. I chose it because I first learned about painting on fabric at NYU. Our studios at that time were on the very floor where the Triangle Fire took place.")

These memories are no longer solitary.

The fabrication of the memorial was born from the labor of the hands of more than four hundred participants and over one hundred volunteers. Over a hundred years after the fire, we gathered to reveal our personal relationship to Triangle and recognize all it had done for us. We build the memorial today for all that it continues to do for us today.

The act of remembering reframes memory, reconstructing it with each recollection. Similarly, our relationship with a vessel of memory held in the hand, or a vessel of memory built tall on the schist of Manhattan, changes each time we encounter it. The Triangle Fire Memorial is designed to hinge on this fulcrum, pivoting between present and past—and tilting into the future. In remembering the Triangle fire, we reframe our relationship to that which the fire brought to the forefront over a hundred years ago. We also reframe our relationship to our own present. And yet as a thing in the world, the memorial is barely there. Its material is light, absence, space, memory. It works as a catalyst. The Triangle Fire Memorial was designed in keeping with a personal ethic of materiality and memory. Its presence on the urban landscape is but a sliver of sky—thin cuts into the chunks that make Manhattan. But what it *does* is potent. In remembering, we reframe ourselves. With our passage to and across the Triangle Fire Memorial, the memorial reflects who we are now and changes who we may become. The Triangle Fire Memorial *is* what it *does*. It changes us. It changes what we do, how we work. It changes how we remember. It takes the deeply personal and private and thrusts it into public collective remembering. It manifests meaning from our current circumstance. It reminds us that we can, at times, make change happen, that we can nourish this change. This memorial does not remember people who died going to war; it remembers people who died going to work. It pays respect to immigrants looking to make a better life—the simple American promise that was betrayed. In this way, I think of it as a memorial for peace.

Remembering Is Too Often Done Alone

My parents immigrated to the United States from Korea. My father came alone, with twenty dollars in his pocket, and slept on a couch in the waiting room of the hospital where he was to begin his first residency. My mother, too, came alone, on a scholarship. It was the sixties— my brave young parents. At first, they each sought an American future for themselves, alone. Once they met and married, they tried to become American together. We lived in the suburbs. We had a camper van and a

Figure 17.2. Richard Joon Yoo, Uri Wegman, and Peter Homestead (the Triangle Fire Memorial's project manager) with the large-scale model of "Ribbon," cut from the same canvas used in the Collective Ribbon itself, October 2019. Photo by Richard Joon Yoo; courtesy of the photographer.

ranch house with a barbecue grill in the backyard. Bicycles were strewn across pungent freshly mowed lawns. At nightfall, we played games of kick the can with the neighbors. My parents gave me a childhood from a Norman Rockwell painting.

They were Korean. They spoke their native tongue only between themselves, a secret layer of our family conversation from which I was excluded. It was difficult to get them to talk to me of their past. When pressed, they would describe scenes of war. My mother remembered being carried on her father's shoulders when a bridge they were about to cross was bombed before their eyes. My father would speak of his time as a young medic in the Korean army. Whenever I got hurt playing, his first question was, "Is everything intact?" I understood that his early adulthood must have been littered with lost limbs.

My parents sought to leave their history.

But it is not possible to leave your history. As my parents grew older, their dressers overflowed with remnants from the past, lives of which I knew nothing: brothers and sisters and cousins and their children thousands of miles away, cascading through the twentieth century; parents and grandparents and uncles and aunts shrouded in mystery; history lost across borders. I would feel the texture of a tapestry that was kept neatly folded in the back of their lowest drawer, or peer into a black-and-white photograph of children in school uniforms, their poses rigid as they waited through long exposures, and I would bewilder at the opacity of these memories. It was like looking into a mirror, the reflection of myself after suffering amnesia. But in place of the mirror was this photo or scrap of paper, or the scarf with an orange-and-blue flower-blossom print. I felt the texture at the ends of my fingertips—is this my history?

It is not. I do not possess this memory. The memory unleashed through the touch of a one-hundred-year-old fabric is not mine; it is my mother's. Looking at this photograph, in which I meet the gaze of a child I never met but somehow am part of, is like locking eyes with any child on the street for a single long, still breath, a sharp inward gasp. We share the street and the sky in that moment—and then we are gone.

When my father peers into that photograph, does he imagine who was standing behind the camera?

I grew up surrounded by a world of things and places and things of places, all containing a silent tempest of memory. These photos and this creased, thinned-out scarf were tucked away for decades, with many other such things that will not speak. Displayed on the mantel was a strange set of wooden totems arranged on a narrow base, colorfully painted and carved from wood. When I was six years old, I decided the two tallest totems were my parents. The next two were my twin sisters. And one was me. But there was one extra totem. Who could this one be? Is this us? This bronze bell and hammer with deep metal lips and crevices at the corners, purchased on a serpentine bridge over a waterfall in Korea, is now coated by a black patina of time. What has the ringing of this bell brought on? I hit it with the hammer and listen intently as the ring rolls down to silence. There's something timeless about the ring and decay of a bell.

My relationship to my history is through the witnessing of those who are remembering—my mother, my father. The poignancy of their recollections was to me more real than what they held in their hands as they remembered. And so, my connection to the Triangle fire is through a desire to focus on memory as a process, an action, a catalyst that can change us. We project meaning onto our personal world of objects and the shared world of the built environment. As a young adult, I made sculptures that reduced the emphasis on the object as the "artwork" and focused instead on what the object would do—what it would catalyze. What is a sculpture of a smell, and where can I find it? Where does a lost memory come from? Was it given to me? What makes it mine? What is learning through absence? How do you manifest meaning from disparate events? These questions point to my most heightened and beloved states of mind.

What It Does: Empowerment of Memory

"I had no idea I could do something."

Every cut of thread is embedded with meaning belonging to someone. A fragment from a great-aunt who perished in the fire evokes her wedding dress—she was to marry the week she died. A pillowcase, coarse thread and slightly gray, thinned through time, from a woman's great-grandmother who was a garment worker and witnessed the smoke of the fire bend around her block. Her great-niece wrote, "I imagine here on this pillow is where she rested her head for sleep the morning before, and the night after she witnessed the Triangle fire . . . wondering what was in store for her the next day she was to go to work."

There were those who showed up at the Collective Ribbon event that weekend because they had seen a flyer while buying a ream of fabric. They wanted to see what it was all about. At the event, some approached me to talk about the fire, the memorial, the ribbon.

"I teach American history, but that's all I do."

"My grandparents were Eastern European immigrants and worked in a garment factory, but I didn't know them."

"I am the first woman in my family to get a college degree and a full-time job."

When invited to participate, to sew something into the Collective Ribbon for the Triangle Fire Memorial—*anything*—many would confess, "I had no idea I could do something."

One visitor, who had just learned about the Triangle fire there, cut a patch from his shirt to sew into the Collective Ribbon. Someone contributed the sweater they had knit for their dog. I believe there are three pairs of panties. There is a unicorn, glitter and all, in ribbon D-1, from a five-year-old in my son's classroom at PS 150. What value can I place on each of these things? How can I measure the significance of each fragment to the woman who has her childhood shirt pressed into the metal of the Triangle Fire Memorial?

I tell my children that they have consequence—they *can* have an effect. Nothing is more frustrating than the sense that we have no choice in how our world may become. Over one hundred years of anonymity for the site of the Triangle fire has frustrated many who feel its impact on the world has been quelled. In fact, the effect of the Triangle fire is amplified today. With the Triangle Fire Memorial in place in Manhattan, its presence is bold and wide open to the world. Like you, I can visit with my two sons, Lev and Jonah, point to it, and say, "This is ours. This is yours. The memorial for the Triangle fire belongs to all of us."

"I had no idea I could do something."

Me, neither.

Here is your needle and thread.

Epilogue
Listening to Kalpona

▼

Kalpona Akter

Interviewed by Edvige Giunta, and Mary Anne Trasciatti

I t's still dark when the alarm clock goes off in Teaneck, New Jersey, and in Long Beach, Long Island. It's February 2019. In our still sleeping homes, we move quietly, though we are excited about the upcoming meeting, a conversation via Skype with Kalpona Akter. The idea of including her in *Talking to the Girls* came early in the project, when we were brainstorming our list of ideal contributors. From the beginning, we thought of *Talking to the Girls* as an act of direct and vicarious memory, of witness across time, of acknowledging that trauma does not end in the bodies of the 146 workers who lost their lives that March day of 1911. It spreads—across families, generations, communities, nations. It must be spoken and shared. It must be righted. If this book was to speak of the Triangle fire in a contemporary and transnational context, we had to be in conversation with the woman who has become known worldwide for her courageous advocacy of garment workers, the founder and executive director of the Bangladesh Centre for Worker Solidarity (BCWS), which empowers garment workers, especially women, to fight for safer working conditions, better wages, and the right to form unions. But Kalpona Akter has become more than that. Her name symbolizes the courage of one woman to stand up and use her voice.

We know of Kalpona's strong feelings about Triangle. Although she was born sixty-five years after and thousands of miles away from where the Triangle fire happened, a deep bond connects her to the Triangle girls. In 2011, she was invited by SweatFree Communities and the International Labor Rights Forum to participate in the Triangle Fire Centennial Commemoration in New York City. Her presence signaled the commitment of the Triangle fire community to solidarity with garment workers around the globe. At the time, Bangladesh was already the second-largest apparel manufacturer in the world, with more than 4,500 factories employing 3.5 million people, most of them women.

It is not only the connection between the history of the garment industry yesterday and today, however, that leads us to Kalpona. Deadly sites, like Tazreen and Rana Plaza, have become synonymous with a garment industry that is as indifferent to the safety of its workers as its U.S. predecessors were in the age of the Triangle Factory: crowded factory floors cluttered with scraps of fabric, locked exits, poorly paid workers—mostly young women from rural areas—inadequate fire safety measures, lack of water sources, crowding at the doors, panic, bodies burned beyond recognition. The similarities between the Tazreen Fashions factory fire that occurred on November 24, 2012, in Nischintapur, a neighborhood in Ashulia, a district on the outskirts of Dhaka, Bangladesh, and the fire that killed 146 workers in a ten-floor factory building 101 years earlier in New York City are eerie. Like Blanck and Harris, Tazreen owner Delwar Hossain denied responsibility and was accused of committing additional workplace violations. And like the Triangle fire, the Tazreen fire aroused indignation and prompted demonstrations and labor unions and organizations that demanded better conditions for the workers of Bangladesh, though the outcome did not bring the sweeping changes in legislation that occurred in the United States in the years and decades following the earlier fire. Just five months later, on April 24, 2013, the Rana Plaza building, also in Dhaka, which housed five garment factories, collapsed. Workers had noticed cracks in the building the day before, but authorities ignored their concerns. The collapse killed over 1,100 workers and injured more than 2,500. Whereas Triangle workers felt the force and violence of the U.S. factory system, Bangladeshi workers at Tazreen and Rana Plaza suffered the effects of twenty-first-century global capitalism. These and other labor tragedies have propelled Kalpona's courageous activism.

We get our three-way Skype to work, but it takes a few tries and the connection is not strong enough for the video, which is disappointing. But soon Kalpona's voice, full, warm, vibrant, fills the rooms from where each of us calls. As the book's editors, we have prepared a list of questions, which have emerged out of personal and shared interest in and passion for the history of Triangle and its still powerful reverberations, as well as our eagerness to hear Kalpona tell us about the journey that has led her from working in the factory as a child to becoming an internationally recognized voice for the rights of garment workers.

The two of us have been emailing back and forth, making sure we are covering everything. We want to try to get it all done in one interview, as we appreciate how generously Kalpona is giving us her time. The time difference between New York and Dhaka is eleven hours, and for her the interview comes at the end of a long day. She sits with a cup of tea in a café filled with afternoon sun, while we sit at our desks in our dimly lit home offices, our typed list of questions in front of us. Soon, though, we forget the questions and are drawn into the stories Kalpona shares, as if we are all sitting in the same room.

Kalpona

I learned about the Triangle Shirtwaist Factory fire about fourteen years ago, around 2004 or 2005, when there were a lot of fires in Bangladesh, and I was researching what the global apparel industry looked like previously. The Triangle Shirtwaist fire popped up on an Internet search. I could not believe that kind of fire had happened in a country like the United States and in a city like New York. I had no idea that there were [clothing] factories [in the United States] in those days, and that working conditions were so poor.

The second time I heard about the fire was in 2007 or 2008, when I traveled to the United States to attend a conference organized by SweatFree Communities. I heard a talk about Triangle at Columbia

University. [After the talk], I went to the Triangle Shirtwaist Factory site. There, I met Joe. He was from New York City. He used to be a factory worker. SweatFree Communities brought us together. We stood on the corner [of Washington and Greene]. That was my first time at the site. It was thrilling. It was sad. I felt this connection between the fire that had happened there and the fires in my country, Bangladesh.

When my father, who was the primary earner, became ill, there was no one who could bring home an income. I had to go to work in the factory. It was not very easy for a twelve-year-old to work in a factory when the previous day I was in school. I had no choice. My ten-year-old brother joined me later. That first experience was a culture shock. I had never seen so many people together. I had never heard people yell at others. The supervisor was not only yelling at workers but slapping them, too. I couldn't believe that adults gave me a pair of scissors to cut fabric from the belt area. I hurt my fingers so badly. My brother and I were not the only children working at the factory. There were many more children. The youngest child worker was seven years old. This experience inspired my activism. It taught me that, as a worker, I shouldn't be suffering abuse—that no child should be treated like that.

Being a child worker deprives you of stories. I'm in my forties now. When I hear children talk—children who have a good childhood—I realize that I really don't have anything to share from my childhood. I don't blame my parents at all. They didn't have any choice. My mom worked, but she didn't earn enough to pay a nanny to take care of her babies. My younger sister was two months old. And the country didn't have any medical facilities where my dad could get proper medication and treatment. They had to send me [to work].

When I first started working, I didn't know anything. I thought the factory owners were such nice people. Kind. They gave me a job so I could feed my brothers and sisters. After a few years of work, one month there was a festival. The factory owners wanted us to work overtime without pay, and we said, "No, we can't do that." Out of fifteen hundred workers, ninety-three called for a strike. I was the only young female worker who joined the strike. When we came back after the three-day festival vacation, we learned that we had been fired. Being fired from that shop floor was a turning point for me.

My coworkers heard that the Solidarity Center Bangladesh [American Center for International Labor Solidarity—ACILS] was helping female workers. So they went there and learned about a lawyer who was helping workers who had been fired. They sued the factory owner. They told me that I should join a class on labor law. What the hell is that? What is labor law? I thought. But I joined the class. It changed my entire life. I call this a second birth for me. There, I learned my workday is supposed to be eight hours. I should not be forced to work overtime. My workload shouldn't be doubled. There is a minimum wage. There are safety issues. Something beautiful I learned is that I have the right to organize and the right to join a union. And I thought, Ooh, let's do that!

And so the next day I started whispering to my coworkers. During lunch break we had a small meeting and I shared with them [what I had learned]. In the coming days, we started organizing on our shop floor to form a union. I was one of the lucky ones who got over 90 percent of membership for our union. But membership is not the end. We submitted our application [for recognition of the union] to the government department. They rejected it, due to bribes, corruption and, of course, the influence of the factory owners.

When I was organizing on my shop floor, I went to my mom one evening with a sad face and told her, "I'm so young. Can I *do* this?" And she said something amazing that has inspired me and will keep inspiring me all through my life. She said, "If there is injustice, someone can always stand up and speak up. If there is someone, then why not you?" For a mom in Bangladesh, in those days, to tell her teenage daughter this—I mean, this was so incredible. When I became a union president on my shop floor, I was barely fifteen and a half, or sixteen. This is when my fight started. I got [fired and] blacklisted. It was a stupid idea for the factory owners to fire me. They shouldn't have done that. I will always keep fighting in one factory or in one industrial area. Now, I'm fighting nationally and globally for workers' rights!

These days [the fight] is growing everywhere. Many people and organizations have supported me: the Solidarity Center, the Worker Rights Consortium, International Labor Rights Forum, SweatFree Communities, USAS (United Students Against Sweatshops), the Canadian unions, the steelworkers, Public Service Alliance of Canada, the Clean Clothes Campaign, the International Labour Organization (ILO) in Geneva. I am also on the Advisory Board of the Remember the Triangle Fire Coalition.

When I was a teenager, I attended a conference to stop child labor, organized by the ILO in Italy. I got a sense that my voice was not just local; it had become international. In 1997, I went to the United States and spoke at the UN. I was barely twenty. My activism went really global starting in 2005, and more and more in 2009 and 2011 and later years. Global action [intensified] after Tazreen and Rana Plaza. It wasn't constant, it wasn't crazy, but it was global. I'm not talking about workers only in Bangladesh; I'm talking about workers in all production countries. Every sector. What they are facing. Retaliation. Inequality wages.

Figure Epilogue.1. This is the photo Kalpona Akter included in the job application submitted to the factory where she started to work as a sewing machine helper when she was twelve years old. Photographer unknown; photo courtesy of Kalpona Akter.

[As part of my global activism] in 2011, I attended the one-hundred-year anniversary of the Triangle Shirtwaist Factory fire.

If you ask who inspired me, [I'd say] factory workers struggling in countries like mine. They all fight a great fight. They all have great stories. Some get the chance to tell them. Some do not. The women inspire me, too, like those who organized before the Triangle Shirtwaist Factory fire, like Clara Lemlich: "I have something to say." She is one of my idols. A hundred years ago, now almost 120 years ago, when you barely had even telephones, fighting for your rights, doing the strike, being on the picket line, even when many people did not support you—that was extraordinary. And, of course, my mom is my idol, too.

Just think about those 146 lives. Dozens of them could have done wonders if they had lived. They could have become activists like Clara Lemlich. They were victims of greed. They were never considered as human, [just] another [piece of] equipment in the factory. From the Triangle Shirtwaist fire to Tazreen Fashions to Rana Plaza, the heroes are the workers who raised their voices, [like the workers] of Rana Plaza who said, "We don't want to go inside this factory because we saw a crack in the building that can collapse anytime." [But] they were forced to be in that factory. They had to keep working because the factory had another shipment.

I have learned that there is a political connection, from the Triangle fire to Tazreen and Rana Plaza. In 120 years of this industry, only one thing has changed—the place. They keep killing workers everywhere. They harass and retaliate against the workers. The industry has never taken any voluntary initiative to make sure that our workers do not die. One hundred twenty years after the Triangle fire, we had to lose over fifteen hundred workers at Tazreen and Rana Plaza to get the Accord on Fire [and] Building Safety [in Bangladesh]. The accord was signed by the companies because shareholders and investors sent a letter to brand retailers that said, "You gotta sign." This is not enough for Bangladesh. We also need [a similar accord] in other producing countries—Pakistan, India, Cambodia, South America, everywhere clothes are produced.

Every time we tried to make brand retailers responsible for all these disasters and bad working conditions, they would say, "No, no, no, we weren't there." We could not provide any evidence. During the Tazreen Fashions fire, workers jumped from a nine-floor building. Like the Triangle workers, they jumped to save their lives. And like the Triangle workers, they jumped to their death. After, we couldn't prove which brands and retailers had outsourced [with Tazreen]. So, finally, this idea came to me. I knew that as soon as the fire stopped, they would be cleaning up the evidence. I took a risk with two of my coworkers. I pretended I was a journalist. I had a camera with me. I went inside and started cutting the logos [and taking pictures of the logos and my face]. I shared these pictures with workers in other parts of the world. This is how you need to expose these brands. Otherwise, they will just clean their hands and say, "I wasn't there." We did the same thing with Rana Plaza. We were helping the workers out of the rubble. At the same time, we were documenting.

Even one hundred years later, people in New York, the unions— they did not forget about those workers who lost their lives in the Triangle fire. [When I attended the Centennial Commemoration in New York,] I was thankful, thankful to all the people, all the organizations, because this is not happening here, in Bangladesh. I'm glad that the Triangle fire commemoration happens every year and that you keep fighting for the Triangle memorial. But this is not happening in every country. The people who died in 1990 are not remembered here. [At the Triangle commemoration,] oh my God, I had goose bumps. I was going through every sequence. I was seeing the fire in front of me. I was seeing every person. I was seeing their souls. They were seeing from somewhere that people still remember them. The respect that people were giving. The respect that children were giving. And [people] from the government also joined. This is how you need to respect those lives. This is how.

I have become part of the U.S. labor movement, as well. I am so honored to be part of all this activism around the Triangle fire and the memorial. I will be glad to be there [the dedication of the Triangle Fire

Figure Epilogue.2. Poster for the Centennial Commemoration of the Triangle fire.
Photo courtesy of the Remember the Triangle Fire Coalition.

Memorial]. I keep the Triangle close to my heart because this is what I'm fighting for—to have a safe working place.

When I worked in the factory, there was a fire, as well. It was a five-story building. The fire started on the fifth floor. The management kept us locked in the production floor, which was originally on the third floor. We were crying, shouting to leave the factory. But we weren't allowed to. They forced us to stay. And after two or three hours of crying and shouting, they let us go. There was one staircase and about eight hundred workers leaving the factory at the same time. The staircase wasn't wide enough, and half was blocked by the merchandise. Many of us got stampeded. We were lucky no one died. Many workers were severely injured and had to be in the hospital for weeks. So I think I can still feel the workers who were in the Triangle fire. They were stuck in the building and couldn't get out. I can feel that. I can feel how desperate they were to save their lives, to see their loved ones, to go to their families. I can see it.

The Triangle fire changed the whole labor movement. You saw that fire happen. You saw that people died. You saw that burned building. That history will teach you that you can make a change. You can still step up and fight back when you lost your village, when you lost your sister. You can [fight to] make sure that you can enjoy the benefits [of a safe workplace and a union]. You can [fight to] make a world where many people can enjoy those benefits, too.

When I cry for the people who died in the Triangle Shirtwaist Factory fire, I also feel angry. This happened 108 years ago, in New York. And people, they stepped up, they fought back. And this is what I need to do. Triangle is a symbol to me: "Who is responsible for this?" The greedy business system, the corporations. And we need to make them change.

Acknowledgments

▼

When we first conceptualized this book, in 2015, we knew we wanted the personal experiences of our contributors to be a key component of the writing. As we started to receive proposals, we defined the scope of the book and came to a clearer and more focused understanding of the role of the personal in the Triangle fire reflective narratives we would include. While historically based, this book should not be read as an authoritative historical narrative of the Triangle fire, for which other texts exist. This work is informed by the authors' subjective experiences and points of view. It draws on historical narratives, archival sources, oral histories, family memories, and personal experiences. It relies on the principles and strategies of creative nonfiction, including, in some cases, imaginative reconstruction, to convey the subjective nature of each author's relationship to Triangle history. We are deeply grateful to our nineteen contributors for their willingness to dig deeply, and at times painfully, into the many ways the history of the fire and its reverberations are embedded in their memories. They worked patiently and tirelessly to write, and rewrite, essays that told their own distinct Triangle stories but also coalesced around an expansive narrative of the meaning of Triangle's legacy. All the essays are published here for the first time.

We are enormously grateful to Lynne Elizabeth, director of New Village Press, for embracing our project with enthusiasm, interest, and passionate commitment. Her trust in the importance of this book has sustained and inspired us. Our deepest appreciation to Abigail Grimminger, editorial and publicity assistant at New Village Press, who, with Lynne, offered precious insights and vital guidance as we revised the manuscript, prepared it for submission, and worked through all the stages of production. We thank Carol Edwards, our copyeditor, for her meticulous work. Three anonymous readers for New Village Press offered encouraging praise and invaluable suggestions that have helped make this a better book. Our agent, Malaga Baldi, believed in this book and was determined to find a good home for it. We are profoundly grateful for her passion and commitment.

The dedication and generosity of family members of Triangle workers have sustained this book and we are honored to count some of them among our contributors. We always thought of *Talking to the Girls* as a book that would embody the spirit of the Triangle community. In that spirit, we acknowledge the many people to whom we have turned for help on matters concerning the history of the fire. Their activism inspired us long before we started this book. By answering our questions, they have helped us again and again. Our thanks to Sherry Kane, whose knowledge of the history of Triangle commemorations was an invaluable resource; to Emma Baeri, for her insights into the history of Triangle fire memory in the Italian feminist movement; to Luisa Del Giudice, for providing guidance on questions related to editing oral histories; to Massimiliano Vintaloro, for inspiring us with his dedication to uncovering and sharing the story of the Italian workers of Triangle. Jennifer Guglielmo's work has inspired us over the years; we are also grateful to her for suggesting potential contributors and being such a great resource for historical questions. Janet Zandy's groundbreaking scholarship in the field of working-class studies, and especially her work on the poetry of the Triangle fire, was a key point of reference in our work long before we decided to do this book. In addition, we would like to thank Fawzia Afzal-Khan, Letizia Airos, Vinny Alvarez, Nancy Azara, Emily Bass, Marcella Bencivenni, Rachel Bernstein, Robin Berson, Meg Browne, Roy Campolongo, Phyllis Capello, Mary Cappello, Carmelina Cartei, Valeria Castelli, Esther Cohen, Peter Covino, Anna Maria Crispino, Maria Rosa Cutrufelli, Nan Enstad, Jane Fazio-Villeda,

Rabbi Michael Feinberg, Elena Frigenti, Helen Geglio, Mary Giaimo, David Gonzales, Steven Greenhouse, Brendan Griffith, Mary Ann Hacker, Peter Homestead, Rose Imperato, Charles Lauster, Annabella Lenzu, Rob Linné, LuLu LoLo, Stephanie Longo, Erik Loomis, Tracy Mann, Ernesto Martinez, Gina Pollara, Kym Ragusa, Caterina Romeo, Edgar Romney, Elissa Sampson, Andi Sosin, Joel Sosinsky, Linda Stagno, Gioia Timpanelli, the late Ed Vargas, John Viola, Uri Wegman, Karen Weiser, Dan Levinson Wilk, and Julia Wolfe.

A number of organizations sustained our Triangle fire work that preceded this book. A special thanks to Casa Italiana Zerilli Marimò at New York University, and its director, Stefano Albertini. It was thanks to Dr. Albertini's vision and generous hospitality that we were able to organize, as members of the Collective of Italian American Women (later Malia), the ninetieth commemoration of the Triangle fire in 2001. In March 2015, we organized panels on the Triangle fire at the Italian Cultural Institute and the John D. Calandra Italian American Institute, CUNY. Our gratitude especially to Donatella Boldini, Anthony Tamburri, Joseph Sciorra, and Rosangela Briscese for hosting these events. We wish to acknowledge the Italian American Studies Association for hosting a session on the Triangle fire in 2015. We consider the collective work of memorialization by Toponomastica Femminile in Italy as complementary to the work of this book. We appreciate the work of the Triangle Fire Memorial Association, especially its founders, the late Vincent Maltese and Senator Serphin Maltese and his wife, the late Constance Maltese: The Association has brought the history of the fire to schools and communities in an exemplary manner. We are deeply grateful to the Kheel Center for Labor-Management Documentation & Archives at Cornell University—and especially Wesley Chenault—for granting permission to reproduce several photographs that appear in the book and for being an essential archival source for the history of the Triangle fire, a source to which we and our contributors turned again and again before and during the making of this book.

Governor Andrew Cuomo and Senator Elizabeth Warren offered powerful reminders of the relevance of the lessons of the Triangle fire for today's world. Laura Boldrini, president of the Italian Chamber of

Deputies, was the first Italian elected official to visit the site of the fire to pay tribute to the workers, especially those southern Italian women immigrants too long forgotten by their native country. Our immense gratitude to board members and volunteers of the Remember the Triangle Fire Coalition and especially founder Ruth Sergel.

Several people read our introduction. Joanna Clapps Herman, who has been a stalwart supporter of this project and first suggested that New Village Press would be a perfect home for our book, read and commented on the introduction with the keen eye of the writer. Kevin Baker's extraordinary knowledge of the history of the fire served us well as we identified and described key historical moments of Triangle history. Regina Tuma's careful reading through the critical lens of social psychology helped us frame and clarify our argument. Nancy Caronia's comments helped us rethink our opening. Donia Ayoub proofread the introduction with great care. Joshua Fausty's detailed comments helped us strengthen and focus our argument. Fraser Ottanelli read the introduction multiple times and helped us clarify key concepts.

Claudia Giunta generously offered her help and suggestions as we turned this project into a book.

Edvige would like to thank New Jersey City University for awarding her a sabbatical leave in the fall of 2019 and course release time to work on this book. She would like to thank her students, especially those from her Triangle fire classes (2017–2021) at NJCU. Their commitment to exploring the Triangle fire in projects that often delved deep into the powerful connection between personal and academic has inspired and continues to inspire her. In particular, she would like to thank Etrita Abdulahu, Gabrielle Arroyo, Donia Ayoub, Nada Banoub, Olivia Boules, Cassandra Casella, Ebony Chillin, Glenroy Clarke, Melanie Colon, Sadik Erisen, Samantha Garcia, Julia Havilland, Dominique Jean, Natalie Mendez, Elizabeth Miller, Mayada Muhareb, Erika Perez, Natasha Persaud, Johanna Rihera-Puma, Emily Sierra, Jennifer Torres, and Sabrina Vargas. She is grateful to Annie Lanzillotto for being so open and generous to her Triangle fire students. Her appreciation to former provost and senior vice president at NJCU Dan Julius for his support of her work as a teacher and scholar of the Triangle fire. Her deepest thanks to Steve Darwin for his endless support and constant interest in her work. Her daily conversations with her friend and writing partner Joanna Clapps Herman have sustained her every step of the way. Her gratitude to her husband, Joshua Fausty, for his help and support of her work and for the enlightening conversations about this project. He first suggested that she should teach a course exclusively on the Triangle fire at NJCU, a pedagogical experience that has deeply affected her work on this book. Many friends and family, near and far, have made it possible for her to do this work through the sense of love, connection, and purpose they have given her. Her children, Emily Cutts, who at age thirteen attended the ninetieth commemoration and was inspired to write the novella "Michelina's Journey," and Matteo Giunta Fausty have been a source of strength, courage, and determination, as have her niece Dalila Urbano and her son-in-law, Michael Feltis. Becoming the great-aunt of Samuele Fasano has heightened her belief in the importance of remembering and passing on stories, which is at the heart of this book.

Mary Anne Trasciatti is grateful to Hofstra University for supporting and uplifting her Triangle work in a variety of ways. She thanks her students, especially Eileen Follano, for their participation in Triangle commemorations, including singing labor songs. Thanks also to Catherine Cerrone for sharing her insightful comments about the presence of Triangle in popular culture. Her eighth-grade social studies teacher, the late Burt Koza, set her on the path to becoming a teacher-scholar-activist. His memory continues to guide her. Thanks to Lisa Merrill for providing companionship at Triangle commemorations and sharing the joy of bringing Hofstra students to the event over the years. Christine Noschese, Phil Dalton, Paulette Brinka, and Matt Sobnosky have offered encouragement, camaraderie, and laughter, which sustained her throughout her Triangle odyssey. Her deepest gratitude to fellow board members of the Remember the Triangle Fire Coalition for showing her the true meaning of solidarity. Her partner, Fraser Ottanelli, has been an unfailing source of support and strength. He is a true comrade.

Her daughter, Bridget Caslowitz, sons Michael and Sam Caslowitz, daughter-in-law Erin Stymacks Caslowitz, and granddaughter Sophie Ruth Caslowitz remind her every day why the work matters.

Our collaboration in the editing of the essays, the cowriting of the introduction and part of the epilogue, and the process of handling the myriad aspects involved in the making of this book has been a true gift. Through these years of intense work, we have forged a life-sustaining collaboration and friendship, the benefits of which we have felt deeply in our lives. Working together to complete this book during the COVID-19 pandemic has given us a sense of connection and community that has deepened our appreciation of the work we have done in memory of the Triangle workers.

Edvige Giunta and Mary Anne Trasciatti
Teaneck, New Jersey, and Long Beach, New York
March 13, 2021

The Literature of the Triangle Fire

▼

William Gunn Shepherd's eyewitness account of the Triangle fire, published in *The New York World* on March 26, 1911, became the first written account of what David Von Drehle has called, in the subtitle of his 2003 history, *The Fire That Changed America*. Shepherd's powerful narrative is part of a vast body of literature that has been generated in the 111 years since the fire. From the outset, newspaper accounts of the tragedy, its aftermath, the funerals, and the trial were the main form of written commentary. But other written texts have been produced over the century—to remember, reflect, and understand the significance of the fire. The centennial commemoration has inspired literary and artistic works that retell and re-present the fire. In addition to historical narratives, a diverse body of literature, which includes works of fiction, poetry, drama, film, song, and documentary, even illustrated and graphic narratives, testifies to the fire's continued impact on people's hearts and imagination. This body of creative work considers Triangle as a collective event that has at its center the lives and vicissitudes of working-class people and their families and communities. It taps into the historical, ethical, and symbolical meaning of the Triangle fire.

The single-authored books that have become classics of Triangle history pulse with collective spirit. At the center of Leon Stein's 1962 book, *The Triangle Fire*, the first full-length historical account of the fire, are the oral history interviews he conducted with survivors. These interviews have become an essential source for anyone delving into Triangle history. Triangle is at the heart of Annelise Orleck's 1995 *Common Sense and a Little Fire*, a collective biography of early twentieth-century immigrant women activists, all of whom were touched by the tragedy. In *Triangle: The Fire That Changed America*, Von Drehle, too, includes the personal stories of Triangle workers, even as he situates the fire within an early-twentieth-century U.S. social and political context. Richard Greenwald's *The Triangle Fire, the Protocols of Peace, and Industrial Democracy in Progressive Era New York*, published in 2005, connects the 1909 Uprising, a 1910 strike, and the Triangle fire to make a case for cooperation between labor, industry, and the state in the pursuit of social and economic justice. Jennifer Gugliemo's 2010 *Living the Revolution: Italian Women's Resistance and Radicalism in New York City, 1880–1945* examines the little-known but significant role of Italian immigrant women, including garment workers, in the turn-of-the-century labor movement and socialist and anarchist circles. In her 2016 book, *See You in the Streets*, Ruth Sergel explores, through reflections on her own artistic and political practice, the power of Triangle memory to inspire art and social transformation through collective action.

The stories of the women and girls who came from southern Italy and Eastern Europe, surviving hunger, persecution, and the dreadful journey to America, have inspired several novelists. These authors have drawn from historical research to depict characters who live, work, and sometimes die within the larger social fabric of the world in which the fire happened. At times, in reimagining the fire, novelists, while also using historically based figures, create contemporary characters who have been affected by the fire. This is the case in Katharine Weber's *Triangle*, Susan Meissner's *A Fall of Marigolds*, and Rachel Wesson's *Orphan Train Disaster*. Weber's novel tells the story of Esther Gottesfeld, a fictional survivor of the fire. In the novel, Esther's granddaughter searches for the truth about what happened that March 25th. Meissner entwines the story of a 9/11 widow with that of a young woman who witnessed and was traumatized by the Triangle fire. In Wesson's novel, the Triangle fire is not the central event of the narrative, but it appears within the larger canvas of the lives of a gallery of characters in early-twentieth-century New York City. In this novel, a number of Triangle workers and their family members are referred to by their actual names. Sometimes, characters are pieced together through fragments of historical figures. Weber's Triangle survivor has the last name of the author's grandmother, who worked at Triangle two years before the fire. The three young women protagonists of Margaret Haddix's *Uprising* are an Italian immigrant, an Eastern European Jewish immigrant, and the daughter of a wealthy New Yorker, each representative of an important group of actors in Triangle history. Blanck's daughter also appears in the novel's narrative frame. In Kevin Baker's *Dreamland*, Blanck and Harris are renamed after contemporary neoconservative writers John Podhoretz and William Kristol. Politicians, performers, gangsters, union organizers, and a Triangle factory worker also populate Baker's novel, which journeys back and forth between Coney Island and the Lower East Side. In these novels, New York City's historical sites come alive as the stage on which the vicissitudes of the characters and the larger events surrounding the fire unfold. Although Triangle is not at the center of Alice Hoffman's *The Museum of Extraordinary Things*, it's interwoven with its plot. The novel is set in Coney Island's Dreamland, an amusement park that burned to the ground on May 27, 1911, only two months after the Triangle fire. These novelists have turned to the fire not as a singular, self-contained event, but as a portentous historical moment that reverberates with multiple layers of meaning—emotional, social, historical.

In the hands of skilled teachers, young adult novels, such as Haddix's *Uprising* and Mary Jane Auch's *Ashes of Roses*, encourage a new generation's interest in Triangle history. These books re-create the world in which Triangle workers lived and the events that culminated in the fire. They make the story accessible to young readers by focusing on teenage characters who lived through or died during the horrific fire. Both Haddix and Auch draw from historical sources to create places and characters, and to depict through storytelling the economic, social, and political forces at play during that time.

An even younger readership is addressed by a handful of children's books, such as *Brave Girl: Clara and the Shirtwaist Makers' Strike of*

1909, by Michelle Markel; *Fire!*, by Barbara Diamond Goldin; *Fire at the Triangle Factory*, by Holly Littlefield; *Lucy Fights the Flames*, by Julie Gilbert, which is published in a series called Girls Survive. These authors face the challenge of presenting the terrifying story of the fire in a manner that is suitable for children. They do so by focusing on interethnic friendship, struggle, resilience, and survival, all of which are part of the Triangle story.

Several poets have written about the fire, from Robert Pinski ("Shirt") to Mary Fell (*The Persistence of Memory*) to Donald Kentop (*Frozen by the Fire*) to Chris Llewellyn (*Fragments from the Fire*). The year of the centennial, Julia Stein published an anthology of poems, *Walking through a River of Fire: One Hundred Years of Triangle Factory Fire Poems*. Many Triangle women poets focus on sisterhood as that which binds the Triangle girls among themselves, and also connects women and girl workers across time and place. Carol Tarlen's "Sisters in the Flames" relies on the second person to bring to the page the sorrow and mourning that move the poet. Triangle is on Phyllis Capello's mind as she evokes the last day of the workers who died in the 1993 Kader toy factory fire in Thailand. Whether a poet addresses the "girls, girls, teenage immigrant girls"—as Annie Lanzillotto does—or honors the "Girl Talk" between the Triangle girls and "the Chinese girls, the Indonesian girls, /the Vietnamese, the Taiwanese/Girls. Girls" in Paola Corso's poem, Triangle poets affirm the power of witness, which enables the poet to transcend individual experience and ethically embrace the experiences of others. Triangle poetry thus provides a space for the expression of collective grief and solidarity. There is a commitment, a passion, that runs through Triangle poetry. Working-class studies scholar and writer Janet Zandy recognized this commitment and passion, which has been central to her own work and life. Writing about the poetry inspired by the fire, Zandy wrote in a 1997 foundational article: "What these poets have in common is a sense of kinship with the women who lost their young lives and a sense of outrage over the injustice done to them." It is this kinship that runs through the diverse body of Triangle literature.

Key images of the fire became imprinted in the memory of its witnesses and have become over time part of collective memory. These images appear, juxtaposed with interviews with family members, activists, and scholars, in HBO's *Triangle: Remembering the Fire* and PBS's *Triangle Fire*, two historical documentaries that were released for the centennial. Other documentaries feature the fire prominently, though they focus on broader events and issues (Ric Burns's *New York: A Documentary Film*, Gianfranco Norelli and Suma Kurien's *Pane Amaro/ Bitter Bread: The Italian American Journey from Despised Immigrants to Honored Citizens*), specific historical figures (Mick Caouette's *Summoned: Frances Perkins and the General Welfare*), or other labor tragedies (Costanza Quatriglio's *Triangle*).

In works of drama, music, dance, and performance, artists have provided a space for the reenactment of Triangle memory, often in ways that highlight the choral quality of the event. Annabella Lenzu's untitled choreographed procession for the Triangle centennial brought to the street a visualization of a mourning ritual. Elizabeth Swados and Cecilia Rubino's oratorio *From the Fire*, Bev Grant's *Ballad of the Triangle Shirtwaist Fire*, Julia Wolfe's oratorio *Fire in My Mouth*, Massimiliano Vintaloro's musical *Fire!*, Marco Savatteri's musical *Camicette Bianche*, Ruth Rubin's "Ballad of the Triangle Factory Fire," and Francesca Incudine's song "No Name" all provide compelling illustrations of the ties between memory and community that have permeated Triangle history and activism.

Talking to the Girls: Intimate and Political Essays on the Triangle Shirtwaist Factory Fire, the first anthology on the Triangle fire, acknowledges its debt to this diverse literary tradition.

APPENDIX 2

Contributors Reflect on Their Processes

▼

WITNESSES

Chapter 1
Another Spring
Annie Rachele Lanzillotto

My essay draws from my personal experience as an artist/activist in New York City (2007–2019) and during a trip to Sicily (2018). Conversations with activists, artists, and family members of Triangle victims and survivors informed my work, as did conversations with Ester Rizzo and the women of Toponomastica Femminile in Licata, Sicily. I thank Ester, her husband, Vanni, her father, Antonino, and Stefania Taviano, who hosted me while I conducted research in Sicily. My conversations with Diane Fortuna about her great-aunt Daisy Fitze Lopez and her book, *They Were Legal: Balzac y Lopez: The History of an Hispanic Family*, were instrumental to the writing of my essay. Fortuna shared sources such as photos and newspaper clippings, as did Jane Fazio-Villeda, great-granddaughter of Joe Zito. Ester Rizzo shared birth certificates and other documents. My gratitude to Paola Corso, LuLu LoLo, Rose Imperato, and Ruth Sergel, who commented on early drafts of the essay, and to Phyllis Capello, who first told me about Triangle.

Chapter 2
The New Deal Began with My Grandmother, Frances Perkins
Tomlin Perkins Coggeshall and the Reverend Charles Hoffacker

This essay links Tomlin Perkins Coggeshall's grandmother, whom he lovingly remembers from his early years, with the transformational public figure whose legacy continues into the twenty-first century. Over many years, Coggeshall has read publications and consulted archival sources about his grandmother and engaged in conversations with many people who knew her or studied her. This essay results from an ongoing collaboration between Coggeshall and the Reverend Charles Hoffacker. Hoffacker first raised the topic of the importance of conversions in the life of Frances Perkins, especially how witnessing the Triangle fire was a pivotal incident in her conversion to the world and the fulfillment of her calling. Coggeshall readily endorsed this perspective on his grandmother's spirituality. These studies of Frances Perkins have served as key sources in the authors' collaboration in this essay: Kirstin Downey, *The Woman Behind the New Deal: The Life and Legacy of Frances Perkins—Social Security, Unemployment Insurance, and the Minimum Wage*; Tom Levitt, *The Courage to Meddle: The Belief of Frances Perkins*; George Martin, *Madame Secretary: Frances Perkins*; and Donn Mitchell, *Tread the City's Streets Again: Frances Perkins Shares Her Theology*.

Chapter 3
The Triangle Factory Fire and the City of Two Who Survived
Ellen Gruber Garvey

I have drawn from personal and family memories in writing this essay, including conversations with Frances Goldin, Sally Goldin, and Ellen Marks that took place between December 2017 and December 2019, in person and by telephone, and conversations with Peter Burmeister that took place between October 2017 and January 2021, by telephone and by email. I repeatedly consulted the United States and New York State census records and steamship records digitized on Ancestry.com. In addition, the website of the Kheel Center for Labor-Management Documentation & Archives at Cornell University, including the transcript of the trial, and articles in the *Jewish Daily Forward* have been primary sources. Chana Pollock checked the Yiddish version of the *Forward* article that covered Abraham's testimony to confirm that he was referred to as "H. [hey] Bernstein" in Yiddish, as well. I have also drawn from Leon Stein's *Triangle Fire*, David Von Drehle's *Triangle: The Fire That Changed America*, and Ruth Sergel's Street Pictures website. *The New York Times* reviewed *Morning Star*, the 1940 play about the fire. *Curbed New York* reported in April 2018 on the Trump Tower fire that killed a tenant. The Lo-Down website reported in February 2018 on the opening of the Frances Goldin Senior Residence.

Chapter 4
Girl Talk
Paola Corso

This essay draws primarily from personal and family memories. Other sources include Leon Stein's *Triangle Fire* and David Von Drehle's *Triangle: The Fire That Changed America*, as well as the Frances Perkins Center's website and the Clean Clothes Campaign's website for the Rana Plaza factory collapse in Bangladesh. In addition, I have used eyewitness and survivor testimonies from various accounts of the Rana Plaza collapse.

FAMILIES

Chapter 5
A Legacy of Grief: In Search of Rosie Weiner
Suzanne Pred Bass

The Kheel Center for Labor-Management Documentation & Archives at Cornell University, *The Triangle Fire* by Leon Stein, and *Triangle: The Fire That Changed America* by David Von Drehle are resources I return to whenever I am seeking information about the Triangle Fire. The invaluable conversations I had with my mother, Mary Pred, and my great-aunt Katie Weiner were with me throughout the writing of this essay. In addition, my cousin and friend Don Weiner provided key information, as did Michael Hirsch. Finally, all that I accomplish is in large measure due to the love and support of Lane.

Chapter 6
My Father, Isidore Abramowitz
Martin Abramowitz

To write this essay, I have relied for the most part on personal memories and personal effects, such as photographs. I have also used information found in Leon Stein's *Triangle Fire*, David Von Drehle's *Triangle: The Fire That Changed America*, the Kheel Center for Labor-Management Documentation & Archives at Cornell University, and the 1910 census records.

Chapter 7
The Two Roses: A Great-Niece Remembers
Annie Schneiderman Valliere

This essay draws from personal and family memories, including interviews with my father, Herb Schneiderman, conducted in Maine (2008 and 2009), interviews with my aunts (Lois King in New York in 2010 and Florence Dobrer in New York in 2011 and in South Carolina in 2012). I spoke with my sister, Rachel Schneiderman, in Gulfport, Florida, in 2016, and my cousin, Lisa Klein, in Philadelphia in 2020. Important to this essay was a 2005 conversation and a 2021 email with Annelise Orleck, and an interview with Elizabeth Hart in Maine in 2020. Sources include Rose Schneiderman's memoir, *All for One*; Pauline Newman's letters in the Rose Schneiderman Papers: (WTUL) and its Principal Leaders at Tamiment Library/Robert F. Wagner Labor Archives at New York University; the Leonora O'Reilly Papers in the Papers of the National Women's Trade Union League of America (NWTULA) at the Library of Congress; *The New York Times*; annual reports of the NYWTUL, and *Life and Labor*, a journal of the NWTUL. In addition, I relied on Leon Stein's *The Triangle Fire*, Annelise Orleck's *Common Sense and a Little Fire*, Melvyn Dubofsky's *When Workers Organize*, and Gary Endelman's *Solidarity Forever: Rose Schneiderman and the Women's*

Trade Union League. I would like to thank Antony Polansky, author of *The Jews in Poland and Russia*, vol. 1, *1350–1881*, for helping me with Polish Jewish history, and Michael Koncewicz, research scholar, Tamiment Library & Robert F. Wagner Labor Archives, New York University, who graciously helped me with photos.

Chapter 8
Triangle in Two Acts: From Bubbe Mayses to Bangladesh
Annelise Orleck

This essay grew out of a lifetime of stories told by my grandmother and her daughter, my aunt, the veracity of which, as I suggest in the piece, was always open to question. I began by talking about my grandmother and then moved on to examine the way my understanding of the Triangle fire was shaped first by her, then by my research over thirty years as a professional historian. From there, I turned to my burgeoning friendship with Bangladeshi garment union leader Kalpona Akter, whom I first met at the Triangle Centennial Commemoration in 2011. Through various drafts, I explored these personal relationships against the background of broader research on several of my books that bear on Triangle particularly and the women workers' movements I have written about professionally.

TEACHERS

Chapter 9
Teaching the Triangle Fire to Middle School Students
Kimberly Schiller

This essay draws from my memories as well as family stories of my mother, Carolyn Fevola, Governor Mario Cuomo, Division Avenue High School teacher Ms. Judith Evans-Gallagher, Professor Marilyn Klee at Adelphi University, and my beloved friends Jane LaTour and Rachel Bernstein from the New York Labor History Association. In addition, I referenced several texts, including *Ashes of Roses*, by Mary Jane Auch; *To Kill a Mockingbird*, by Harper Lee; *The Giver*, by Lois

Lowry; *The Tale of Despereaux,* by Kate DiCamillo; *Eragon,* by Christopher Paolini; and "The New Colossus," by Emma Lazarus.

Chapter 10
Remembering the Triangle Fire in California
Laura E. Ruberto

This essay draws from personal memories, especially of various exchanges, including with my daughter, Alma Goldstein Ruberto, artist Melanie Shapiro, colleagues Shawn Doubiago and Elizabeth Wing, and numerous students, colleagues, and visitors at Berkeley City College. Telephone and email conversations with Evelyn Velson, Arnold Passman, and Tim Z. Hernandez were also helpful. The main primary written source on the Los Gatos plane crash is Tim Z. Hernandez's *And They Will Call You.* I also relied on Ruth Sergel's *See You in the Streets;* Joanna Clapps Herman's essay "Filatrici: Stitching Our Voices Together"; Woody Guthrie's song "Plane Wreck at Los Gatos," with music by Martin Hoffman; Shanna Hullaby's photographs taken in Berkeley; and some journalistic articles. I am grateful to Luisa Del Giudice, Persis Karim, and Joseph Sciorra, each of whom read and commented on earlier drafts of this essay. I am especially thankful to Tim Z. Hernandez, who commented on a draft and generously shared his research with me.

Chapter 11
Teaching the Girls: The Triangle Fire as Affective History
Jacqueline Ellis

This essay draws from online articles, social media posts, and visual sources—including video and photographs—to explore historical and contemporary girls' activism. I also reflect on many of the texts I have used to teach women's history and girlhood studies classes at New Jersey City University. Annalise Orleck's *"We Are All Fast Workers Now": The Global Uprising Against Poverty Wages,* Meredith Tax's essay "The Uprising of the Thirty Thousand," and David Von Drehle's *Triangle: The Fire That Changed America* are also key to the research that frames this essay.

MOVEMENTS

Chapter 12
Solidarity Forever!
May Y. Chen

I wrote this essay to remember and reflect on many years of personal experiences, people, and events that have shaped my career and life. Family members, community organizing projects and people, and workers and activists in the labor movement provided rich source materials. I consulted different primary and secondary source materials from the ILGWU records at the Kheel Center for Labor-Management Documentation & Archives at Cornell University, *Amerasia Journal* from the UCLA Asian American Studies Center, and images and videos from Visual Communications Media in Los Angeles. I was also inspired by participating actively with Esther Cohen, Lana Cheung, and others in the 2017 oral history project We Built New York: Honoring Chinese Workers, which was published online by PBS in 2018.

Chapter 13
Remembering Family: Labor Activism and the Triangle Fire
Michele Fazio

This essay draws from personal and family memories as well as an earlier published essay, "The Recovery of a Family History: Who Was Raimondo Fazio?" In addition, Janet Zandy's essay "Fire Poetry on the Triangle Shirtwaist Company Fire of March 25, 1911"; Rudolph J. Vecoli's essay "Who Was Raimondo Fazio? The Documentary Record"; Simone Cinotto's *The Italian American Table: Food, Family, and Community in New York City*; Michael Miller Topp's *Those Without a Country: The Political Culture of Italian American Syndicalists*; Jennifer Guglielmo's *Living the Revolution: Italian Women's Resistance and Radicalism in New York City, 1880–1945*; Marcella Bencivenni's *Italian Immigrant Radical Culture: The Idealism of the Sovversivi in the United States, 1890–1940*; and the websites of the Library of Congress's Chronicling America and the Kheel Center for Labor-Management Documentation

& Archives at Cornell University have been primary sources for much of the research on which this essay relies. I wish to thank Nancy Caronia and Carla Simonini for their insightful feedback on earlier drafts. I am especially grateful to my relatives for their willingness to collaborate with me on reconstructing our family history.

Chapter 14

They Were Not There: A Rumination on the Meaning of the Triangle Shirtwaist Fire to Black Garment Workers in Early-Twentieth-Century New York City

Janette Gayle

This essay draws from manuscript and archival sources, oral interviews, and from my experience as an Afro-Caribbean immigrant woman living in the United States. Initially, I struggled to write this essay because there were no Black women employed in the garment industry at the time of the Triangle Shirtwaist Factory fire. However, while I could not tell that story, I could tell the equally compelling one of why they were absent. This story involved the initial rejection they faced in their quest to gain employment in the New York City garment industry and how they struggled to overcome this rejection. I could tell the story of Black women's efforts to gain jobs in the garment industry in the waning years of World War I. My research took me to the Schomburg Center for Research in Black Culture (SCRBC), where records such as those of the American West Indian Ladies Aid Society, the Bermuda Benevolent Association, and the Beach-Thomas Family Papers showed the centrality of social networks in helping newly arrived immigrants settle into the Black community, and also threw light on their efforts to find and adjust to work in the industry. Two oral interviews with Black garment worker Maida Springer Kemp, one conducted by Elizabeth Balanoff in 1978 as part of The 20th Century Trade Union Woman: Vehicle for Social Change Oral History Transcripts, and the other by Daniel Katz in 2005, were instructive: I learned about the excitement with which Black garment workers participated in the ILGWU Dressmakers' Strike in August 1933 and signed up en masse to join the union. Finally, my research led me to the ILGWU records located at the Kheel Center for Labor-Management Documentation & Archives at Cornell University. These invaluable papers showed the union's efforts to organize Black garment workers and their participation in the union, where, perhaps for the first time, they learned about the Triangle Shirtwaist Factory fire.

MEMORIALS

Chapter 15
Chalk and Smoke, Fabric and Thread:
Reflections on Feminist Commemoration and the Triangle Fire
Ellen Wiley Todd

This essay draws from personal memories as well as conversations with Ruth Sergel in New York and Berlin over the last decade, documentation on the Shirtwaist Project from Lulu Lolo and Annie Lanzillotto, generously provided in 2010, and correspondence with Harriet Bart and her director Julie McGarvie that took place in December 2020. In addition, the Kheel Center for Labor-Management Documentation & Archives at Cornell University; the Archives of American Art at the Smithsonian Institution, Washington, D.C.; the Wirtz Labor Library, U.S. Department of Labor, Washington, D.C.; and the Loomis Chaffee School Archives, Windsor, Connecticut, have provided primary sources.

Chapter 16
And They Returned Home:
Italy Remembers the Triangle Fire Women
Ester Rizzo Licata

While drawing from personal experiences to write this essay, I have consulted the archives of the Uffici dei Servizi Demografici in the following Italian towns: Licata, Casteldaccia, Marineo, Bisacquino, Sambuca di Sicilia, Cerda, Mazara del Vallo, Sciacca, Cerami, Sperlinga, Noto, Casamassima, Bitonto, Armento, Polignano a Mare, and Striano. The documents I found in these archives allowed me to identify the places of birth of the Italian victims, their exact first and last names, the names of their parents, and, in some cases, the addresses of the homes where they were born. The essay is shaped by the deeply emotional impact that this research has had on me.

Chapter 17
The Fabric of Memory
Richard Joon Yoo

The work I write about in "The Fabric of Memory" was shaped by many forces throughout my life: my personal writing and reflection, my work on the texture of memory in the everyday while studying art in Chicago, and my concern with identifying the meaningful ways I relate to the built environment as an architectural designer and teacher. I want to thank Uri Wegman, a most incredible collaborator; my mother and father, who have always given me a chance; Lev, Jonah, and Oriana, who are my greatest joys; the Tornado; and the incredible folks at the Remember the Triangle Fire Coalition: You all are a constant inspiration to me.

Epilogue
Listening to Kalpona
Kalpona Akter
Interviwed by Edvige Giunta, and Mary Anne Trasciatti

The editors interviewed Kalpona Akter on Skype in February 2019. Kalpona's answers to the editors' questions were transcribed by the editors, who omitted their questions from the transcript to give greater space to Kalpona's voice. In place of the questions, a short introduction by the editors frames their encounter with the Bangladeshi activist. This interview was first edited by them to shape it into one extended narrative. Kalpona has read, reviewed, and edited the final version.

Bibliography

Archival Collections and Online Databases

Archives of American Art, Smithsonian Institution, Washington, D.C. Evelyn Longman Batchelder Collection, Loomis Chaffee School Archives, Windsor, Connecticut.

ILGWU records. Kheel Center for Labor-Management Documentation & Archives, Martin P. Catherwood Library, Cornell University.

Luigi Antonini Correspondence. Courtesy of the ILGWU. Local 89. 5780/023. Kheel Center for Labor-Management Documentation & Archives, Martin P. Catherwood Library, Cornell University.

Remembering the 1911 Triangle Factory Fire. Kheel Center for Labor-Management Documentation & Archives, Martin P. Catherwood Library, Cornell University. See https://trianglefire.ilr.cornell.edu/.

Rose Schneiderman Papers, Series V: Pauline Newman Letters, TAM. 018, Tamiment Library & Robert F. Wagner Labor Archives, New York University.

Selected Digitized Correspondence of Eleanor Roosevelt 1933–1945, Schneiderman, Rose (1 and 2), Franklin D. Roosevelt Presidential Library and Museum. See http://www.fdrlibrary.marist.edu /archives/collections/franklin/?p=collections/findingaid&id=504.

Triangle Fire Open Archive. See http://open-archive.rememberthe trianglefire.org/.

Uffici dei Servizi Demografici Licata, Casteldaccia, Marineo, Bisacquino, Sambuca di Sicilia, Cerda, Mazara del Vallo, Sciacca, Cerami, Sperlinga, Noto, Casamassima, Bitonto, Armento, Polignano a Mare, e Striano.

United States Census, 1910. See http://www.familysearch.org.

Wirtz Labor Library, U.S. Department of Labor, Washington, D.C.

Articles, Books, and Documents

"100th Anniversary of the Triangle Shirtwaist Factory Fire," March 25, 2011. See https://www.democracynow.org/2011/3/25/100th _anniversary_of_the_triangle_shirtwaist.

"120,000 Pay Tribute to the Fire Victims, Army of Workers, Most of Them Women, March Through the Downpour of Rain." *New York Times*, April 6, 1911. See https://www.nytimes.com/1911/04/06 /archives/120000-pay-tribute-to-the-fire-victims-army-of-workers -most-of-them.html?searchResultPosition=1.

"32 Killed in Crash of Charter Plane." *The New York Times*, January 29, 1948.

Ahmed, Farid and Tom Watkins. "After 16 Days Buried in Bangladesh: 'Save Me!'" CNN (May 11, 2013). https://www.cnn.com/2013/05 /10/world/asia/bangladesh-building-collapse.

"America's Largest Frescoes Picture Social History and Achievements of Garment Industries and Unions." *Justice* 22 (July 15, 1940).

Annual Report 1908/09–1918/19 of The Women's Trade Union League of New York. New York: Women's Trade Union League. See https:// babel.hathitrust.org/cgi/pt?id=coo.31924003675117&view=1up &seq=1.

Anderson, Jervis. *A. Philip Randolph: A Biographical Portrait*. New York: Harcourt Brace Jovanovich, 1973.

Antonini, Luigi. *Dynamic Democracy*. New York: Eloquent Press Corporation, 1944.

Atkinson, Brooks. "The Play: Molly Picon Acts Her First English-Speaking Part on Broadway in 'Morning Star.'" *New York Times*, April 17, 1940.

Auch, Mary Jane. *Ashes of Roses*. New York: Square Fish, 2015.

Baeri Parisi, Emma. "Una Storia Impostorica," unpublished essay.

Baker, Kevin. *Dreamland*. New York: HarperCollins, 1999.

"Bangladesh Collapse Left Many Amputees." NBC News (June 20, 2013). https://www.nbcnews.com/news/photo/bangladesh -collapse-left-many-amputees-flna6c10393995.

"Bangladesh rescuer: 'I cut off limbs to save lives.'" BBC News (May 3, 2013). https://www.bbc.com/news/world-asia-22384529.

Beasely, Kate Lynn, "'Who Will Protect the Working Girl?': The Effect of the 1909 Shirtwaist Strike and Triangle Factory Fire on Early Twentieth Century Labor Organizations." Master's thesis, University of Oklahoma, 2017. See https://shareok.org/bitstream/handle /11244/325049/BeasleyKL2017.pdf?sequence=1.

Bencivenni, Marcella. *Italian Immigrant Radical Culture: The Idealism of the Sovversivi in the United States, 1890–1940.* New York: New York University Press, 2011.

Benin, Leigh et al. *The New York City Triangle Factory Fire.* Charleston South Carolina: Arcadia Publishing (Images of America), 2011.

Bodnar, John. *Remaking America: Public Memory, Commemoration, and Patriotism in the Twentieth Century.* Princeton, New Jersey: Princeton University Press, 1992.

Boston Women's Health Book Collective. *Our Bodies, Ourselves.* Boston: New England Free Press, 1971.

Brown, Kathleen M. *Good Wives, Nasty Wenches, and Anxious Patriarchs: Gender, Race, and Power in Colonial Virginia.* Chapel Hill: University of North Carolina Press, 1996.

Calvino, Italo. *The Castle of Crossed Destinies.* New York: Harcourt, Brace & Company, 1976.

Chen, Michelle. "'When We Made Mistakes in Our Sewing, They Slapped Us' Bangladeshi Garment Workers Are Still Struggling to Win the Safe and Humane Workplaces They Deserve." *The Nation* (December 21, 2015). https://www.thenation.com/article/archive /when-we-made-mistakes-in-our-sewing-they-slapped-us/.

Cinotto, Simone. *The Italian American Table: Food, Family, and Community in New York City.* Urbana: University of Illinois Press, 2013.

Clapps Herman, Joanna, "*Filatrici*: Stitching Our Voices Together." In *Embroidered Stories: Interpreting Women's Domestic Needlework from the Italian Diaspora,* edited by Edvige Giunta and Joseph Sciorra. Jackson: University of Mississippi Press, 2014, 106–118.

Clark, Jessie, and Gertrude E. McDougald. *A New Day for the Colored Woman Worker*. New York: C. P. Young Co., 1919.

"Closet with Wedding Clothes Is All That Is Left of Yetta Goldstein." *Forverts*, March 28, 1911. See https://forward.com/symphony /publish/articles/136170/.

Cronaca sovversiva (Barre, VT.), April 2, 1910. See https://chronic lingamerica.loc.gov/lccn/2012271201/1910-04-02/ed-1/seq-4/.

Daly, Emma. "Rana Plaza Factory Collapse Still Plagues Survivors." *Human Rights Watch* (April 22, 2015). https://www.hrw.org/news /2015/04/22/witness-rana-plaza-factory-collapse-still-plagues -survivors.

DeSalvo, Louise. *Vertigo: A Memoir*. Introduction by Edvige Giunta. 1996. New York: The Feminist Press at the City University of New York, 2002.

DiCamillo, Kate. *The Tale of Despereaux: Being the Story of a Mouse, a Princess, Some Soup, and a Spool of Thread*. Somerville, MA: Candlewick Press, 2015.

Diner, Hasia R. *In the Almost Promised Land: American Jews and Blacks, 1915–1935*. Baltimore: Johns Hopkins University Press, 1977.

Doss, Erika. *Memorial Mania: Public Feeling in America*. Chicago: University of Chicago Press, 2012.

Downey, Kirstin. *The Woman Behind the New Deal: The Life and Legacy of Frances Perkins—Social Security, Unemployment Insurance, and the Minimum Wage*. New York: Anchor Books, 2009.

Dubofsky, Melvyn. *When Workers Organize*. Amherst: University of Massachusetts Press, 1968.

Du Bois. W. E. B. "The Class Struggle." *The Crisis: A Record of the Darker Races* 22, no. 4 (August 1921).

"Elizabeth Warren, at Washington Sq. Park Rally, Promises to Take on Corruption." *New York Times*, September 16, 2019. See https:// www.nytimes.com/2019/09/16/us/politics/elizabeth-warren-nyc -rally-speech.html.

Ellis, Jacqueline, "Working-Class Women Theorize Globalization." *International Feminist Journal of Politics*, March 10, 2008.

Endelman, Gary Edward. *Solidarity Forever: Rose Schneiderman and the Women's Trade Union League*. New York: Arno Press, 1982.

Enstad, Nan. *Ladies of Labor, Girls of Adventure: Working Women, Popular Culture, and Labor Politics at the Turn of the Twentieth Century*. New York: Columbia University Press, 1999.

Epstein, Rebecca, Jamilia J. Blake, and Thalia González. *Girlhood Interrupted: The Erasure of Black Girls' Childhood*. Washington, D.C.: Center on Poverty and Inequality, Georgetown Law, 2016. See https://www.law.georgetown.edu/poverty-inequality-center/wp-content/uploads/sites/14/2017/08/girlhood-interrupted.pdf.

Fairclough, Alice Brown. "A Study of Occupational Opportunities for Negro Women in New York City." Master's thesis, New York University, 1929.

Fazio, Michele. "The Recovery of a Family History: Who Was Raimondo Fazio?" In *In Our Own Voices: Multidisciplinary Perspectives on Italian and Italian American Women*, edited by Elizabeth Giovanna Messina, 77–86. New York: Bordighera Press, 2003.

"Fire Questionnaires." Papers of the Women's Trade Union League and Its Principal Leaders, Leonora O'Reilly Papers, Library of Congress Manuscript Division, Washington D.C.

Fortuna, Diane. *They Were Legal: Balzac y Lopez, The History of an Hispanic Family, New York 1901–1960*. Bloomington, IN: AuthorHouse, 2011.

Freeman, Ira Henry. "Sprinkler Bill Assailed as 500 Remember Triangle Disaster." *New York Times*, March 26, 1961. See https://www.nytimes.com/1961/03/26/archives/sprinkler-bill-assailed-as-500-remember-triangle-disaster.html?searchResultPosition=1.

Friedan, Betty. *The Feminine Mystique*. New York: W.W. Norton, 1963.

Garvey, Marcus. "The Negro, Communism, Trade Unionism and His (?) Friend." In *The Marcus Garvey and Universal Negro Improvement Association Papers, September 1924–December 1927*, edited by Robert A. Hill. Berkeley: University of California Press, 1995.

———. *The Philosophy and Opinions of Marcus Garvey*. Compiled by Amy Jacques Garvey. Dover, MA: Majority Press, 1986.

Gee, Emma, ed. *Counterpoint: Perspectives on Asian American*. Los Angeles: UCLA Asian American Studies Center, 1976.

"Girl Strikers Firm: Waistmakers Undaunted by Failure of Arbitration." *New-York Tribune*, December 13, 1909. See https://chroniclinga merica.loc.gov/lccn/sn83030214/1909-12-13/ed-1/seq-3/.

Giunta, Edvige. "The Reality of a Bridge." *i-italy*, May 23, 2014. See http://www.iitaly.org/magazine/focus/op-eds/article/reality-bridge.

Gli Italiani di New York, Speciale Sezione Commemorativa del XX Anniversario dell Unione dei Dressmakers Italiani, Locale 89— I.L.G.W.U., 11 Novembre, 1939, Windsor Theatre, New York City. New York: Labor Press, 1939.

Goldin, Barbara Diamond. *Fire! The Beginnings of the Labor Movement*. New York: Viking Juvenile, 1992.

Gompers, Samuel. "The Cooper Union Meeting of 1909." See https://trianglefire.ilr.cornell.edu/primary/testimonials/ootss_Samuel Gompers.html.

González, Emma. "A Young Activist's Advice: Vote, Shave Your Head, and Cry Whenever You Need To." *New York Times*, October 5, 2018. See https://www.nytimes.com/2018/10/05/opinion/sunday /emma-gonzalez-parkland.html.

———. "Parkland Student Emma González Opens Up About Her Fight for Gun Control." *Harper's Bazaar*, February 26, 2018. See https://www.harpersbazaar.com/culture/politics/a18715714 /protesting-nra-gun-control-true-story/.

Goren, Arthur Aryeh. "Sacred and Secular: The Place of Public Funerals in the Immigrant Life of American Jews." *Jewish History* 8 (1994): 269–305.

Gornick, Vivian. *The Situation and the Story: The Art of Personal Narrative*. New York: Farrar, Straus and Giroux, 2001.

Greenberg, Cheryl Lynn. *"Or Does It Explode?": Black Harlem in the Great Depression*. New York: Oxford University Press, 1991.

Greenwald, Richard A. *The Triangle Fire, the Protocols of Peace, and Industrial Democracy in Progressive Era New York*. Philadelphia: Temple University Press, 2005.

Guglielmo, Jennifer. *Living the Revolution: Italian Women's Resistance and Radicalism in New York City, 1880–1945*. Chapel Hill: University of North Carolina Press, 2010.

Gunderson, Jessica. *The Triangle Shirtwaist Factory Fire*. Mankato, MN: Capstone, 2006.

Haddix, Margaret. *Uprising*. New York: Simon & Schuster, 2007.

Hernandez, Tim Z. *And They Will Call You*. Phoenix: University of Arizona Press, 2018.

Hoffman, Alice. *The Museum of Extraordinary Things*. New York: Scribner, 2014.

House Special Committee on Un-American Activities (1938–1944). *Investigation of Un-American Propaganda Activities in the United States: Hearings Before a Special Committee on Un-American Activities, House of Representatives, to Investigate (1) the Extent, Character, and Objects of Un-American Propaganda Activities in the United States, (2) the Diffusion Within the United States of Subversive and Un-American Propaganda That Is Instigated from Foreign Countries or of a Domestic Origin and Attacks the Principle of the Form of Government as Guaranteed by Our Constitution, and (3) All Other Questions in Relation Thereto That Would Aid Congress in Any Necessary Remedial Legislation*. 75th Congress, 3rd sess.–78th Congress, 2d sess., on H. Res. 282, 1938–1944, 1649–2166. Washington, D.C.: U.S. Government Printing Office. See https://babel.hathitrust. org/cgi/pt?id=mdp.39015073451760&view=1up&seq=8&q1 =appendix.

Hyman, Linda. *Ernest Fiene: Art of the City, 1925–1955*. New York: ACA Galleries, 1981.

Hyman, Paula. "Beyond Place and Ethnicity: The Uses of the Triangle Shirtwaist Fire." See https://jwa.org/triangle/hyman.

Katz, Daniel. *All Together Different: Yiddish Socialists, Garment Workers, and the Labor Roots of Multiculturalism.* New York: New York University Press, 2011.

Kim, E. Tammy. "Bangladeshi Factory Owner, Out of Jail, Accused of More Worker Abuse." *Aljazeera America,* August 21, 2014. See http://america.aljazeera.com/articles/2014/8/21/bangladeshi -factoryowneroutofjailaccusedofmoreworkerabuse.html.

Kine, Edith. "The Garment Union Comes to the Negro Worker." *Opportunity* 12, no.4 (April 1934): 107–10.

LaborArts, et al. We Built New York: Honoring Chinese Workers. See https://www.pbs.org/wnet/chasing-the-dream/series/we-built -new-york-honoring-chinese-workers/.

Lazarus, Emma. *The Poems of Emma Lazarus.* Edited by Susan L. Rattiner. Mineola, NY: Dover Publications, 2015.

Lee, Harper. *To Kill a Mockingbird.* New York: HarperCollins Publishers, 2002.

Levitt, Tom. *The Courage to Meddle: The Belief of Frances Perkins.* Privately printed, 2020.

Littlefield, Holly. *Fire at the Triangle Factory.* Minneapolis: Carolrhoda Books, 1996.

Litvack, Ed. "Coming Home 50 Years Later: Residents Settle in at the Frances Goldin Senior Apartments." See http://www.thelodownny .com/leslog/2018/02/coming-home-50-years-later-residents-settle -in-at-the-frances-goldin-senior-apartments.html.

Llewellyn, Chris. *Fragments from the Fire: The Triangle Shirtwaist Company Fire of March 25, 1911.* London: Puffin, 1987.

Loomis, Erik. *Out of Sight: The Long and Disturbing Story of Corporations Outsourcing Catastrophe.* New York: The New Press, 2015.

Lowry, Lois. *The Giver.* New York: Houghton Mifflin Harcourt, 1993.

Mahin, Chris. "60th Anniversary of 'Plane Wreck at Los Gatos (Deportee).'" Chicago & Midwest Regional Joint Board of UNITE HERE. See http://www.indybay.org/newsitems/2008/01/30 /18475895.php.

Markel, Michelle. *Brave Girl: Clara and the Shirtwaist Makers Strike of 1909*. New York: Balzer + Bray, 2013.

Martin, George. *Madame Secretary: Frances Perkins*. Boston: Houghton Mifflin, 1976.

"Mass Meeting Calls for New Fire Laws." *New York Times*, April 3, 1911. See https://www.nytimes.com/1911/04/03/archives/mass-meeting-calls-for-new-fire-laws-metropolitan-opera-house.html ?searchResultPosition=1.

McCarthy, Julie. "Bangladesh Collapse: The Garment Workers Who Survived." NPR Morning Edition (July 10, 2013). https://www.vpr .org/post/bangladesh-collapse-garment-workers-who-survived #stream/0.

Mead, Rebecca, "Joan of Arc and the Passion of Emma González." *The New Yorker*, March 26, 2018. See https://www.newyorker.com /culture/cultural-comment/the-passion-of-emma-gonzalez.

Meissner, Susan. *A Fall of Marigolds*. New York: Penguin. 2014.

Miller, Kelly. "The Negro as a Workingman." *The American Mercury: A Monthly Review* 6 (November 1925): 310–13.

Mitchell, Donn. *Tread the City's Streets Again: Frances Perkins Shares Her Theology*. Princeton, NJ: Anglican Examiner Publications, 2018.

Morales, Ed. "Emma González: La nueva cara of Florida Latinx." *Washington Post*, March 1, 2018. See https://www.washingtonpost.com /news/post-nation/wp/2018/03/01/emma-gonzalez-la-nueva-cara -of-florida-latinx/?noredirect=on&utm_term=.4e23995d1dbc.

Morgan, Robin, ed. *Sisterhood Is Powerful*. London: Penguin Books, 1970.

"Morgue Is Full of Our Victims." *Forward*, March 15, 2011. Originally published in the *Forverts*, March 26, 1911. See https://forward.com /news/national/136207/the-morgue-is-full-of-our-victims/.

Motlagh, Jason. "The Ghosts of Rana Plaza." *Virginia Quarterly Review* 90.2 (Spring 2014). https://www.vqronline.org/reporting-articles /2014/04/ghosts-rana-plaza. "Mourning Zone Created by the Factory Fire: Scene of Disaster and Homes of the Victims." *The*

Evening World, March 28, 1911. See http://chroniclingamerica.loc
.gov/lccn/sn83030193/1911-03-28/ed-1/seq-2/.

National Women's Trade Union League of America. "Fire in Factories."
Life and Labor Bulletin 1 (January 1911): 31. See https://babel
.hathitrust.org/cgi/pt?id=uc1.b3859487&view=1up&seq=41&q1
=newark.

National Women's Trade Union League of America. "Fire Protection."
Life and Labor Bulletin 1 (June 1911): 180–81. See https://babel
.hathitrust.org/cgi/pt?id=uc1.b3859487&view=1up&seq=191&q1
=newark.

Nessen, Steven. "Family Keeps Memory of Hero Triangle Fire Elevator
Operator Alive." WNYC, March 24, 2011. See https://www.wnyc
.org/story/119910-family-keeps-memory-triangle-fire-elevator
-operator-alive/.

New York (State) Legislature. Joint Committee Investigating Seditious
Activities, and Clayton Riley Lusk. *Revolutionary Radicalism: Its
History, Purpose and Tactics with an Exposition and Discussion of
the Steps Being Taken and Required to Curb It, Being the Report
of the Report of the Joint Legislative Committee Investigating Seditious
Activities, Filed April 24, 1920, in the Senate of the State of New York.*
Albany: J. B. Lyon, 1920. See https://catalog.hathitrust.org/Record
/001134234.

"NY Governor Andrew Cuomo June 4 Press Conference Transcript."
See https://www.rev.com/blog/transcripts/ny-governor-andrew
-cuomo-june-4-press-conference-transcript.

Ogle, Jacob, "Leading a Revolution: Emma González." *The Advocate,*
May 22, 2018. See https://www.advocate.com/people/2018/5/22
/leading-revolution-emma-gonzalez.

Orleck, Annelise. *Common Sense and a Little Fire: Women and Working-Class Politics in the United States, 1900–1965.* 2d ed. Chapel Hill:
University of North Carolina Press, 2017.

———.*We Are All Fast Food Workers Now: The Global Uprising Against
Poverty Wages.* Boston: Beacon Press, 2018.

————. *Rethinking American Women's Activism*. New York: Routledge, 2014.

Overy, Richard, ed. *New York Times: Front Pages 1851–2013*. New York: Black Dog and Levanthal Publishers, 2013.

Paolini, Christopher. *Eragon*. New York: Penguin Random House, 2005.

People of the State of New York v. Isaac Harris and Max Blanck. Trial Transcript, December 1911. See https://digitalcommons.ilr.cornell.edu/triangletrans/.

Perkins, Frances. "Reminiscences." Interview by Dean Albertson. Oral History Archives at Columbia University, Rare Book & Manuscript Library. See http://www.columbia.edu/cu/lweb/digital/collections/nny/perkinsf/transcripts/perkinsf_1_1_131.html.

Petrovsky-Shtern, Yohanan. "Military Service in Russia." See https://yivoencyclopedia.org/article.aspx/Military_Service_in_Russia.

Polonsky, Antony. *The Jews in Poland and Russia*. Vol. 1, *1350–1881*. Liverpool: Liverpool University Press, 2009.

Quan, Katie. "Memories of the 1982 ILGWU Strike in New York Chinatown." *Amerasia Journal* 35 (2009): 76–91.

Rabatz, Marilyn, and Walter Rabatz. *Evelyn Beatrice Longman Batchelder* (exhibition catalog). Windsor, CT: Loomis Chaffee School, 1993.

"Rana Plaza." See https://cleanclothes.org/campaigns/past/rana-plaza.

Randolph, A. Philip. "Negro Labor Organizers." *The Messenger* 5, no. 6 (June 1923).

Richards, Yevette. *Conversations with Maida Springer: A Personal History of Labor, Race, and International Relations*. Pittsburg: University of Pittsburgh Press, 2004.

Rizzo, Ester. *Camicette Bianche. Oltre l'8 marzo*. Palermo: Navarra Editore, 2016.

Robinson, Carol, "Mom, Family Heartbroken After Daughter's Promising Life Ended in Shooting at Huffman High" See https://www.al.com/news/birmingham/2018/03/mom_family_heartbroken_after_d.html.

Robsom, Steve. "Bangladesh Survivor Reshma Akhter Changed Dead Colleagues Clothes in Trapped Rubble." *Daily Mail UK* (May 19, 2013). https://www.dailymail.co.uk/news/article-2322391/Bangladesh-survivor-Reshma-Akhter-changed-dead-colleagues-clothes-trapped-rubble.html. "

"Rose Schneiderman." *New York Daily News,* August 13, 1972. See https://img2.newspapers.com/clip/44634516/daily-news/.

"Rose Schneiderman," *New York Times,* August 14, 1972. https://www.nytimes.com/1972/08/14/archives/rose-schneiderman.html.

"Rose Schneiderman Dies at 88; Pioneer Women's Union Leader," *New York Times,* August 12, 1972. https://www.nytimes.com/1972/08/12/archives/rose-schneiderman-dies-at-88-pioneer-womens-union-leader.html.

Rose Schneiderman to Rachel Schneiderman, February 23, 1960; personal collection of Annie Schneiderman Valliere.

Rosenfeld, Morris. "The March of Tears: Half a Million People in Mourning." *Forward,* March 15, 2011. Originally published in the *Forverts,* April 6, 1911. See https://forward.com/articles/136163/the-march-of-tears/.

Saaritsa, Sini, Janne Hulkkonen, and Carry Somers. "Rana Plaza—The Survivors' Stories." Fashion Revolution.org (2018). https://www.fashionrevolution.org/rana-plaza-the-survivors-stories/.

Samu, Margaret. "Evelyn Beatrice Longman: Establishing a Career in Public Sculpture." *Woman's Art Journal* 25 (Fall 2004/Winter 2005): 8–15.

Schlesinger, Benjamin. *Report of General Executive Board to the Sixteenth Biennial Convention of the International Ladies' Garment Workers' Union.* May 1, 1922. ILGWU Convention Records on Microfilm, 1900–1929, Collection Number: 5780/080 mf., Kheel Center for Labor-Management Documentation & Archives, Cornell University.

Schneiderman, Rose. *All for One.* New York: Paul S. Eriksson, 1967.

———. "We Have Found You Wanting." See https://trianglefire.ilr.cornell.edu/primary/testimonials/ootss_RoseSchneiderman.html.

Selkin, Michael. "Lion about Lunch." *Columbia Daily Spectator*, September 19, 1960. See http://spectatorarchive.library.columbia.edu/cgi-bin/columbia?a=d&d=cs19600919-01.2.20.

Sergel, Ruth. *See You in the Streets: Art, Action, and Remembering the Triangle Shirtwaist Factory Fire*. Iowa City: University of Iowa Press, 2016.

"Socialists Have A Woman's Day." *New York Times*, February 28, 1910. See https://www.nytimes.com/1910/02/28/archives/socialists-have-a-womans-day-speakers-at-carnegie-hall-all-women.html?searchResultPosition=15.

Spero, Sterling D., and Abram L. Harris, *The Black Worker: The Negro and The Labor Movement*. 1931. Reprint, New York: Columbia University Press, 1959.

Sprague, Leah W. "The Woman Behind the New Deal." See https://francesperkinscenter.org/.

Stein, Julia, ed. *Walking Through a River of Fire: One Hundred Years of Triangle Factory Fire Poems*. Introduction by Jack Hirschman. CC. Marimbo, Berkeley, CA., 2011.

Stein, Leon. *The Triangle Fire*. 1962. Reprint, New York: Carroll & Graf Publishers, 1985.

Stevens, Matt, "'Skinhead Lesbian' Tweet About Parkland Student Ends Maine Republican's Candidacy." *The New York Times*, March 18, 2018. See https://www.nytimes.com/2018/03/18/us/politics-maine-republican-leslie-gibson.html.

"Strikers Reject Advance." *New York Sun*, March 2, 1912. See https://www.loc.gov/item/sn83030272/1912-03-02/ed-1/.

"Surviving the Bangladesh Factory Collapse." *Times-Republican* (April 30, 2013). https://www.sachem.ca/news-story/2550381-a-world-that-suddenly-explodes/.

Thomas, Dana. "Why Won't We Learn from the Survivors of the Rana Plaza Disaster?" *New York Times* (April 24, 2018). https://www.nytimes.com/2018/04/24/style/survivors-of-rana-plaza-disaster.html.

Tax, Meredith, "The Uprising of the Thirty Thousand." In *Unequal Sisters: An Inclusive Reader in U.S. Women's History*, edited by Vicki Ruíz and Carol DuBois. 2d ed. New York: Routledge, 1994.

"Texas Pool Party Incident: Teen in Video Says Officer Was Provoked by 'Rudeness.'" See https://www.theguardian.com/us-news/2015 /jun/08/texas-pool-party-police-dajerria-becton-eric-casebolt-rude.

Todd, Ellen Wiley. "Remembering the Unknowns: The Longman Memorial and the 1911 Triangle Shirtwaist Fire." *American Art* 23 (2009): 61–81.

Topp, Michael Miller. *Those Without A Country: The Political Culture of Italian American Syndicalists*. Minneapolis: University of Minnesota Press, 2001.

"Triangle Boss a Witness." *Forward*, March 15, 2011. Originally published in the *Forverts*, March 26, 1911. See https://forward.com /articles/136253/triangle-boss-a-witness.

Vecoli, Rudolph J. "Who Was Raimondo Fazio?: The Documentary Record." In *In Our Own Voices: Multidisciplinary Perspectives on Italian and Italian American Women*, edited by Elizabeth Giovanna Messina, 87–98. New York: Bordighera Press, 2003.

Von Drehle, David, *Triangle: The Fire That Changed America*. New York: Grove Press, 2004.

Walker, Ameena, and Alissa Walker. "Trump Fought Law Requiring Retrofit of Sprinklers in New York City High-Rises." See https:// ny.curbed.com/2018/4/9/17215222/trump-tower-fire-nyc-death -sprinklers.

Weber, Katherine. *Triangle*. New York: Picador, 2006.

Wesson, Rachel. *Orphan Train Disaster*. Self-published, 2020.

"Woman Sues Wirt for Anarchy Charge." *Atlanta Constitution*, October 17, 1934.

"Woman Unionist to Quit Post Here." *New York Times*, April 7, 1949. See https://www.nytimes.com/1949/04/07/archives/woman -unionist-to-quit-post-here-rose-schneiderman-recalls-events .html?searchResultPosition=1.

Woolman, Mary Schenck. *The Making of a Girls Trade School: Being the Organization, Work, Problems, and Equipment of the Manhattan Trade School for Girls, New York City.* New York: Columbia University Press, 1909.

Wrong, Elaine Gale. *The Negro in the Apparel Industry.* Philadelphia: University of Pennsylvania, Wharton School of Industrial Research, 1974.

Zandy, Janet. "Fire Poetry on the Triangle Shirtwaist Company Fire of March 25, 1911." *College Literature* 24, no. 3 (1997): 33–54. See http://www.jstor.org/stable/25112327.

Film and Video

"11-year-old Naomi Wadler's Speech at the March for Our Lives Rally (Full)." NBC News, March 24, 2018. See https://www.youtube.com/watch?v=C5ZUDImTIQ8.

"Edna Chavez—March for Our Lives (Full Speech)." Community Coalition, March 28, 2018. See https://www.youtube.com/watch?v=BinNvKznltA.

"Emma González Gives Speech at March for Our Lives Rally." CNN, March 24, 2018. See https://www.youtube.com/watch?v=hDEc4ImIVHk.

"Florida Student to NRA and Trump: 'We Call BS.'" See https://www.cnn.com/videos/us/2018/02/17/parkland-florida-student-emma-gonzalez-anti-gun-rally-fort-lauderdale-full.cnn.

Ida B. Wells: A Passion for Justice. Directed by William Greaves. San Francisco: California Newsreel, 1989.

Made in Thailand. Directed by Eve Laure-Moros and Linzy Emery. New York: Women Make Movies, 1999.

"MLK Jr.'s Granddaughter Surprises Rally Crowd." See https://www.cnn.com/videos/us/2018/03/24/mlk-jr-granddaughter-sot-march-for-our-lives-nr.cnn.

The True Cost. Directed by Andrew Morgan. Los Angeles: Life Is My Movie Entertainment, 2015.

Triangle Fire. Directed by Jamila Wignot. Alexandria, VA: PBS Distribution, 2011.

"Young Gun Control Activist Naomi Wadler Visits Ellen." *The Ellen Show,* April 4, 2018. See https://www.youtube.com/watch?v=L3d GFt96H8Y.

Music

"8 marzo." Movimento Femminista Romano, *Anti delle Donne in Lotta 2,* Vedette Albatros, 1976.

"Are My Hands Clean?" Sweet Honey in the Rock, *Live at Carnegie Hall.* Flying Fish, 1987.

"No Name." Francesca Incudine, from the album Tarakè, 2018.

Websites

Accord on Fire and Building Safety in Bangladesh, https://bangladesh accord.org.

Chronicling America: Historical American Newspapers, Library of Congress, https://chroniclingamerica.loc.gov/.

Clean Clothes Campaign, https://cleanclothes.org/.

Food Chain Workers Alliance, https://foodchainworkers.org/.

Frances Perkins Center, https://francesperkinscenter.org/.

Migrant Justice, https://migrantjustice.net/.

Street Pictures, https://streetpictures.org/streets/.

Woody Guthrie, https://www.woodyguthrie.org/.

About the Editors and Contributors

Martin Abramowitz, born in Brooklyn, New York, in 1940, is the son of Triangle Waist Company cutter Isidore Abramowitz. Martin's professional career included leadership positions in public welfare and Jewish community organizations in New York, Jerusalem, Montreal, and Boston. After he retired in 2006, he served for several years as a volunteer consultant to the board for the New England region of the Jewish Labor Committee. He has written and lectured on the history of Jews in Major League Baseball. In collaboration with the American Jewish Historical Society and the National Museum of American Jewish History, he has produced comprehensive and popular sets of Jewish Major Leaguers baseball cards. He is coauthor of *The Jewish Baseball Card Book* (2017). Martin has also "produced" Isidore Abramowitz's four grandchildren and nine great-grandchildren. Since 2016, he has served on the board of directors of the Remember the Triangle Fire Coalition.

Kalpona Akter is the founder and executive director of the Bangladesh Center for Workers Solidarity. In 2020, the U.S. Department of State awarded her the Special Faces of Exchange Award for her contributions to workers' rights in Bangladesh and globally. In 2016, she was awarded the Human Rights Watch's Alison Des Forges Award for Extraordinary Activism. She has traveled around the world as an advocate for garment workers and was a featured speaker at the 2011 official centennial commemoration of the Triangle fire in New York. She started working at a garment factory when she was a teenager and has devoted her life to fighting for safety in the workplace and for the rights of workers to be represented by unions.

Suzanne Pred Bass is the great-niece of Rosie Weiner, who died in the Triangle Shirtwaist Factory fire, and Katie Weiner, who survived the fire. She has served as an executive board member of the Remember the Triangle Fire Coalition since its inception in 2008. She spoke as a family representative at the 2011 Triangle Fire Centennial Commemoration and appeared in the HBO Documentary *Triangle: Remembering the Fire*. She has spoken at the Tenement House Museum, the Eldridge Street Synagogue, the Italian Cultural Institute of New York, and other venues. Her writing appears in *See You in the Streets: Art, Activism, and Remembering the Triangle Fire* by Ruth Sergel. She has a private practice as a psychotherapist and was the founder and artistic director of the Todd Mountain Theater Project, which supported the development of new plays for seventeen years. She and her husband, Lane, divide their time between New York City and upstate New York.

May Y. Chen's union career began in the ILGWU Immigration Project, where she advocated for fair immigration policies and helped thousands of union members resolve immigration problems and become U.S. citizens. She worked in the union's Education Department, coordinating English, civics, and labor training classes. Her work was profiled in Marcia Rock's 1994 documentary *City Originals: Women Making It Work*. For more than twenty-five years, she was involved with the garment workers' union in New York City (Local 23-25 Workers United/SEIU). Her essays have appeared in *Union Voices* and *Counterpoint: Perspective on Asian Americans*. May was founding officer and board member of the Asian Pacific American Labor Alliance (APALA), commissioner for President Obama's White House Initiative on Asian Americans and Pacific Islanders, and general executive board member of the Coalition of Labor Union Women. She serves on the Advisory Board of the Remember the Triangle Fire Coalition.

Tomlin Perkins Coggeshall is Frances Perkins's only grandchild. In 2009, with a group of dedicated volunteers, he founded the Frances Perkins Center, a nonprofit that preserves her legacy and carries on her work at her family homestead in Newcastle, Maine. After attending the Middlesex School, in Concord, Massachusetts, he studied biology and botany in college, graduating with a B.S. from the University of Maine in 1980. In addition to working with the Frances Perkins Center, he focuses on the transition from fossil fuels to clean energy resources, especially hydrogen and fuel cells as a better form of "battery" to deliver electric energy for mobile applications (cars, buses, trains, ships, trucks, etc.), with water vapor as the only "exhaust."

Paola Corso, a New York Foundation for the Arts Poetry Fellow and Sherwood Anderson Fiction Award winner, is the author of eight books of poetry and fiction set in her native Pittsburgh, where her southern Italian immigrant family worked in steel mills. Her recent books include *Vertical Bridges: Poems and Photographs of City Steps* (2020), which explores her family's ethnicity and working-class background; *The Laundress Catches Her Breath* (2012), winner of the Tillie Olsen Award in Creative Writing; and *Once I Was Told the Air Was Not for Breathing* (2012). A 2018 Triangle Fire Memorial Association awardee, she has been invited to read her poetry about garment and steel workers in universities across the country. Her writing has appeared in *The New York Times, The Christian Science Monitor, Women's Review of Books*, and numerous journals. A literary activist, Corso is cofounder of Steppin Stanzas, a grant-awarded poetry and art project celebrating city steps and the early immigrants who built them. See www.paolacorso.com.

Jacqueline Ellis grew up in Peterborough, England. She is a professor of Women's and Gender Studies at New Jersey City University. She is the author of *Silent Witnesses: Representations of Working-Class Women in the United States* (1998) and coeditor of *Transformations: The Journal of Inclusive Scholarship and Pedagogy*. Her most recent article, "Nurturing Anger: Race, Affect, and Transracial Adoption," was published in *WSQ*. Her scholarship on cultural representations of gender and working-class identities has appeared in *Feminist Review, International Feminist Journal of Politics*, and *History of Photography*. Her personal essay, "Palindrome," appeared in *Mutha Magazine* in 2020. She is working on a creative nonfiction book, "Palindrome: A Multiracial Family History." She lives in Montclair, New Jersey.

Michele Fazio is professor of English and co-coordinator of the Gender Studies minor at the University of North Carolina at Pembroke, where she teaches courses on contemporary U.S. ethnic literature, service learning, and working-class studies. The film she coproduced, *Voices of the Lumbee* (2014), received the Studs Terkel Award for Media and Journalism and the North Carolina Folklore Society Brown-Hudson Award. She has served as president of the Working-Class Studies Association and coedited the *Routledge International Handbook of Working-Class Studies* (2021). Her research on family history, community, and memory has been exhibited at the Harvard Law School Library and the American Labor Museum. Through the support of a BMI Woody Guthrie Research Fellowship and a Massachusetts Historical Society Fellowship, she is working on a book project on the cultural legacy of Sacco and Vanzetti.

Ellen Gruber Garvey lives in New York, where she appreciates the ever-changing traces of the past. Her two prizewinning books, *Writing with Scissors: American Scrapbooks from the Civil War to the Harlem Renaissance* (2013) and *The Adman in the Parlor: Magazines and the Gendering of Consumer Culture* (1996), were both published by Oxford University Press. Her work on publishing, writing, editing, suffrage, African American history, and immigration has appeared in numerous journals, collections, and blogs, including CNN, *The Washington Post*, *The New York Times* Disunion blog, *Slate*, the *Forward*, and *The Root*. She blogs about scrapbooks at www.scrapbookhistory.wordpress.com. She has given many public talks on scrapbook history and on women's bicycling through the public speakers programs of the New York and New Jersey Council for the Humanities. She currently works on making her scholarly writing useful in nonacademic realms. She is a Professor Emerita of English at New Jersey City University.

Janette Gayle is an assistant professor of history at Hobart and William Smith Colleges. She earned an M.A. in Afro-American Studies from UCLA and a Ph.D. in history from the University of Chicago. Her work lies at the intersection of African American, women's, and labor history and explores the interconnected histories of migration, civil rights, and workers' rights. Her current book project, "Sewing Change: Black Migrant Dressmakers and the Struggle for Rights in Early-Twentieth-Century New York City," examines the role that black dressmakers from the American South and the British West Indies played in the civil rights and labor movements as they transitioned from home-based production to the garment industry and membership in the ILGWU. She teaches courses in African American, labor, and women's history and is affiliated with the Africana Studies Program at HWS.

Edvige Giunta, who was born in Sicily, is a regular contributor to Italian American studies and a founder of the field. Her books include *Writing with an Accent: Contemporary Italian American Women Authors* (2002), and five coedited anthologies: *The Milk of Almonds* (2002), *Italian American Writers on New Jersey* (2003), the MLA publication *Teaching Italian American Literature, Film, and Popular Culture* (2010), *Embroidered Stories* (2014), and *Personal Effects* (2015). Her literary nonfiction and poetry appear in such journals as *Assay, Barrow Street, Creative Nonfiction*, and *Mutha Magazine*. At New Jersey City University, where she is professor of English, she has trained scores of students in the art of memoir and teaches a course on the Triangle fire that she developed. The recipient of a Triangle Fire Memorial Association award, she has been profiled by the Italian public broadcasting company, RAI, as well by *The New York Times* and other publications. She has taught memoir workshops for communities in the United States and Italy.

The Reverend Charles Hoffacker is an Episcopal priest who lives in Greenbelt, Maryland, a community established as part of the New Deal. From 2012 to 2014, he was interim rector of St. Monica and St. James Episcopal Church in Washington, D.C. St. James Church was Frances Perkins's parish during her Washington years. Since 2013, he has served as a board member of the Frances Perkins Center. His article "Frances Perkins: The Saint Behind the New Deal" appeared in the May 4, 2014, issue of *The Living Church*. While enjoying an active retirement, Father Hoffacker ministers in various ways, including as a writer, independent scholar, and activist.

Annie Rachele Lanzillotto is an author, poet, performance artist, actor, director, songwriter, and activist who has promoted audience participation in hundreds of performances everywhere, from the Arthur Avenue Retail Market to the Guggenheim Museum. While sheltering in place alone during the COVID-19 pandemic, Lanzillotto embarked on a solo "Decameron" to tell one hundred original stories in her podcast, "Annie's Story Cave." Lanzillotto's books include *Hard Candy: Caregiving, Mourning, and Stage Light, Pitch Roll Yaw* (2016); *L is for Lion: An Italian Bronx Butch Freedom Memoir* (2013), a finalist for the LAMBDA Literary Award; and *Schistsong* (2013). Lanzillotto was on the founding board of the Remember the Triangle Fire Coalition. See annielanzillotto.com and StreetCryInc.org.

Annelise Orleck is professor of history, Women's, Gender, and Sexuality Studies, and Jewish Studies at Dartmouth College. She is the author of five books on poor and workingwomen's activism, immigration, race, and gender: *Common Sense and a Little Fire: Women and Working-Class Politics in the United States, 1900–1965* (1995); *Soviet Jewish Americans* (1995); *Storming Caesar's Palace: How Black Mothers Fought Their Own War on Poverty* (2005); *Rethinking American Women's Activism* (2014); and *"We Are All Fast Food Workers Now": The Global Uprising Against Poverty Wages* (2018). She also coedited, with Alexis Jetter and Diana Taylor, *The Politics of Motherhood: Activist Voices from Left to Right* (1997) and, with Lisa Hazirjian, *The War on Poverty: A New Grassroots History, 1964–1980* (2011). Orleck is founder and copresident of Dartmouth's AAUP chapter. She has published in popular media, including *Salon, Jacobin, The Guardian, Ms., Bitch Media*, UPI, *The Los Angeles Review of Books*, and *The Conversation*. She has long been involved in struggles for labor justice, a living wage, academic freedom, tenure equity, and against sexual violence and sexual harassment in the workplace.

Ester Rizzo Licata was born and lives in Licata, Sicily. She is an award-winning author whose book, *Camicette bianche: oltre l'8 marzo* (2014), is the first book on the Triangle fire published in Italy. She teaches women's literature at UNITRE and CUSCA, two institutions of continuing education for older adults. She regularly writes for *Malgrado tutto* and *Vita-mine vaganti*. She is actively involved in many organizations that focus on women's rights and history, including the Commissione Donne Pari Opportunatà and Toponomastica Femminile. She has spearheaded a large commemorative initiative by Toponomastica Femminile in the Italian hometowns of workers who died in the Triangle fire. She has edited *Le Mille: i primati delle donne* (2016). Her most recent books are *Le Ricamatrici* (2018) and *Donne Disobbedienti* (2019).

Laura E. Ruberto is associate professor of humanities at Berkeley City College. She was a Fulbright Faculty Scholar to Italy (2006) and a Mellon/ACLS Faculty Fellow (2020–2021). Her research focuses on Italian and Italian American film, material culture, and cultural theories of migration. She is the author of *Gramsci, Migration, and the Representation of Women's Work in Italy and the U.S.* (2007); her coedited collections include *Italian Neorealism and Global Cinema* (2007), *New Italian Migrations to the United States*, vol. 1: *Politics and History Since 1945* (2017), and vol. 2, *Art and Culture Since 1945* (2017). A book series editor for Fordham University Press, she serves on the editorial boards of *California Italian Studies* and the *Italian American Review*.

Kimberly Schiller is a veteran English teacher. She graduated from Adelphi University with a Masters in Secondary Education and currently teaches middle school English. Kimberly began her career on the Lower East Side of Manhattan, and has been teaching in Huntington, New York since 2005. Throughout her years as a teacher, Kimberly has taken over two-hundred students to the site of the Triangle fire. Because of her work, she has been honored with an award of recognition from the Triangle Fire Memorial Association. Kimberly serves on the executive board to the New York Labor History Association and as District Vice President for her local union, the Associated Teachers of Huntington. Kimberly was involved with political action and history early on because of her trail-blazing mother and supportive father. She and her encouraging husband have vowed to do the same with their two children, Annalee and Billy. They have both already attended their first rally and marched with their mother down Fifth Avenue in the Labor Day parade.

Ellen Wiley Todd is associate professor emerita of art history, Cultural Studies, and Women and Gender Studies at George Mason University, and a former museum studies course instructor for the Smith College program in Washington, D.C. She is the author of *The "New Woman" Revised: Painting and Gender Politics on Fourteenth Street* (1993). She has been writing and presenting on the Triangle fire and on Ernest Fiene's murals in New York's High School of Fashion Industries. Her work considers how individual producers and groups, and viewers of their work, have engaged with historical memory and the politics of visual representation. Her writings on the Triangle fire include "Photojournalism, Visual Culture, and the Triangle Shirtwaist Fire," published in *Labor: Studies in Working Class History of the Americas* (2005), and "Remembering the Unknowns: The Longman Memorial and the 1911 Triangle Shirtwaist Fire," published in *American Art* (2009).

Mary Anne Trasciatti teaches rhetoric and directs the Labor Studies program at Hofstra University. She is president of Remember the Triangle Fire Coalition. Since 2010, she has helped organize the annual official Triangle fire commemoration. She has led the project to build the Triangle Fire Memorial, scheduled for dedication in 2022. Funded by a $1.5 million grant from the state of New York and more than $500,000 in contributions from labor unions, ethnic organizations, and individuals, it will be the first labor memorial and one of only a handful of memorials to women in New York City. Her work on the memorial has been the subject of articles in *The New York Times* and *Newsday*. She wrote the foreword for *My Life as a Political Prisoner: The Rebel Girl Becomes "No. 11710"* (2019), the prison memoir of radical labor activist Elizabeth Gurley Flynn, and is coeditor of the forthcoming anthology *Where Are the Workers?: Labor's Stories at Museums and Historical Sites.*

Annie Schneiderman Valliere, a native of Washington, D.C., is a Maine-based retired social worker and a great-niece of Rose Schneiderman. She has spent more than a decade researching and writing a biography of Rose. Annie was awarded the Eichleberger-Linzer Grant from the Franklin D. Roosevelt Presidential Library in Hyde Park, New York. She has traveled from Maine to Washington—including a visit to the Roosevelt House in New York—to deliver captivating talks on Rose. Annie gave presentations about Rose at the conference "Frances Perkins and the Progressive and New Deal Eras" and as a part of the 2019 Maine Suffrage Centennial. She has written articles on Schneiderman, the Uprising of the 20,000, and the Triangle fire for the *Oxford Encyclopedia of American Business, Labor, and Economic History.* In 2015, she published an article on her great-aunt's suffrage activism for the Turning Point Suffragist Memorial Association.

Richard Joon Yoo is an architectural designer and artist. He studied art at the School of the Art Institute of Chicago and architecture at the Southern California Institute of Architecture (SCI-Arc). He has taught at SCI-Arc and Woodbury University in Los Angeles, and currently teaches at Pratt University and the Center for Architecture Science and Ecology at Rensselaer Polytechnic Institute. His work focuses on memorials and monuments, specifically the ability of the built environment to heighten the present and provoke the future through the careful positioning of memory, context, and material. In collaboration with Uri Wegman, he won the international design competition for the Triangle Fire Memorial. In March 2019, in collaboration with the Remember the Triangle Fire Coalition, he and Uri Wegman hosted the Collective Ribbon project.